YESTERDAY

A Memoir of a Russian Jewish Family

BY MIRIAM SHOMER ZUNSER,
EDITED BY HER GRANDDAUGHTER,
EMILY WORTIS LEIDER

Harper & Row, Publishers
New York, Hagerstown, San Francisco, London

1918

Cop A

Photographic reproductions by Elizabeth Crews.

Designed by Gloria Adelson

Library of Congress Cataloging in Publication Data

Zunser, Miriam Shomer.
    Yesterday : a memoir of a Russian Jewish family.
    1. Bercinsky family. 2. Jews in Pinsk, White Russia—Biography. 3. Shaikevitsch, Nochim-Mayer, 1849–1905—Biography. 4. Authors, Yiddish—Biography. 5. Zunser, Miriam Shomer. 6. Pinsk, White Russia—Biography. I. Leider, Emily Wortis. II. Title.
DS135.R93P56   1978   947'.652   78–2150
ISBN 0–06–012553–5

78 79 80 81 82 10 9 8 7 6 5 4 3 2 1

In Memory of Helen Zunser Wortis

Contents

Editor's Acknowledgments

I would like to thank my aunt, Florence Zunser Saltz, for generously sharing memories and records; Charles Madison, for translating from Yiddish and for providing invaluable background information; my father, Joseph Wortis, for discovering letters and other memorabilia. Esther Enzer of the Yiddish Theater Collection, Museum of the City of New York, was most helpful, as were Dina Abramowicz and Marek Web of the YIVO Institute for Jewish Research. Jesse and Mary Zunser offered reminiscences and help in tracking down newspaper columns. David Arkin sent essential materials from Los Angeles. My husband, William Leider, has believed in and supported this project from the start.

To my children:

You wanted me to tell you the story of my family. Here it is. At least, here are the tales I can retrieve from my own memory and those recalled by the few surviving members of the large family your great-grandfather reared.

When Uncle Dave died he took with him into everlasting silence stories of wisdom and of mirth. When Aunt Haiye died she took along the same tales colored in romantic hues. Aunt Dvayreh, could she tell those stories, would no doubt turn them into legends of bitterness. Coming from your grandmother Dinneh they are—well, you know how she tells things in her large roving way, spicing her stories with bits of shrewd observation, egotism and imagination. If all of your great-grandfather's children had lived to recount what they saw and heard, you would no doubt have had as many more versions of the things that happened. As it is, there are only a few left now. If I wait a little longer these few will also vanish, and even my own memories will fade. So let me begin.

MOTHER

YESTERDAY

ONE

Reb Michel

YOUR GREAT-GRANDFATHER had twenty-four children, all by
the same wife. The first child was a daughter, Rochel-Leah.
The second was a son, Mayshe. Then came a series of eight
girls, among them your grandmother Dinneh and Haiye and
Faygle, who died when she was seventeen. The names of the
others I do not know. Then came another son, Avrom; then
more girls and boys of whom I remember only five in the
order of their ages: Dvayreh, Fraydel, Menye, David and
Joshua.

Your great-grandfather was fourteen years old when he
married. Your great-grandmother was twelve. When she
was fourteen she had her first child. There was a good reason
why these young people were married at so early an age.
They lived at the time when Nicholas I was Czar of all the
Russias. This man, who has gone down in history as a despot, imposed a military service of twenty-five years upon his
Jewish subjects, the service to begin when a youth was eighteen. To carry out a determined policy of Russification,
however, and to break the Jew from his faith, the powers
declared that "preparatory training" for military service

would have to begin at a much earlier age; say at ten or twelve. Accordingly, little boys, sometimes as young as seven or eight, were snatched from their homes, actually torn from their mother's arms, and placed under the "guardianship" of a *diadka* ("little uncle"). This endearing term was usually applied to a peasant who lived hundreds of miles from any Jewish settlement and who treated his ward as a criminal whose will was to be broken, by physical means if necessary. This meant that a boy would be taken away from his parents before he had reached his teens, that he would be bullied, starved, beaten and broken, and that he would return, if he returned at all, when he was a middle-aged man.

Nicholas I's twenty-five-year decree, issued in 1827, wrought havoc in Jewish life, causing suffering that cannot easily be described. Old and young, rich and poor were involved in a struggle of tragic terror.

Agony of a special kind was visited upon young married people. A young husband would be taken from his home and sent no one knew where. For endless years the wife would not know what had become of him. She would not know whether she was a wife or a widow, whether or not her children were orphans, or if she could allow another man to be a father to them. The distress caused by this uncertainty was so keen that many a young man divorced the wife of his bosom before entering into the service. For a people who built their lives upon the home and its sanctity, this was a calamitous fate.

When the terror of the decree was at its height, in 1834, a rumor was spread that to allay the hardships of these young people, married men would no longer be conscripted. The rumor was false, but it brought about the period known to Jews as the *beholoh*—a Hebrew word meaning fright or panic. Men feared they would be conscripted before it was too late. That caused the immediate marriage of thousands of young children.

Thus it happened that your great-grandmother Yentel at the age of twelve had her hair matted with syrup and sugar, then her head shaved and a wig placed upon it to signify that she was a married woman. (There are several folk explanations for the custom, the two favorite being that after marriage a woman should not, by her charms, entice other men; that the hair is given to the "evil one" so that he may not demand all of the bride.)

Great-grandmother Yentel was a woman of short stature. At the age of twelve she was so small that when she was brought to the synagogue for her own wedding, she could not see what was going on. After the marriage ceremony she had to be lifted up and placed upon the window sill to get a view of the festivities.

The first glimpse she had of great-grandfather Michel came when he dropped the veil over her face before she was led under the *chuppe* (wedding canopy). But she did not in the least mind all this, for she did not know what it was all about, and, what is more, she was not especially bright or sagacious. She had just been brought in from the village of Yaneve, where she had spent her little life wandering in the fields, playing jacks and occasionally helping her mother about the house. When, for some reason, she was chosen to marry Michel, who was a very promising boy, she acquiesced quickly, as a good girl should, and looked forward with glee to a ride in the hay cart all the way to the town of Pinsk. Her marriage did not prevent her from playing jacks in her father-in-law's yard when nobody was looking or from secreting her rag doll in her bridal chamber where, some seventy years later, she died of a broken heart because

Michel could no longer answer her impetuous call.

Michel and Yentel were married in the year of the *beholoh,*
1834. Two years later the first of the procession of their
twenty-four children was born. I mean to tell you the stories
of only those of the twenty-four who survived into manhood or womanhood. There were not many, ten in all. The
rest were claimed by the many scourges of infantile life that
were rampant in Europe until your own generation. The
lives of the ten, born over a period of forty years, lead me
from remote days in Russia, now only recorded in history,
to your own day here in America.

Great-grandfather Michel was an extraordinary man. You
may yourselves have noted the veneration, the awe, with
which grandmother, Aunt Menye or Uncle Dave spoke of
him; I will refer to him, in his maturity, as Reb Michel. That
is how he was spoken of in his own day. He would most
certainly have been outraged to hear himself referred to
simply as Michel, except by his wife or some very close
friend.

Reb is a reverential title meaning Mister or Sir. It is by no
means and at no time generally applied. No mere man in the
street is addressed as *Reb,* unless of course you say *Reb Yid*
—"Mr. or Sir Jew," which is a very common appellation.
Otherwise the term is applied to men who are supposed to
have Talmudic learning, and not to people with a secular
education only.

When great-grandfather Michel at one time wanted to
pay a special compliment to Yentel's remarkable older sister
Zlate, he said that one might speak of her as *Reb Zlate.* This
was a tribute, indeed, coming from Reb Michel Bercinsky to
a mere woman.

2

Reb Michel's personality became manifest when he was a little more than sixteen. It expressed itself in a daring which caused a rift between him and his father. That occurred shortly after Michel's first child was born, and when his father, Tzodek-Mayshe Bercinsky, bought him out of the hands of the conscripting agents for the sum of a thousand rubles. It was a big price to pay since Tzodek-Mayshe was a poor man; but he could not let his bright young son go into the army. It was not only the thought of the physical torture and long separation that plagued him, but the possibility of the young man's being weaned away from Judaism. The air was full of "Russification." The Czar had determined it; he would have the Jews discontinue their resistance, abandon their mode of life, their way of thinking, and become Russians.

The Pale of Settlement had been a long-established institution. Within its boundaries the Jews had been confined by previous Czars. Now there came one who would drive them out of the peace they had found for themselves into a terrifying world. "Russification" was dreaded. It was to be shunned in every way. If you used the language of the enemy, you laid yourself open to his onslaught.

Michel was then living with his wife at his father's house. The story goes that the home folk noticed that Michel would disappear for hours at a time. No one knew where he went. After watching him closely, the women discovered that he made his way by stealth to the attic of the house. What could he be up to? The women put their heads together. There was much whispering and speculation. No one dared to tell Michel's father. The head of the house, the pious man of learning, should not be bothered with trivialities. But his mother, Shayndel, became uneasy. She set a watch upon her son.

One day when Michel vanished in his strange way, she sent a servant up to the attic, ostensibly to hang the wash that would not dry out-of-doors. The woman was told to observe closely what Michel was about. Quietly she stole up the ladder. Silently she set down her burden. For a few minutes she stood dumbfounded and watched; then she hastened down breathlessly. Michel was sitting over strange-looking books, reading and writing. A pall fell over Shayndel. Secret reading and writing meant trouble of the most serious kind. Tzodek-Mayshe would have to be found and told at once.

Michel's father hastened home. He, too, crept up the rickety ladder. Besides suspicion, a great hope was in his heart. Perhaps his son was a secret saint. Perhaps he was studying some sacred volume of mystic lore which was to be kept from the vulgar eyes of the many. Nevertheless he pounced upon the unheeding lad and tore the volume from his hand. It was printed in Russian.

The tragedy in the attic soon spread throughout the house, indeed, throughout the town. Reb Tzodek-Mayshe's son Michel was reading "profane literature," *goyish*—things Gentile. Verily, he was deserting the faith of his fathers.

The rest of the household was spared the arguments between father and son, but when these were done and Michel would not relinquish his right to know the language of the Czar, Reb Tzodek-Mayshe tore his garments, put ashes on his head, and sat on the floor reciting the prayer for the dead. He had lost his son.

Michel and his small family left his father's house. His kin were forbidden to talk to him. He had brought shame upon his father's name. It was not until many years later that father and son wept in each other's arms in joy and forgiveness. I will tell you how that happened.

3

In the course of several years Michel Bercinsky became popularly known as Michel the Scribe. He was not a scribe of holy books, one who is designated as a *sofar,* but a writer of legal briefs, documents, appeals and the like. The young man had persevered. He had learned the Russian language, studied Russian law and government, and was becoming known as a clever negotiator of the law, in spite of the fact that he had no academic training.

There was no doubt that Michel was making something of himself. Tall, handsome, hawk-nosed, with flashing brown eyes and a commanding personality, he had captured the imagination of his townspeople. They had profound faith in him and his word was their assurance. In later years belief in him became so great and his word so convincing, that, as Uncle Dave joyously related, when Michel Bercinsky stamped his foot and called a man *bock!* (goat) the man bleated meekly, *Meh. . . .*

In the town of Pinsk there was a very old *shul* (synagogue). I use the word because I like its sound and the picture it brings to my mind. It was said to be a thousand years old, and one of the oldest in all Europe. It seems that sometime in the remote past, the ground upon which the *shul* was built belonged to the church. As evidence of and because of this assumption, the church authorities of the city required that a yearly rental or property tax of some three hundred rubles be paid into the coffers of the church by the Jewish community. It was so arranged that the time for the payment of the tax coincided with the Jewish high holidays. Thus it came to pass that year after year, with the approach of the holy days, the *shul* would be closed and padlocked until the tax was paid. This naturally caused distress in a community where three hundred rubles was an enormous amount of money and the raising of it a formidable task.

One year the community could not raise the required amount and the *shul* remained closed throughout the holy days. When I tell you that the old building was the center of the spiritual and emotional life of the town, and that the holy days were the pivotal point of the year, you will understand what the padlocking of the *shul* meant.

Michel Bercinsky took this very much to heart and very clearly into his head. This business of the tax would have to be looked into. The closing of the *shul* was an outrage. Surely the age and long use of the edifice should entitle the community to some privilege.

The young man started an investigation, approaching all sorts of people and putting his nose into all sorts of places. Everywhere he was told that he was butting his head against a stone wall. The church was powerful, the Jewish community helpless. Besides, who was he to question a custom that had been established for generations?

But Michel took to reading musty old volumes in the town hall. How he got access to these books nobody knew or bothered to ask. Then he took to writing voluminous documents which he sent off with *éclat* to the governor at Minsk and, finally, to St. Petersburg itself.

Then there came a startling announcement. Michel Bercinsky was summoned to St. Petersburg to argue the case of the Pinsk*er* (belonging to Pinsk) *shul.* The town was dumbfounded. It was also shocked and annoyed. Such folly! Fight against the church! It was dangerous and stupid. The man should not be allowed to go. Clearly he was out of his mind.

But go he did. The stubborn fellow emptied his house of all he possessed. Silver, linen, furniture, clothes—all went into pawn. Even Yentel's silver Sabbath candlesticks were not spared. With all arrangements made, Yentel was the only one who saw Michel off on the post-chaise which was to take him on his perilous journey. Even if she did not understand what he was talking about, the fat little woman had faith in her husband.

There were months of anxiety, and of silence. The man had been swallowed up by the unknown world into which he had ventured. Yentel's life was a vale of tears. Suddenly a message from St. Petersburg! From Michel! He had won his case! The community would never again have to pay a tax on the *shul.*

Once again the town was dumbfounded, but this time it broke into cries of jubilation. After weary weeks of traveling, the victorious advocate of his people's rights finally arrived, and the town turned out in a body to greet him. Among the thousands who came, Michel saw his old father. Men and women wept at the meeting of the two. So did Michel and old Tzodek-Mayshe. Father and son had found and forgiven each other.

You are probably curious to know how Michel performed the miracle of freeing the *shul* from its taxes. It was simple enough once you dug to the bottom of the matter. He proved that though the land upon which the *shul* was built had indeed at one time belonged to the church, it had been used as a cemetery, and, as such, under Russian law was not taxable property; the church, therefore, could not collect.

All the household goods Michel had pawned for his venture in St. Petersburg were redeemed and brought back to him by pawnbrokers and townspeople alike. No one would take a *groschen* from him for the chattels he had pledged in the interest of the community. The town also voted him a handsome monetary compensation. But he would have none of it; instead, he named his own reward. He asked, and received for life, a seat at the eastern wall of the *shul.* It is a place of honor and one much desired by religious Jews— *shul*-goers. To him also was granted the privilege of reading *Maftir* (a portion of the Bible read on Sabbaths and holidays), an honor every respectable member of the community coveted for himself.

4

One day Pinsk was startled by the news that thieves had broken into Reb Michel's house and had carried away everything on which they could lay hands. The town had hardly recovered from the shock when it received the still-more-astonishing news that the stolen things had been returned. These were found heaped on the doorstep of Reb Michel's house in keeping with a thief's promise that Michel Bercinsky would never be robbed. How did this happen?

Pinsk, like a great many Russian towns, was infested with gangs of thieves. There was no one to take them into custody. They went about their business snatching goods and making a general nuisance of themselves. Nobody did anything effective about getting rid of them.

Idiots and harmless lunatics were also allowed to wander about the town at their ease. Every town could boast its own maniac. *Der shtodt meshugener* (the town lunatic) was a familiar figure on its leading streets. He was jeered at, pelted with rubbish by boys, thrown out of houses which he attempted to enter; otherwise nobody paid any attention to him. The maniacs were allowed to wander at large because there were no proper asylums to take care of them, and the thieves were allowed to ply their profession because nobody cared to turn them over to the tender mercies of the prison officials. Apparently the good people preferred to be robbed of their earthly possessions rather than have their conscience burdened with the knowledge that, for the sake of a bit of merchandise or a handful of silver, a man had been brutally beaten or publicly flogged. If the thief was a Jew it was worse still. In prison he would be segregated from Jewish life and so exposed to every possible breach of its observances.

The town suffered and the thieves were thriving when Michel Bercinsky came upon the scene. Although he had come into prominence, the thieving gangs took little notice of him. They knew how spineless the so-called community leaders could be where police and officialdom were concerned.

Then there came a day when Pinsk rocked with excitement, and the condition was no longer to be borne. The retired old general's horse had been stolen! True, the Polish doctor's racing specimen had disappeared a month before and various other horses had vanished during the last six months; but the general's horse! A man's coat would be taken "from right off his back" in broad daylight, and one could no longer be sure that he owned anything that he did not have his hand on. The town turned to Michel. Would he undertake to rid the place of thieves? Michel said he would.

When my mother told this story, I was ready for a vision of Reb Michel stepping forth like the Pied Piper of Hamelin, with the thieves of the town trailing him in a merry dance right to the very waterfront. But nothing of the kind was forthcoming. In a matter-of-fact way Michel started studying the manner in which the horses had disappeared. He felt confident that the horse thief with all his daring was the brains, the leader of the gang.

The "study" showed that the horses had been stolen at night directly from their stables. It also showed that the stable locks were not tampered with in the ordinary way. Instead, they were crushed and twisted as if by a gigantic hand. As all the locks were broken in the same way, it was clear that all the horses had been stolen by the same person. Continued investigation revealed that these animals were sold in the open marketplaces of nearby towns. Michel concluded that the thief must be a powerful man, a good walker (since to avoid being recognized he would have had to come on foot from the towns in which the horses were sold), and that he must have had the opportunity of studying the horses before he stole them. Not every animal could be counted upon to make a swift journey through the night to a neighboring town.

Suspicion fell upon a young man, Danielke by name, who was quite an infamous character. Danielke is a diminutive for Daniel; in Yiddish such suffixes as *e, ke, le, el* are diminutives tacked on to names of people or things for reasons of affection, familiarity or derision.

In Pinsk when one said Daniel*ke,* the *ke* implied a feeling of dread. This was so not only because the fellow was an irascible young giant who could do one bodily harm, but because, though he sauntered about town much at his leisure, nobody knew just what he was about.

Danielke lived on the outskirts of the town. Behind his house stretched a green field where the town's cows and horses were turned out to pasture. With suspicion fixed on the young giant, it was easy to see how he could study the horses and pick his prey deliberately. Michel set a day-and-night watch upon the young fellow until he was seen at work. Danielke's method was a simple one. He crushed the lock in his mighty hands, led the horse quietly from the stable, mounted and rode out of town to sell the animal elsewhere. In a few days he returned and stared the townspeople down brazenly.

Soon it was definitely established that Danielke was the ringleader. Siberia loomed for him. Of all punishment, Siberia was the most fearful. It meant months of walking across the frozen steppes. It meant bleeding feet on icy soil; chains, flogging, starvation, death, perhaps by slow torture.

The word *Sibir* (Siberia) sent a shudder of horror down the spine of the town of Pinsk. Danielke knew the place and he knew its people. Siberia was too great a punishment to be meted out to any man, no matter what his crime. Who in the town would be ready to inflict it upon any one of its sons? No one, Danielke guessed, not even that new leader, Michel Bercinsky.

And Danielke was right. Michel had not the sternness to send him to Siberia. While the young hoodlum strode about with his hands in his pockets defying the town to do its worst, Michel racked his brains trying to find a way out of the difficulty. He finally decided: Danielke would have to be conscripted into the army.

That was not as easy to accomplish as you may suppose. Danielke was the only son of a widowed mother and as such was exempt from military service. The struggle which ensued filled the town with awe. Michel had his life at stake, Danielke his freedom. Danielke might as well lose his freedom for murder as for theft, and Michel feared for his life.

Michel had a thousand people sign a petition to the governor of the township setting forth reasons why Danielke should be conscripted into the army. It was drawn, accepted, and acted upon. Danielke was taken into the army and removed from the town. But before leaving he managed to get word to Reb Michel—a word of warning and a threat that this was not the end.

Reb Michel was fond of walking out of town on Sabbath mornings. He loved to wander about the fields on the outskirts of the city. One morning, thus engaged, he saw a familiar figure in the distance—Danielke! The man was supposed to be safe in some military barracks in Minsk; but there he was, large as life. Danielke saw Reb Michel at the same moment. Both men halted.

Then the two started across the field, approaching closer and closer. Michel steeled himself. He was big and strong, but no match for Danielke. They were fifty feet apart. Thirty —twenty—Would Danielke leap? He was still coming on. Perhaps he feared that Michel would raise a cry if he showed any sign of intended violence. Perhaps he wanted to come near enough for a quick stranglehold on his adversary. Whatever it might have been, Michel went forward to meet his foe. When Michel was within three feet of him, Danielke stopped and surveyed him with cold murderous eyes; he seemed ready for action.

Then Michel said in a firm voice, "I see you are going on a long journey abroad."

Danielke instantly knew the import of that. Michel, knowing him to be a deserter, suggested that he leave the country and implied by his friendly tone that he would not hinder his escape.

"You have relatives abroad, I believe, who will be glad to see you," Michel continued.

Danielke was still speechless. A maze of conflicting emotions appeared on his face. Michel watched the effect of his words.

"A very wise decision, my boy. As for your mother, you need have no worry about her. I will continue to take care of her as I have been doing since you went away."

Michel had hit Danielke's soft spot.

"She loves you very dearly, Daniel, and you must see that no harm comes to you, for her sake." Danielke's head was bowed. "Well, good luck to you," Michel concluded and added meaningfully, "And see that you leave no evidence of having been here."

With that admonition Michel proceeded on his way. For the next five minutes he feared that a flying rock might split his head open, but he did not turn or look back. Apparently Danielke had accepted his advice. Michel never saw him again.

The ringleader was gone. The thing to do now was to impress the lesser thieves that the city jail was ready for them if they continued their practices. The difficulty lay in finding a messenger who could carry the word of punishment into the camp of the disgruntled hoodlums.

Reb Michel's sleep was disturbed one night by what he thought was someone moving about in the living room. He got out of bed to investigate. The living room was pitch dark and no one seemed to be about. To assure himself that the silver closet was intact, he groped his way across the room, opened the closet door and felt about for the familiar objects. Suddenly his hand came in contact with a head. He quickly grabbed it and pulled. The head and the man belonging to it emerged from the closet. There was a quick struggle in the dark, and the thief, held captive, was led into the dimly lit entrance hall.

Michel recognized the man as one of Danielke's gang. Holding him securely, Michel gave the man an earful of what thieves were hereafter to expect. He painted a fearful picture, and then dragged the man to the door, opened it wide and said, "Run, before I call the police!" The thief ran a few paces and reeled over in excitement. Humbly grateful that he had not immediately been subjected to the punishment he had just heard described, he called back tremulously, "Reb Michel, never need you close your doors! Never again will anyone rob you!"

Thus it happened that when some years later thieves who did not know Michel came to Pinsk and robbed him of his chattels, these were brought back and piled high on the threshold of his door.

5

When Tzodek-Mayshe died, Michel, though not the eldest son, became the head of the house. Brothers, sisters, uncles, cousins, and aunts swarmed around him with complete trust, seeking not only counsel, but everything else that harassed human beings could demand.

Michel was a born autocrat. He loved to lead and have his way. He rejoiced in responsibility. Assuming the leadership of his tribe, he went to work. He bought an inn for his older widowed brother Laybush; "the city scales" for his ne'er-do-well younger brother Berel; found a husband, provided a dowry and promised *kest* for his sister Sarah, and kept the whole family and many more in his house until each was able to manage for himself.

But some of Michel's arrangements require a word of explanation. Pinsk lies on the Pina River. Freight boats bearing cargoes of wheat, grain, and lumber stopped at its shores to unload, and to take in exchange flour, oil, and soap. This was by no means a daily occurrence. When a barge or freight boat arrived, the young people of the town would turn out

then rest in bed as comfortably as her baby did. The windows and the door posts were hung with printed charms to ward off the "evil" ones from entering the room, and the walls were hung with similar devices. The midwife attended her patient quietly, not permitting anyone to enter the room for fear of the "evil eye." When someone insisted upon seeing her charge, the old woman would wrap a cloth about Yentel's head and tell her to moan. The visitor would be told that all was not at all well with Yentel, that the bright glow in her cheeks was due to fever. No sooner was the visitor gone than off came Yentel's cloth and the old woman's hands were describing mystic circles about her head. Three times the circles were drawn, and three times she imbibed with eager lips the air about Yentel's head. Thus she sucked in whatever evil might have been left about her patient, and out she spat it with a vengeance in the opposite direction. Being fed on delicious concoctions of milk, butter, honey and eggs, Yentel would be on her feet again in a few days and toddling about the house as if nothing at all had happened. A little time later while a wet-nurse took care of the new infant, Yentel would send specimens of the spots on her linen to the rabbi, to see if she were clean enough for her ritual bath, and so for cohabitation with her husband.

Offspring being the great achievement of one's life, you can readily understand the pride with which Michel regarded his growing family. I don't know how he took the death of so many children. None of the Bercinsky family ever commented on this grief, though everything else about him was thoroughly discussed. About Yentel it was said that she had no special love for any but one of her brood. In return, none of her children except the loved one had much affection for her. Haiye, Dvayreh and Fraydel disliked her. My mother, Dinneh, softened

toward her only when she herself was an old woman.
Dave looked upon her philosophically, disregarding her
faults and virtues. Avrom said, "Speak no evil of the
dead." Joshua had contempt for her mentality. Once he
chided her at the top of his voice: "Fifty years you have
been sitting in front of this clock (a rare large-faced specimen that hung opposite her chair in the living room),
and you still can't tell the time!" Which was perfectly
true. The only one who had a word of love for her was
Menye, Yentel's twenty-second and favorite child.

6

Michel's rise to power was a matter of wonderment to the
town. To begin with, there was the matter of his career. Who
ever heard of a Jew, self-educated, without degrees or di-
plomas, holding a position in legal matters? Remember that
this was in the time of Nicholas I. Michel not only prepared
briefs and wrote appeals, but he argued cases in court and
upset the best-trained minds arrayed against him. And it
was not usually on points of law that he upset them, as in
the case of the *shul,* but rather on those of common sense and
quickwittedness.

There was, for instance, the business of a promissory note
upon a man's house, which the man swore he knew nothing
about. The note was brought in for collection and Reb
Michel's client came running to him saying that the note was
fraudulent. He had never given such a note. Never thought
of borrowing money on his house. The house was the only
thing in the world he possessed. He counted upon it for
marrying off his daughters or perhaps securing his own old
age. But there was the claimant, Simche, with the note in his
hand, and the poor man's signature clearly written upon it.

The case was argued in court, claimed and counterclaimed. The claimant brought witnesses. True, they were not all that could be desired, but then the other man had nothing but his word to offer and Michel Bercinsky to defend him. But Michel was a power to reckon with.

The trial dragged on. A hundred times the facts were restated. The poor homeowner brought his wife and daughter to court, not to testify but to weep. He asked Simche to state what the money was needed for. The claimant grew indignant. He protested with a great show of superiority that it was not his wont to pry into the affairs of people who came to him begging for money. He was very righteous and the court was impressed, especially since there was the defendant's signature, plain as day.

Michel paced the courtroom. He asked again for a look at the note. Then he demanded that the claimant stand up, face the court and once again tell the exact year, month, day and hour the note was signed. Simche did so in smooth, even tones. Michel dashed up to the window and held up the note to the light. There on the watermarked paper the date of its manufacture was clearly discerned. It was fully a year and a half later than the time of the supposed signing of the note.

Today we would think nothing of such a trick. We take it for granted that legal documents are drawn on paper bearing the date of manufacture. But in Michel's day that had not yet been established, and in Pinsk no one ever thought of referring to the paper itself when the legality of documents was discussed. In New York City any sensational story, no matter how extravagant, is a passing wonder. In Pinsk the little matter of the fraudulent note thrilled its inhabitants for many years.

Reb Michel's triumph added much to the popularity he already enjoyed. It brought him clients and money, and it

helped him win a seat in the *duma,* or town council, a place
rarely given to a Jew.

How he emptied his pockets because of personal vanity,
in the interest of the poor, or for the honor of his children,
and how Simche avenged himself for his public humiliation,
I will tell you presently.

7

When I was a little girl, I used to visit grandfather's house.
I don't ever remember going with mother but I do remember
going with my sister Rose. We were both about the same
size and age. We clasped hands and walked down the "narrow little lane" to reach grandfather's house. Coming within
sight of it, we often found curious oxcarts drawn up in front
of the gate. They were made of large planks of wood, peasant carts, crudely put together. They had large wheels and
the animals pulling them held their heads low, weighed
down by the heavy harness. Presently their owners appeared from out of grandfather's house. They were curious
people with long hair which was cut off straight all around
their heads and fell in thick fringes about their necks. They
wore coarse long garments which resembled yellowish
woolen sacks, tied about the middle with a cord or some sort
of sash. They had no shoes but something which we called
laptches or *postoles,* a sort of foot covering without heels, made
of cloth or felt. These were kept in place by lacing them to
the rag-covered legs, as far up as the knees. The peasants
wore little leathern bags about their necks, in which they
kept their coarse tobacco and copper coins. They reeked
terribly of the weed and of some other strong smell which
is hard to define. They talked in loud voices, opening their
mouths wide, and showing their tongues as they spoke.

Their voices sounded hollow, and they blew out their words as one would if he had a hot potato in his mouth. Sometimes they would sit on the pavement or in their carts to eat. Doing so they would remove their huge caps for a moment, cross themselves and dig for their food into the bags (*torbas* they were called) which they wore slung about their shoulders. Rose and I would watch them take a big bite of coarse black bread and a little bite of a whiter kind of bread for a relish.

These were the peasants of the surrounding country, Reb Michel's best and most reliable clients. At the time we knew them as such, grandfather was an old man past seventy and his practice had been greatly reduced. But in his heyday his peasant clientele was something to wonder at. On market days when they drove into town to sell their products, they came in crowds to grandfather's house. One wanted to adjust an inheritance, another to dispute a tax claim; a third had an argument with a neighbor over the boundary line of his field, while many wanted to make sure that the men buying their hay or potatoes or eggs were not cheating them. Their faith in Reb Michel was boundless. Affectionately they called him "our old one," referring not to his age, but to his sound judgment.

Many of the peasants were rich enough to pay for Reb Michel's services in red-backed ten-ruble bills, though most could pay only in farm products. Many others paid what they could and brought along gifts: a sack of meal, a pail of honey, a basket of eggs or a load of potatoes. As a result, his larder was bursting with plenty, and the cellar of the house was stored with barrels of apples, potatoes, sauerkraut and pickles of grandmother's own making. The storehouse in the yard was full of sacks of flour and meal, baskets of dry beans and peas and everything else that a great household would need. Even in my day—that is, when Rose and I came visiting—we saw the great closets in the anteroom stacked with jars of rendered chicken fat, jam and preserves, and cupboards full of wheaten products—bread, rolls, *kuchen* and cake. I remember grandmother Yentel standing before those packed shelves on Thursdays, distributing enormous white rolls and loaves of white Sabbath bread to the poor of the town, who came all day in a steady procession to collect their portion for the coming Sabbath.

On Friday nights, that is on the eve of the Sabbath, the family assembled about the enormous table in the *salle*, as the living room was called. How big that table was I really cannot say. If you remember how many children there were, if you remember, too, that when they were married their number was doubled, tripled and quadrupled, and that grandfather would never sit down at a Sabbath meal without having a couple of *orchim*—guests—at his board, you will have some idea of how large that table had to be.

In my memory that table lingers as something vast and glorious. I remember one Purim day peeking into the *salle* for a glimpse of the table. There it stood in its tremendous length across the room; six, eight, twelve shimmering silver candlesticks all lit up with wax candles. Chairs and chairs and chairs around that table and upon it—but here one must take breath—upon it, that vast Purim *kaylitsch,* the twisted white loaf of six strands made especially for the occasion, which no one but Yentel could braid together. In achieving this miracle she kept on adding to the length of the strands as she went. How the bread was ever placed in the oven for baking, I do not know. All I remember is that a procession of people carried it on a board, like so many stretcher bearers, across the hall from the dining room, where it was made, into the kitchen, where it disappeared from sight, only to reappear again on the vast table, looking shiny and golden brown, its many little adorning crowns studded with raisins. Cutting the Purim *kaylitsch* was an honor bestowed only upon grandfather. He went about the task with great ceremony, while thirty or forty pairs of eyes gazed upon him with awe.

That was in my time. Back in his glory, and at one period in particular, his table actually extended into the courtyard of his house and wound around it. There was a year of famine in the town. The crops had failed; the fields were parched; the cattle were starved. There was nothing to eat. People who had stored away provisions kept them secretly for their own use. Those who had nothing begged in vain. People were falling in the streets for want of food. It was then that the extension of Reb Michel's table began.

The constant additions to the original house had at last produced a courtyard of large enough dimensions to please its owner. It was flanked by the original but enlarged domicile on one side and by a more modest house on the other; the storehouses and barn formed the back enclosure, while out in front was a high picket fence with a great double gate. When the famine fastened upon the town, Reb Michel in characteristic and dramatic fashion announced in *shul* that in the courtyard of his house those who were hungry would be fed. Unmindful of what was going to happen to his own family if the famine continued, he ordered that his cellars and storehouses be opened and that what these contained be prepared for the hungry. Sacks and bags, boxes and barrels were dragged into the open.

Rough tables were constructed and placed in rows about the courtyard. Temporary stoves were built under the open sky and the great copper cauldrons used for festive occasions were put to daily use. For weeks every servant and member of the house was busy cooking yellow cornmeal and serving it with fresh bread and butter to the famished hundreds.

When the famine passed, Reb Michel was, as you may well believe, a greater favorite than ever. Jew and Gentile alike admired his magnanimity and yielded to the charm of his personality. He was truly the leader of the town. In the town council, which consisted of eight people, most of them Christians, he was at this time chosen as *golva,* or head. There was no monetary compensation for a member of the *duma,* but it was the highest honor the town could bestow on one of its inhabitants.

Along with his popularity, envy of him arose among less-favored members of the community, and the hatred his enemies had for him became all the more intense. This group included Getzel Tsichovsky, a lawyer of much ability, as well as our friend Simche, the man Michel had publicly exposed.

What perplexed the people who envied him was this: here was a man who, despite his lack of training and wealth, and in the very face of his avowed Chassidism, had become the leader of the town. True, he wore a frock coat, his linen was immaculate, and he carried a silver-handled cane and smoked imported cigars; still Bercinsky was an untrained orthodox Jew, a *Chassid,* and he was made the head of the *duma.* It was a thing that academically trained minds could not understand or accept.

There were still others who looked slightly askance at Reb Michel. They were the extreme orthodox or fanatical element. This man Bercinsky was entirely too radical for them. The frock coat, cane and imported cigars were seen from an entirely different viewpoint. He was much too much the man of the "assimilated" world.

The orthodox Jews ignored the fact that the Czar, in his

intense drive for Russification, had ordered that gabardines be discarded, beards and sidelocks cut. They stuck to their ancient form of dress: long gabardines, knee-length trousers, long white stockings, low shoes and large hats. For special occasions the wide-brimmed hats would give way to the *shtreimel*—a great round fur cap. If hoodlums took advantage of the Czar's orders and attacked Jews in the streets, forcibly cutting short their gabardines, beards and sidelocks, it was the duty of the Jew to take the humiliation as best he could but adhere nevertheless to the old traditional costume. Michel Bercinsky would have none of it. True, he did not cut his beard; but, though a *Chassid,* he wore no gabardine, nor long white stockings. An orthodox Jew, he wore no sidelocks and fearlessly hobnobbed with Christians. In the opinion of the fanatical he was every inch a European—a suspicious matter.

If from what I have said you have the idea that your great-grandfather was a man easy to get along with, let me hasten to correct the impression. He was a man of violent temper, of flashing wit and stormy passion. His children feared and adored him at the same time—all except Dvay-reh, who hated him with all the bitterness of her broken life. All his sisters and his brothers, uncles and aunts, nieces and nephews and cousins to the second, third and fourth degree removed, worshipped him.

And there grew up innumerable Michels, because after a certain time every male child born into the family, no matter how remote the relationship, was called Michel for the man who was a hero to them.

You will better understand the force with which his personality projected itself into future generations if you will remember that, according to Jewish tradition, a child may not be named for a living person. All the Michels had to wait until the end of his long life before they could come into being. There are any number of Michels living today in America who were named for the man who dominated distant Pinsk many years ago.

8

It happened that while Reb Michel was at the height of his popularity, conflagrations broke out in various sections of the town. Though there was no such thing as insurance at that time, the fires were obviously of suspicious origin. Pinsk was built of wood. Not only dwellings, but churches, synagogues and public buildings were made of local lumber. Even the sidewalks, where there were any, were merely planks of wood nailed across extended beams. No wonder then the city was in a panic when fires were reported everywhere. The *pazharne komande*—the volunteer fire brigade— rushed with buckets and barrels from one section of the town to another. The fires started so frequently that reports were carried to the governor of the province, who decided to take the matter in hand. One day his personal representative came down in state, all the way from Minsk, to have the matter investigated.

The town was excited. The governor's personal representative! The citizens turned out to meet the envoy and to help in the investigation. Questions and answers, noise and confusion, seemingly nothing was gained. Finally the townsfolk gathered in the marketplace. People were asked to speak up. Perhaps some clue to the incendiaries would be found.

Up stepped Simche. He knew who was responsible for all this evil. He pointed to Michel Bercinsky. There stood the man whom thieves would not rob! The man who permitted

Danielke to escape. The man who in the midst of famine had enough to feed the poor of the town in his own private courtyard, out of his own private pocket!

There was a roar of excitement from the populace.

A few days later, after some secret sessions, the governor's representative left Pinsk. The town was quieted, but passions seethed underneath. In secret corners, in whispered conversations the crowds talked in nervous expectation. People knew Reb Michel. They also knew Simche. But the man had dared to make a public accusation before government officials! What did he know? Who was to be involved? It was the Czar's government they were dealing with now, a devastating power which had little patience with and less mercy for Jews.

I cannot describe the gloom that fell upon Reb Michel's house. To this day members of the family, referring to that period, lower their voices and speak with bated breath. Life was a matter of waiting for the fall of doom. In the silent house the curiously audible clock seemed to be ticking off the hours which approached catastrophe. For two weeks this went on. Then—and here the Bercinsky taletellers raise their eyebrows and wet their lips in ominous expectation—on Yom Kippur night when, after a day's fasting, the family had gone to bed, someone knocked at the door.

You must understand that in Pinsk any knock on one's door was significant. People did not ask permission to enter each other's houses. They just walked in and said, "Good morning" or "God help" or simply "Peace." A knock on the door meant officialdom, or trouble of some other nature.

The door was opened. In walked the police captain, who heretofore had been a very good friend of Reb Michel's. He was followed by two strangers, government officials newly arrived from Minsk. They were curiously polite. Would *Gos-*

podin (Russian for "Mister") Bercinsky be good enough to get dressed and accompany the gentlemen? With good grace Reb Michel dressed, lit his fine cigar, put on his coat. An officer approached him. "You are under arrest," he said.

Outside the door, a closed carriage drawn by a pair of horses was waiting. It was the mail cart that went to Minsk. After a trip of many days, during which the horses were changed many times, they arrived in that city, the capital of the province, where Reb Michel was put into prison on a charge of arson.

For five weeks he sat behind bars while the wheels of Russian justice turned in their slow and notoriously incompetent fashion. The Jewish population of Minsk was in a state of excitement. Michel Bercinsky's name and importance had reached this community through the interrelationship of the merchants and *Chassidim* of that city and Pinsk. Much to the surprise of the prison officials, the foremost Jewish citizens of the town—bankers, merchants, rabbis and scholars—came in a steady procession to the prison cell, bringing not only words of cheer but gifts of every kind, including great trays of food.

Meantime Pinsk was in turmoil. Who knew how long the investigation would go on? Something would have to be done. Getzel Tsichovsky was appealed to, but he and his followers moved not an eyelash. Tsichovsky's opportunity to be the leader of his community had come at last, so why should he bestir himself to bring back the man who would take that leadership away? The extreme orthodox element, always frightened by government action, stroked their beards cautiously—what could they in their helplessness do for Reb Michel, the man of the modern world? Simche and his crowd were of course jubilant. But the common people of the town rose to their hero's defense. They could not call

protest meetings, but the congregation gathered in the *shul.*
Black candles were lit, prayers were offered and Divine
guidance invoked.

Finally the town determined a form of action: a petition
to the governor beseeching him to set aside all suspicions
and charges, setting forth Reb Michel's character and standing and Simche's possible reason for indictment. It was done.
The petition, bearing countless signatures, was dispatched
to the capital of the province. Jewish Pinsk sat back to wait.

But Yentel could not wait with them. She was disconso-
late. Her Michel had been accused. He was languishing in
prison, and she had to act. Remember that Michel's wife
knew only the hamlet in which she was born and the house
in Pinsk to which she was brought as a child. Remember,
too, that she had always been surrounded and protected by
scores of people, that she had no education whatsoever, and
that she knew nothing at all of the ways of the world. Yet
this ignorant little woman, with child as usual, found her
way not only through officialdom, but into the very house
of the governor of the province. Yentel wanted no briefs of
right or wrong. She cared not a whit for investigations. She
wanted her husband, her Michel.

Once in the governor's presence, Yentel threw herself at
his feet and, in the quaint Polish of her village, implored his
aid. So tellingly did she plead that the great man stooped,
raised her to her feet and kissed her brow. "Do not weep or
worry, my dear little woman," he told her, "your husband
will be restored to you."

To this day my mother, whose version of the story I am
giving you, sheds tears of compassion when she tells the tale
of the governor's sympathy for Yentel.

I do not mean to detract from the effectiveness of Yentel's
effort when I tell you that by the time she reached Minsk,

the petition with its many signatures was already in the
governor's hands, and that investigation brought no evidence to substantiate Simche's charges. Michel was indeed
restored to his wife and to Pinsk, where he returned in
triumph.

A short time later Reb Michel's cup of happiness brimmed
to overflowing when Yentel, after having presented him
with eight girls in succession, gave birth to a boy, his second
son, Avrom. The circumcision ceremony was the occasion
for a great feast in which the entire town participated. The
celebration lasted for two weeks and was capped with the
presentation to the *shul* of a gold-embroidered *porocheth*—the
ornamental curtain suspended before the sacred Ark of the
Law. On it was triumphantly recorded the birth of the long-
awaited second son, who sixty years later was destined to
die of starvation in a wartime breadline.

9

Two startling things happened shortly after Michel's return and the celebration of Avrom's birth. One was the great
conflagration of Pinsk; the other was Simche's end.

The fire started in the same unknown manner as the many
I have already mentioned. This time, however, the primitive
fire brigade with its water barrels and comic fire extinguish-
ers did not succeed in stemming its course. A great wind had
fanned the flame into a furious blaze. Block after block of
houses was consumed. When the fire reached the vicinity of
Reb Michel's house, the poor and humble who felt bereft
during the period he was away gathered about his house and
vowed that it should not burn. With buckets, pitchers and
pots of all description they surrounded the building, climbed
its roof and poured water upon its walls. Others linked

themselves into a chain, passing the water from the well in the yard to the people on the roof. The house did not burn.

Simche's end was this: he was suspected of starting the great fire as well as the many lesser ones, all of which he had probably planned with the intention of fixing the blame on Reb Michel. Now it was Reb Michel who was leading the investigation, and evidence was accumulating. There was no avenue of escape from impending Siberia but one: death. Dreadful though it was, it had the possibility of involving the man he hated more than anything else in the world. So Simche did a fearful thing. In the dead of night he stole into Reb Michel's yard. He stood over the well and cut his own throat with a cobbler's knife. His body and the knife were found the next morning in the well.

It was Simche's wife who told of his motive, of the oath he had taken that he and Michel should be damned together in eternity. And it was Simche's friend, the cobbler, who told of the missing knife after Simche's little visit.

10

On Fridays there was a tremendous bustle in grandfather's house. Floors were scrubbed, silver polished, shoes blackened, clothes brushed. The Sabbath was at hand and everything must be made to shine. I remember one particular Friday:

My grandmother is standing by the smaller table in the dining room where on weekdays all except grandfather take their meals. (He alone always eats in the *salle*, at the very large table.) She is rolling out a vast sheet of yellow dough. Because she is short and cannot reach far over the table, she circles it, rolling the dough from every side. She keeps on rolling until the entire tabletop is covered by the thin yellow sheet. She looks at it contentedly, throws a white cloth over it to keep the flies off and waddles off through the door. I run out of the room, across the anteroom into the entrance hall, across the hall to the kitchen, where I stop at the door. Such a variety of wonderful odors! The Sabbath meals are being prepared. Nothing else in the world can smell that way. I open the door cautiously and slip into the room. Someone is throwing big logs into the oven getting it ready for baking. I catch a glimpse of its depth. It is vast, deep and half round. A bright fire is burning in it. All around the kitchen on tables and benches are huge earthenware pots and all manner of pans. Old Sosche is cooking a cauldron full of *gefullte* fish on the *pripechuk* (a contraption in front and to one side of the oven used for quick cooking over an open fire). Sosche's daughter, Channa, is pounding sticks of cinnamon in a brass mortar, clanging the pestle against its sides; Itche, Channa's son, is bringing in more wood for the fire; a tall man with a little gray beard, the town's water carrier, is carrying in buckets of fresh water and emptying them into the water barrel. Someone is grating horseradish on a huge grater. Before I can get a chance to see what all the others are about, someone gets hold of me and puts me out of the room. Nobody has time to be bothered by children *erev Shabas* (on the eve of the Sabbath). Everybody is anxiously watching the clock. Nobody may touch fire after the sun sets or all of the next day. All the cooking must be done for this and the holy Sabbath day before the Sabbath candles are lit, so the people in the kitchen are working feverishly. In fact, they have been up most of Thursday night scaling fish, salting meat, plucking fowl, cutting vegetables and baking bread.

I sit down on the steps leading into the courtyard and allow the Sabbath smells to envelop me. The pungent fragrance of the *gefullte* fish, the odor of dill dropped into the chicken broth, the smell of the newly baked *challe* (special white Sabbath loaves) and *kichlach* (yeast cakes filled with chopped almonds, raisins and cinnamon). I know, too, that soon they will be putting the *tzimmes, tscholent* and *kugel* into the oven. *Tzimmes* is a dish of carrots cooked with a bit of fat meat, sugar and dumpling. *Tscholent* is a combination of meat, potatoes and beans. *Kugel* means either a sphere or a pudding. When it goes into the *tscholent* it is both. It is made of flour, fat, raisins, nuts and loads of other things, molded into a ball and cooked right in with the *tscholent.*

As soon as the *kichlach* and *challe* are out of the oven, the *tzimmes* and the *tscholent* will go in. The oven will then be closed, plastered over and sealed tight until the next day when the family is assembled for dinner. When the huge earthenware pots come out of hiding, the food will be cooked to perfection. The *tzimmes* will be rich red, the *tscholent* will be the gold and brown of copper, and the *kugel* will be a glittering mass of ambrosia.

I am still on the stairs waiting for grandmother Yentel. She is nowhere to be seen. Channa runs out of the kitchen and into the dining room. I follow her and behold a miracle performed. She takes the golden sheet of grandmother's making, rolls it into a long tube. A sharp glittering knife appears, and Channa goes to work with a will, reducing the thing to a million shreds. The way the knife follows her rapidly retreating fingers without cutting them off is something to wonder at, but it goes on and on until the last solid bit of the tube is done. The golden sheet has been reduced to a heap of noodles!

But here comes grandmother. She looks so queer with a strange cap on her head, her face hot and red. She has just returned from the "ritual bath" where she has been cleansed and scrubbed and where she was obliged to duck three times under water while a prayer was said over her.

Later I learned that all Jewish women are obliged to cohabit with their husbands after having taken the ritual bath. I also learned that grandmother Yentel and most women of Pinsk immediately looked up into the sky upon leaving the bathhouse and passed the bearded bathhouse keeper without looking at him. This was in order that they might have an exalted child and not one resembling the first living object they might happen to encounter. Since the bathhouse keeper was always at the door, he invited the snubs so generously handed out to him.

But now my grandmother is clean and fresh for the Sabbath. In a little while she will appear in her Sabbath best, ready for *shul* and the lighting of the Sabbath candles.

It is Saturday, at twilight. The Sabbath is about to end, but the peace of the day is still in full possession of grandfather's house. The men are in *shul.* The young people are walking by the river's edge. Because no work is permitted on the Sabbath, by man, woman or beast, the peace is complete. The servants are either sleeping, sitting idly on the garden steps or visiting their kin. Only old Sosche, the aged servant who has been in the house for fifty years, lingers in the kitchen. She watches the family with tender regard. Someone may want a glass of tea. Since no fire may be kindled on the holy day and the samovar could therefore not be set up, she has an earthenware jug full of hot water ready in the depths of the still warm oven.

For some reason there is no one but grandmother Yentel in the large living room on the other side of the house. The snow-white Sabbath cloths still cover the tables in the *salle* and in the smaller dining room. Grandmother Yentel sits alone by the smaller table. The back of her chair is placed against the wall so that she faces the clock in the living room. She is dressed in her Sabbath clothes: a black satin jacket buttoned down the front with many little buttons over a black satin skirt; a collar of white ruffled lace sets off her face, which is soft, pink and round. Her eyes are lustrous brown, her eyebrows arched and fine. The hair of her handsome brown wig is parted in the middle, drawn down over her ears. The back of her head is covered by a black lace headgear which falls in graceful folds down to her shoulders. She wears long earrings made of many little diamonds. They are so long and heavy that they have stretched the lobes of her ears to an unusual length. Her cherished possession is her necklace of true pearls, which she wears wound three times about her throat. Because one must not carry anything on the Sabbath, her large white handkerchief is fastened under the belt of her jacket.

Grandmother Yentel sits in her chair, a short, round figure, her plump white hand resting on the table. The twilight deepens. It is dusk now. She turns her head slowly and glances out of the window to see if the first star of the evening has yet appeared. With it will come the end of the Sabbath. She waits. Presently a little light twinkles in the sky. Swaying softly Yentel chants in a low, sweet voice:

> *God of Abraham, Isaac and Jacob*
> *Guard your beloved nation Israel from all evil.*
> *The beloved holy Sabbath is passing*
> *And the beloved week is approaching*
> *With fortune and prosperity*
> *With health and blessing. Amen.*

She chants on and on, telling a tale of a cock dressed in gold and silver standing on top of something or other; but the import of the tale escapes me, for the room is dark now, and Dvayreh has told me of goblins and evil ones, and lost stray souls who linger in the shadows of the Sabbath and will not return to their torments until the lights are lit. Then, suddenly, there is joyous commotion on the steps and in the entrance hall. Grandfather and a number of men have come from *shul.* They come in cheerfully calling, "A good week! A good week!"—stressing the "good." Immediately someone brings a light from the kitchen, the *Havdalah* (Sabbath) candle is produced together with the spice box containing herbs from the Orient and a large silver beaker for the blessing of the wine. The candle, prettily colored, is made of six strands, one for each day of the week. Burning together they represent the holy light, the radiance of the Sabbath. The beaker is large, luminous and engraved. The spice box, made of beautiful filigree silver, boasts a steeple and a silver flag. Grandmother sets wine and egg cakes and a bottle of brandy on the table.

With everybody standing around him, grandfather lights the candle. He fills the beaker with brandy, allowing the liquid to overflow its rim. This is for a "full week" to come. Holding the cup on the palm of his hand, he blesses the Creator of the fruit of the vine. Grandmother hands him the spice box. He opens its little door. A curious fragrance fills the air. Something strange, remote, envelops us. Spices from the Land of Israel, we are told. The strangeness is dear to us, the remoteness near, for always, whenever there is rejoicing, we are told of our home, of the Land of Israel from which we have been exiled and where someday we shall return. Grandfather makes a blessing to the Creator of all spices. Other ceremonies follow, indicating the hope of honest toil, and the everlasting faith in God.

Finally the moment we children have been waiting for arrives. Grandfather dips the lighted candle into the saucer holding the overflow of the *Havdalah* cup. The liquid leaps into a blue flame, through which everybody passes his fingers for good luck. The men do it quickly, catching the flames in their hands and dipping these into their pockets. This was for riches and prosperity in the coming week. Then, still rubbing their hands together, all cry, "A good week! A good week!" The Sabbath is over. The tablecloths are removed; the Sabbath clothes are taken off. Voices, manners, conversations change. Quiet, orderly speech is over. The noisy, prosaic ways of everyday life have returned.

11

Grandfather is pacing the living room. His head is bent, his hands are clasped behind him. He is worrying. Everybody says so. Reb Michel is worrying about money.

No matter how much this man earned, he was almost always virtually penniless. As fast as the money rolled in, out it rolled again. It had to be given away—to the *shul,* to the hospital, to the Hebrew school, for *hachnosses kalleh* (money collected as dowry for some poor girl who otherwise could not get married), for the privilege of being a *sandik* (the honored man in whose lap a newborn boy is circumcised), to teachers for the education of his sons, to friends, to relatives, to this man and that, for household expenses, to Yentel—until not a *groschen* was left in his pocket. While every family in the town borrowed Reb Michel's copper cauldrons to prepare special ceremonial feasts, he himself had to rack his brains to find means for keeping these cauldrons boiling for the daily needs of his family of dependents.

He never knew what people took from him, how much they owed him, or what he owed for those whose notes he had signed. A story is told of how *Arele der Vatnik* (Aaron the cotton-wool seller), a baker of the town, on his deathbed demanded that Reb Michel be brought to him; he could not otherwise die in peace. It seems that Reb Michel was in the habit of giving the poor little notes to be carried to the baker requesting him to give the bearer and his family bread and rolls whenever they needed them, which of course was every day of their lives. Every note ended with the injunction: "charge it to me." The baker not only charged, but overcharged. At the end of many years the accumulated sum Reb Michel had overpaid represented a considerable figure. Now *Arele der Vatnik* was dying; but the man could not go to his peace with that on his conscience.

A similar instance occurred when the wine merchant Ayzer, who had cheated Reb Michel as Arele did, while supplying a host of people with wine for Passover for a period of years, sobbed out his confession. The occasion, however, was not the wine merchant's own imminent death but that of his daughter, who was laboring in childbirth. Ayzer believed that she was being punished for his sins and hastened to Reb Michel to confess his theft and to seek forgiveness. The daughter recovered, but poor Ayzer had to face the community for many years as a self-confessed thief.

Reb Michel's heedless giving troubled his aged friend, Reb Zimel Blucher. This old man was wise and good and quite out of patience with Michel's reckless generosity. No amount of talking could induce the younger man to keep his palm closed. So Reb Zimel took to borrowing money for himself. He put on a sorry air and demanded ten rubles one day, fifty another. Once he asked for a hundred, another time for a hundred and fifty. Reb Michel handed out the requested sums, never stopping to ask for a return, never knowing how much money had been borrowed. Reb Zimel stroked his long white beard and held out his hand: "Give, brother, give."

A day came when Reb Zimel found Michel pacing the sidewalk. A sure sign of trouble. What was wrong? Oh, just a little thing: the new wing of the house was about to be completed and Michel had no money with which to finish the roof. The rainy season was at hand, and there was the house with the roof open. It was exasperating to say the least. Michel continued to pace. Reb Zimel lit a cigar, stroked his beard and toddled home. Next day he returned. Michel was pacing the living room. Reb Zimel whispered to his troubled friend: "What would you say if I could get you a few hundred rubles?" What indeed! Michel looked at him with hope.

"Can you really?"

Reb Zimel dug into his pockets and produced twenty-eight hundred rubles, all of which he had taken from Michel.

If you think that this had the effect Reb Zimel had hoped for, you are mistaken. Of course Michel was overjoyed; of course the roof was finished and the house was saved. But the completion of the new wing called for a celebration in honor of God's goodness; and the celebration called for giving, giving—sharing what one had with God and man. That was the philosophy of Reb Michel's life, for he was a true *Chassid*. (A *Chassid* is a follower of the Besht—Israel Baal Shem Tov, the Master of the Good Name [1700–1760], who taught a doctrine of piety, pantheism and cheer. God the omnipresent and omnipotent, with whom one could ever be in communion through prayer, was to be approached not in fear or sorrow but in cheer and joy.)

Well, then, Reb Michel was worrying about money. Purim, the Feast of Esther, was only a few days off, and he did not have the means to meet the demands of the day. He needed some two hundred rubles, and he had no idea where the money was to come from. He kept pacing the room but could reach no solution to his problems. He finished with a sigh and with a deep expression of faith, "God will help," adding, *"Es vet kumen der goy."* This latter phrase, in translation, means simply: "The Gentile will come." It originated with the coming of the peasants, they who brought him all the good things of field and barn. The phrase had now come to mean that the material needs of life would somehow be met. And usually they were. Because grandfather's popularity continued even in his old age, something usually did turn up, and likely as not, the *goy* actually did arrive. Then, as if by a miracle, grandfather became young again. The color rose to his cheeks, his eyes sparkled, and his mood was jubilant, for Purim could be celebrated with the traditional merrymaking.

Purim, as you know, is the celebration that marks the defeat of Prime Minister Haman who, during the reign of King Ahasuerus of ancient Persia, had plotted the destruction of the Jewish people living within its borders. Through the intercession of Queen Esther, he was himself destroyed, together with his ten sons.

The celebration begins on Purim eve, in *shul,* where the story of Esther in the Old Testament is joyfully read to the assembled multitude. (The men sit downstairs, the women up in the gallery.) At every mention of Haman's name there are general cries of derision while the children howl and make as much noise as possible with *gragers*—noisemaking contraptions especially made for the occasion—and the adults beat their pews with sticks as a token of their desire to beat Haman. After the retelling of the tale and the expression of the hope that every modern Haman may meet the fate of the original one, the congregation goes home to the Purim feast.

At grandfather's house this was one of the great occasions. It was then that the festival board reached the tremendous proportions that I have already told you about and that the vast Purim *kaylitsch* was laid out in all its grandeur.

I was scarcely seven when last I saw grandfather at the Purim feast. He was then a little more than seventy years old. He carried himself erect whether sitting, standing or walking. He must have been about five feet ten, and sturdily built. He had a magnificent head; a high, square forehead was framed by long brown hair which was parted at one side and fell in smooth silken strands over his ears, reaching down to the lobes. His beard was not very long, snow white and slightly parted in the middle. His nose was strong, aquiline and proud, his eye flaming, his lower lip rather full and red.

On this Purim he wore a long black satin coat and a high silk skullcap. He sat at the head of the table beating time with his fork, leading the singing, eloquent in gesture and manner. The servant brought in tremendous platters of golden brown *gefullte* fish garnished with carrots and served with horseradish, huge bowls of golden chicken broth full of *kreplach*—"Haman's ears"—triangular patties stuffed with spiced chopped meat. The merriment was boundless, since Purim was one of the two occasions during the year when a Jew might get tipsy if he wanted to without degrading himself in the eyes of his fellow men. The feast went on endlessly. *Homantashen* (Haman's pockets)—large triangular cakes filled with poppyseeds or prunes boiled in honey—were served again and again.

The next day the home celebration was continued in another manner. Friends, family and neighbors sent *shalach-*

mones to one another. These were gifts of sweetmeats made, again, of poppyseeds cooked in honey but rolled out in a sheet and then cut into rhomboid shapes; *monolach,* they were called. Several of these would be spread on a plate together with candy in the shape of vegetables and flowers, cakes or whatever sweetmeats the family could afford. The plate was then covered tightly with a napkin. Children and servants were summoned to carry innumerable plates of such gifts. While these tokens of friendship were being exchanged everywhere, the beggars of the town were having the time of their lives. Purim was their great day. They went about from house to house saying, much in the way children do on Halloween: "Give something for Purim." No sum was too small or large to receive, and nothing could be said to insult them. They came into a house singing:

Heint is Purim	*Today is Purim*
Morgen is ois	*Tomorrow no more*
Git mir a groschen	*Give me a farthing*
Un varft mir arois	*And show me the door*

But "show me the door" is too mild a translation. *"Varft mir arois"* really means "throw me out"; which you could do on this occasion without humiliating the supplicant.

It was for the sake of these beggars and the many others who assumed that role on Purim day that grandfather worried himself to distraction. He had to have plenty of money in small change to distribute at the little table at the door of the dining room. All day long the procession of mendicants continued, and all day long something had to be put into their hands. As everyone knew everyone else in Pinsk, the needs of each beggar were familiar to the disburser. Each man was given according to his need. At the end of the day a couple of hundred rubles were thus distributed. The pleasure of giving at the little table was bestowed upon the eldest of the unmarried children in the house. Down the entire line the privilege went, each married one stepping aside to make room for the next. The only one skipped was Dvayreh, poor Dvayreh, of whom I shall tell you more.

But the greatest fun on Purim day was furnished by the Purim *shpiller*—that is, the Purim players—who portrayed the story of Queen Esther, Mordecai, Haman, King Ahasuerus and Queen Vashti. Don't for a moment imagine that the players were actors in any ordinary sense. They were just any villagers who cared to take part in the performance for the sake of making a few *groschen.* Beggars, cobblers, water carriers, tailor's apprentices all became actors in the drama of Jewish deliverance. They decked themselves out in outlandish finery over their workday clothes, with paper crowns for the king and the queen. They added colorful rags to their costumes to convey the sense of something strange and exotic. Since no woman would think of joining in the Purim *shpiel,* the part of the beauteous Esther was usually played by a beardless youth. Should such be wanting, however, the players were in no way perturbed. The man who had the squeakiest voice would then be called upon to be the queen. If his beard happened to be long, thick, full-blown and unruly, it did not matter much. It was then encased in a large handkerchief (usually a red one) and the mustaches hidden as well as possible. The lovely queen, choking on the beard that filled her mouth, then went on with the play. It was a great sight to see ancient Persian royalty arrayed in all manner of rags, sputtering their lines in a mixture of Yiddish and German—by which the performers sought to dignify their feat.

My brother Abe tells me that many companies of players came to grandfather's house after the feast was over and that they played "Queen Esther," "Joseph and His Brethren," and other so-called biblical plays until the small hours of the morning. I never saw these night performances. No doubt I was fast asleep in somebody's lap long before the *capelles*—as these troupes were called—invaded the house.

What I remember is that on Purim day the troupes of players tore into the house, without knocking at the door, of course, and started their acts without ado. They were not permitted to go on for any appreciable length of time. Aunt Fraydel, whose turn it was then to sit at the little table, stopped one performance after another with a humorous stamp of the foot and a cry of "Enough!" With a handful of small silver the players would be off to the next profitable house, while a new troupe took their place before grandfather's chair, where he sat smoking and rolling with laughter.

For many, many years grandfather Michel and his house have been gone. But he lingers in my memory as one who gave grandeur to everything he touched; his house with all the spiritual things it involved comes back to me with a strange sense of nostalgia and a curious feeling of romance, as of a tale in the long ago.

TWO

Mayshe

THE FIRST of Reb Michel's twenty-four children was Rochel-
Leah. Being a girl, she did not create much of a stir, even
though her mother was only fourteen and her father sixteen
when she was born. Indeed, it is not even generally known
among the Bercinskys that Rochel-Leah ever existed. I
learned that this girl and not Mayshe, a son, was the
firstborn only when I inquired specifically. It was Mayshe
who was always referred to as the firstborn. His name was
on everybody's lips. Mayshe the handsome, Mayshe the
gifted, Mayshe the learned.

Nobody in the family knows very much about Rochel-
Leah, except that she lived and died. Even my mother, who
is the second of the children who survived, does not know
or remember anything but the name of her older sister and
the tragic fact that she died on the eve of her wedding. It
seems, too, that there were several other girls born between
Rochel-Leah and Mayshe, and between Mayshe and Dinneh, my mother. But they died in their infancy, and the loss
of females did not matter much. Mayshe was the important
one—tall and slender, handsome and blonde.

"Blonde? Why blonde?" I asked my mother in surprise. I

have never seen a blonde specimen among all the Bercinskys I knew.

"Was grandfather or grandmother blonde?"

My mother searched her memory. No, grandfather was not blonde, of that she was certain. But grandmother—well, she did not know. Neither did any of the other children. Yentel's head had been shaved smooth as a billiard ball on the day she was married. Since she wore a wig by day and a cap at night, none of the children ever knew the color of their mother's hair.

Anyway, Mayshe was tall and slender, handsome and blonde. And he was dressed like a prince in Israel. The finest of cloth or black satin coats, the daintiest of frilled linen, the softest of patent leather boots and shoes were his. As for his prayer shawl and skullcap, they were made of the best silk obtainable.

And how he was educated! No teacher was too good for him, no expense too great. Torah, Talmud, and the principal commentaries appertaining to them were drilled into his mind by the finest teachers available. I do not know whether grandfather, remembering his own struggles, included secular studies in the program of his son's education, but of one thing I am certain: Mayshe was taught to play the violin.

The picture of Mayshe walking up and down the length of the *salle* playing his violin was indelibly inscribed in the memories of those who remembered him. Such heavenly music! Such sweetness! How could anyone compare the playing of our modern musicians with Mayshe! And while Mayshe played his violin, grandfather, sitting back in his chair puffing at his cigar, listened with rapt attention to the performance of his son—his only son for many years. (You will remember that eight girls arrived in succession before his second son, Avrom, was born.)

In fairy tales we read that when the princess arrived at a certain age, her father sent emissaries all over the land to find a fitting mate for his child. That is about what happened in Reb Michel's house when Mayshe reached his eighteenth year. The *shadchonim* (professional matchmakers) of Pinsk, as well as a number of other emissaries, were instructed to go far and wide to seek a wife for him.

In those days seeking a wife did not mean looking for a girl. It meant searching for a family, for *yiches*—pedigree, or caste, if you will. The girl was really the last thing to be considered. Of prime importance were not only her immediate forbears, but those of generations back, as well as uncles, aunts and kinfolk of all kinds, no matter how distantly related. Everything that happened in, and everybody who was connected with, a family was important in the matter of marriage. Although affluence and influence were considerations of importance, *yiches* usually involved learning and scholarship. The more scholars a family boasted, the greater was its standing. You realize, of course, that "learning" did not mean secular or professional knowledge. Doctors and lawyers were not only exceedingly rare among the Russian Jews of that time, but where they existed they were regarded as outside the Jewish ken. Nor did "learning" concern itself with the arts, sciences or languages of the time. It was entirely confined to Talmudic and biblical literature. Though this knowledge was applied to the Jewish community, it was based on life in Palestine two thousand years earlier. Here was a people holding itself in readiness to take up existence again in a country from which it had been exiled for that length of time. Here were several million people living in the land of the Czars, studying the rules and regulations not of the country in which they lived, but those of an ancient land that would be restored to them with the coming of the

Messiah. Here were thousands of little boys taken out of their warm beds at the break of icy mornings to be hurried off to schools where they would be taught the laws of a nation which no longer ruled, the geography of a land that had been turned into a barren waste, the language of a people who no longer spoke it. And these children would be mercilessly whipped if they did not take these subjects to heart.

Year after year millions of Jews living in mean little Russian ice-bound towns would celebrate planting time in Palestine, and the gathering of its nonexistent harvests. The phrase, "Next year in Jerusalem," which concluded festivities and celebrations of all kinds, expressed their indomitable hope.

Well, Reb Michel had sent out his emissaries to find something extraordinary for his son. For many months the search was on. At last one of the men came home with a breathless report. In the city of Brisk (Brest-Litovsk) there was a glorious family, "kneaded and soaked through" with rabbis. The head of that family was none other than Reb Shlaymke Reb Nochimke's—Reb Shlaymke, the son of Reb Nochim, a distinguished son of a distinguished father. Search where you would, you could not find another such family. Here was a tribe made up entirely of scholars and thinkers. Back through generations it traced its men of learning. And the women? Well, women were women, and what else could they be? They did not matter.

This Reb Shlaymke Reb Nochimke's had a daughter of marriageable age. No one knew anything in particular about her, and no one cared. It was enough that she was a daughter of this very distinguished family. The matchmakers kept traveling to Brisk carrying messages and negotiations between the two houses. Finally an agreement was reached and terms stipulated whereby the houses of Reb Michel of Pinsk and Reb Shlaymke Reb Nochimke's of Brisk would be united. A great gathering was called at Reb Michel's house for the signing of the betrothal agreement.

Since nothing could induce him to part from his beloved son, Reb Michel stipulated that instead of Mayshe's going to Brisk and receiving *kest* at his father-in-law's house, Reb Shlaymke's daughter Henye would come to live in Pinsk and receive two years' *kest* at the house of Reb Michel Bercinsky. The usual custom was reversed, the burden of providing for the young pair being assumed by the groom's instead of the bride's parents. It was arranged that Reb Shlaymke was to provide his daughter with clothes and jewelry befitting her station and that Mayshe was to receive presents according to his rank. All this being sanctioned by the spokesmen of both houses, the betrothal agreement was inscribed in a special document and signed by the proper parties. Then two plates were broken by dashing them to the ground, everybody cried *Mazeltov* (good luck) and Mayshe became a *chossen*—a bridegroom-to-be. At the signing of the agreement the wedding date was set for several months ahead so that both houses might have sufficient time to make preparations for the celebration.

In all this, neither Mayshe nor Henye was consulted. They had neither seen, heard nor communicated with each other in any way. The first news that Mayshe had on the subject of his betrothal came to him when grandfather said: *Mazeltov dir mein sun, du bist gevoren a chossen*—"Good luck to you, my son, you are engaged to be married."

How Mayshe took the announcement is not known. There is no one living now except my mother who remembers those days. Of late she, too, has become hazy, and the days of her youth, though still the most vivid period in her life, are beginning to pale. So we can only surmise how Mayshe the handsome, the talented, the beloved, reacted to the news of his coming marriage. Everything had been done according to tradition. There was no fault to find. Heretofore the best in life had been given to him in full measure. The little world he lived in had been searched to find a bride for him. There could be no shadow of a doubt but that the maiden chosen would be all that a young man's heart might desire. The wedding day loomed large and bright in the distance, and Reb Michel's household was feverishly active.

First of all the place for the celebration would have to be decided upon. It could not take place in Pinsk because Reb Shlaymke Reb Nochimke's was too important a man and could not suffer the indignity of going to the groom's house for the wedding. Nor could it take place in Brisk, because Reb Michel Bercinsky was too proud to go to anyone else's town to attend his son's wedding. It was therefore decided that the celebration would take place somewhere between Pinsk and Brisk. The chosen place was an inn on one of the highways between the two cities.

The shops of Pinsk were ransacked for the finest materials to be made into clothes for Mayshe, and into suits, gowns and dresses for every other member of the family. When the supplies ran short, purchasers were sent to Minsk and even to Warsaw to bring home finery. Tailors and seamstresses filled Reb Michel's house. Finally bands of fiddlers and other musicians were engaged. Reb Michel's copper cauldrons were called in from borrowers' homes and sent to the wayside inn. Cooks and bakers were jammed into covered wagons and sent ahead to start the cooking for the great event.

In the midst of all this frenzied preparation a message arrived from Brisk. It was an urgent plea that the wedding be postponed. The bride-to-be had taken sick! The message did not say just what was the matter with her. Reb Shlaymke begged that the wedding be put off for six months.

There was nothing else to do but comply with Reb Shlaymke's plea. Cooks and bakers were recalled, musicians discharged and clothes laid away. Then there followed anxious months of waiting. Letters were interchanged and Reb Michel was assured that all went well with the *kalleh* (bride-to-be). Before the six months had passed, however, Reb Shlaymke suggested that the wedding be delayed a little longer. In learned epistles he quoted biblical precedents wherein men had had to wait for their destined brides. There was no gainsaying the learned Reb Shlaymke, not only because he quoted scripture, but because a betrothal agreement was a sacred bond that could not be broken. Mayshe had to wait for his bride; and wait he did for a solid year.

At last there were glad tidings from Brisk. All was well. The *kalleh* had fully recovered and the marriage could now take place.

This time not only Reb Michel's house but the entire town of Pinsk burst into excitement. There was indeed cause for jubilation. Not only was Reb Michel's cherished son to be married, but the bride had been rescued from the very arms of the angel of death. Again the cauldrons, cooks and bakers were sent on to the wayside inn. Wagon loads of food followed in their wake, while an army of beggars followed the wagons. The mendicants knew that the "beggars' meal," supplied at every Jewish wedding, would this time amount to a feast. They also knew that since the wedding would be celebrated for a fortnight, for that length of time they could join in the festivities during the day and camp at night in the neighborhood of the inn. For a time it seemed as if all of Pinsk were going to attend Mayshe's wedding; then it was discovered to the great dismay of those concerned that there were two other weddings in the town on the very same day. And what grief the hosts of these other weddings felt when they found that they could procure neither cooks, servants nor musicians. Every one of these had been engaged for the Bercinskys' celebration.

A Jewish *chossen* of that time did not see his bride until the moment when he dropped a veil over her face before leading her to the *chuppe*—the wedding canopy. So it was with Mayshe, who, during all the turmoil of the wedding day, sat nervously by, waiting for that climactic moment.

There had been much whispering and talking in the *kalleh*'s camp, and the talk had somehow reached his own people. Just what it was about he did not know. His father looked grave; so did his mother, but there was no time for asking questions. He had to meet Reb Shlaymke and the elders of that family, he had to meet the hundreds of people who came to greet him, and above all he had to concentrate upon the dissertation he was to deliver before the great assemblage. This practice, imposed upon all bridegrooms, established their reputations in the estimation of their audience. Truly Mayshe had every reason to be nervous. The whole of his wedding day was spent in anxiety. Finally the wedding ceremony began. The *kalleh*, in her quarters of the house, sat in the middle of a room, dressed in her wedding gown, her head covered with a veil which Mayshe would drop over her face. Surrounded by the women who were close to her, she waited for the coming of the *chossen*. While in the main room the wedding canopy was being held aloft by its four bearers, Mayshe, walking slightly in advance of a procession led by his father and mother, came in to meet his bride. Stately, handsome and pale, he stopped before her chair, only to remain standing there transfixed with horror. Henye's face was raw and pockmarked! She had suffered an attack of smallpox.

2

Henye was about ten years older than Mayshe. She had red hair and a pug nose, both very unpopular features in the Pinsk conception of beauty. How she looked before her affliction nobody seems to have known; it was surmised, however, that since she had remained unmarried until the late age of twenty-eight—unheard of for a pious Jewish maiden—she was at no time a great beauty.

When she came home as Mayshe's wife his people did not know what to make of her. They gazed at her raw face and red eyebrows in astonishment. Then there was her curious way of speaking Yiddish in the Brisker dialect, in which *ei* is *ai, au* is *oi*. More curious still were her habits, her manners and her way of thinking.

Here was a woman who, contrary to all traditions concerning the daughter of a great house, always worked. She was either sewing, cooking or embroidering. She made things for herself and for Mayshe, and the great room assigned to them as their own was quaint with all manner of her handiwork. And how she kept washing and scrubbing herself all the time. The water carrier had a hard time providing her with enough water. Then she brought daintily concocted dishes into her room, in the middle of the night. But what was less understandable than anything else was her reading of books in foreign languages. What could a woman be doing reading anything other than the *Ze'enah-U-Re'enah* (a Yiddish paraphrase of the Bible)? And what would any Jew, man or woman, be doing with not only Russian but German books? These languages had hardly penetrated into Pinsk, and here was a red-headed, pug-nosed, pockmarked woman bringing these outlandish things into a pious Jewish house. Curiously enough, Reb Michel, who was entirely against educating his own daughters, in-dulged Henye. He listened to her conversation, smiled at the number of things she knew, and winked knowingly when she picked up a foreign book. He puffed at his cigar and thought deeply about Reb Shlaymke Reb Nochimke's and his strangely emancipated household.

The women of Reb Michel's household, however, did not share his indulgence. To them Henye was not only an enigma, but a nuisance. She was forever criticizing and clashing with them. Instead of being humble, as an ugly woman should be in her husband's home, which was full of beautiful girls, she was proud and fault-finding. It was Henye who first applied the term *yeshuvnize* (peasant woman; ignorant female) to Yentel. The name was applied to that poor woman for the rest of her life by those who sought to punish her.

Henye was having a bad time of it at her husband's house while he, now being a married man, was trying to find ways to earn a living. Mayshe, the handsome and talented, had been taught nothing practical. The two years of *kest* were coming to a close and he had not succeeded in putting him-self on his feet. His father invested thousands of rubles for him in this business or that, but somehow Mayshe could not make things go. It was whispered that the young man's heart and mind were torn by his unfortunate marriage. At this time strange tales of the unhappy life of the young pair were told; of poor Mayshe's brooding; of poor Henye's haughty way of meeting the scorn of the women who disdained her because her husband did not love her.

But a time came when a curious radiance glowed about Henye. She had conceived and was becoming big with child. With greater dignity than ever she was preparing for an event which would put an end to the talk of her being unloved. Perhaps, too, her child would be a son!

Great was the rejoicing when a man-child was born to Mayshe. Reb Michel's house was projecting itself into the future. The circumcision ceremony, which was to make a Jew of the child, would at the same time proclaim the continuance of the tribe of Bercinsky; hence preparations were made which would make the event memorable in the annals of Pinsk. Reb Michel himself would be *sandik* (the man in whose lap a newborn boy is circumcised) to his first grandchild; Reb Shlaymke Reb Nochimke's was asked to come all the way from Brisk for the occasion, and a great many other people were invited to attend.

In prescribed manner the *Brith Milah,* the "covenant of circumcision," as the ceremony is called, was set for the eighth day after the birth of the boy. The night before this event is called the *vach-nacht*—the night of watching. During this time the child must be closely guarded lest evil of any kind befall him. It was on this very night, and in the presence of the watchers, that Henye's man-child died.

A year later the horror of this disaster was wiped away by the birth of her second son. To be sure there was happiness again. But the preparations for the *Brith Milah* were far less ostentatious than those of the previous year. Somehow it was feared that in the first instance the noisy jubilation and extravagant celebration had in some way offended the Almighty. This time the preparations, though ample, were more subdued. The festivities were planned on not nearly so large a scale, and only a hundred or so people were invited to attend the circumcision ceremony. A hushed guard sat

watching Henye's second man-child during the awesome
vach-nacht. But in the morning the child was dead.

Henye's third child met with a similar fate. It too was a
boy, and, it is said, he too died on the eve of circumcision.
Such a thing had never been heard of in Pinsk. All eyes now
turned upon the woman in dread. There could be no doubt
but that a curse rested upon her.

When for the fourth time she grew big with child,
Henye avoided the town and the street and the people of
the house in which she lived. She kept to her room in silent sorrow. Her voice no longer rose among those of the
women in the house, in the *shul,* or in the marketplace.
She crept about the corridors, or out into the garden,
there to hide in the shadows of the trees. Her haughty
manner had at last been broken. She no longer held her
head high. Her ways now were humble and shrinking;
her clever tongue was silenced.

Scarcely daring to groan aloud, Henye gave birth to a
fourth child. Another son! The household hushed its tongue.
No one risked a word for fear of expressing the thought that
was in everybody's mind.

Now, as the dread eve was drawing near, Reb Michel
called the members of his household about him. He towered
above them all while he spoke solemnly. Henye was ab-
solved of all blame. If her children did not live it was so
ordained by a higher power. Who knew toward what end or
for whose sins she was being punished? All evil suspicion
must be cast aside. The will for good must prevail. There was
a newborn infant in the house and he must not be allowed
to die. The greatest forces must be called upon to intervene
between him and that power for good or evil which might
claim him as it had Henye's other sons.

Only the other day my mother for at least the hundredth

time recounted the story of the circumcision of Henye's fourth son. Awe was in her voice, tears in her eyes.

On the day of the *vach-nacht,* in the gloom of the house, Reb Michel summoned his beadle to his side.

"Write," he commanded, "what I tell you to." And he dictated a message to Reb Arele Karliner, the *tzaddik* (holy man) of the town of Karlin, the renowned Chassidic rabbi whose reputation as a miracleworker had spread throughout the realms of Chassidism.

In his message Reb Michel told the holy man of the death of Mayshe's three sons; he poured out his grief and pleaded with the *tzaddik* to come to his aid, to intercede for the innocent newborn babe, and to prevent a branch of Israel from withering before its time. He finished his plea by imploring Reb Arele himself to act as *sandik* for the child. The message was solemnly sealed and carried to the holy man.

Reb Arele responded immediately.

"Tell Reb Michel that I will come," he said. "And in my name let the child be admonished to await the day of his circumcision."

In the presence of his father, grandfather and ten bearded solemn Jews, the child was so admonished. The dreadful *vach-nacht* passed and the boy was still alive.

The next day the hushed, crowded house awaited Reb Arele. At the appointed hour a *Chassid* came running into the house:

"The *Rebbe* is coming!" he shouted.

The crowd stood in silence while the doors were opened to receive the holy man. Presently he appeared, followed by forty *Chassidim.* As they entered the room a thrill ran down the spines of the assembled people. Here were forty fiery-eyed, whiskered men, solemn with the seriousness of the occasion. Reb Arele was clad in a festive collarless gabardine

of pure white satin, bound closely about him by a white
satin sash. The exposed ruddy strength of his neck and chest
contrasted sharply with the white of his garments. His gray
beard framed a radiant face, his bright eyes looking out from
under his *shtreimel*—his great fur cap.

Reb Arele, with solemn greeting, ordered that the ceremony begin.

"Bring in the child," he commanded. He stood in the
middle of the room by the great empty chair which at this
moment was waiting to be occupied by Elijah the Prophet.

The midwife took the boy from its weeping mother. At
the doorstep of the bedroom she turned him over to the
kvater—the young man and woman who would carry him to
the great chair. As they entered the *salle* with the child in
their arms, Reb Arele stepped forward.

Boruch habo! "Blessed be he who arrives," he cried in a
voice that left his listeners in fear.

This salutation was given not to the *kvater,* nor yet to the
baby boy, but to the Prophet Elijah, who was supposed to
enter with him at this moment.

Reb Arele stood aside, making way for the invisible
prophet to seat himself in the great chair. He then ordered
the *kvater* to lay the child in the lap of the Prophet. This
done, the eager watchers trembled while Reb Arele lifted the
infant carefully and made room for Elijah to step down.
Then he sat down in his own chair with the child in his lap.
Finally he addressed awesome words to the babe. He told
him of the privilege of life, of the greatness of the God he
was to serve, of the meaning of the covenant of circumcision. He admonished him not to yield to any evil power, but
to lend himself to the forces of light and life and joy.

The *mohel,* the man who performs the circumcision, then
approached. The child was circumcised according to the law

of Moses and a name was given to him. What that name actually was nobody was told, for before God and man the boy was proclaimed *Alter*—"old one," or "old man." If then, any force threatened Mayshe's newborn son, let him know it was not a child but an *"alter"* he must contend with. Alter did not die.

In the years that followed Henye had another son and then two pretty little daughters. But she was worn and weary by this time. Pinsk, with all the torments she had endured, was no place for her. Nor could Reb Michel's house still the anguish of her aching heart. She longed for her home town, for her friends and family. She showed signs of melancholy. There was nothing else now for Reb Michel to do but part with his beloved son. Mayshe and his wife and their four little children left the city of his fathers, left the home that nurtured him, and went with Henye to live among people he did not know. How he fared there no one really knows, for he rarely wrote home. But from the events that followed, one could guess that his cup was bitter. Henye was growing steadily more melancholy. One day a letter from son to father said, unhappily, that Henye was no more.

Henye had killed herself. She went out into the yard of her house where the woodchoppers were splitting up logs for the winter. She borrowed a hatchet from one of them and split her head open.

Henye's orphaned children were reared by her family, while Mayshe, once the handsome and talented, now broken and bitter, went out alone into the world. He did not come back to Pinsk during his father's lifetime. Perhaps he never forgave his parent for the marriage he had arranged. He wandered out far into Russia and settled in Samara, a very un-Jewish town in the Ural Mountains. There he married again, and there Henye's children joined him. But nobody seems to know much about his bride or how they fared together. Mayshe became merely a memory in Pinsk.

After Reb Michel died, an old man whose white beard showed streaks of yellow came to Pinsk to collect his inheritance. It was Mayshe. Hardly anyone knew him. The two sisters whom he found in the house did not remember him. They were mere children when he had left.

Mayshe took the portion of Reb Michel's estate to which he was entitled and went to Baku, where he was then living. Nobody ever saw him again. Years later it was reported that he was driven out of that town because he was a Jew. He was a very old man by that time. Nobody knows where he went, how he died or where he is buried.

Mayshe, the handsome, the talented, passed like a tormented ghost before the eyes of those who loved him, leaving no trace behind him in Pinsk. There was little by which he could be remembered there. But to this day the songs poor Henye sang to her children may be heard in the town. Perhaps this is because she sang them in so rich and lovely a voice, or perhaps because the songs were different from those commonly heard. They lingered on in people's memories. Even I, who never knew Henye, can sing the song with which she rocked her "old one" to sleep. I heard it from the lips of those who in their day had made the poor woman's life miserable. Freely translated, it goes:

All was asleep,
Midnight it was,
No creature stirred;
Only the moon
Alone in the skies
Roamed among the stars.
And when sleep
With heavy touch
Closed the eyes of mankind

Down from the heavens
In the dead of night
An angel flew to earth,
And, closely enfolded
In his embrace,
He carried the soul
Of an unborn child.

Henye then sang of how the new soul, going to earth, questioned the angel about this flight and asked for an explanation of the many things on earth it had heard about but could not understand. To all of which the angel answered understandingly. Poor Henye! She might have asked the angel a few questions on her own behalf.

When I was a child of five I saw Alter marching with an army brigade through the streets of Pinsk. He was an ordinary infantryman. That was long after his mother had died and his father had wandered out into Samara.

Alter came to see us. A sturdy fellow in his early twenties, he laughed heartily and spoke Yiddish like a *goy* (Gentile). I was impressed by his brown face, his pug nose, his beautiful blue eyes, his curly reddish hair, and his soldier's coat and his knapsack. But above all I was impressed by his boots. Such large, shiny boots! And what a pungent odor they had! I loved that smell and everything else connected with Alter. I think I must have fallen in love with him at the time. Hearty, laughing, delightful Alter! He marched with the soldiers through the streets of Pinsk. Since that time in my childhood I have always been strangely moved at the sight of Russian soldiers marching. Alter was a vision that came to us from somewhere strange and unfamiliar and passed with a troop of singing men through the town. I could not catch the words they sang; but I caught the melody and something that sounded like words; the refrain to me sounded like *Ap la voi, ap la voi, ap la voi tri mo ye.* That was repeated over and over again. Then followed the beat of boots upon the earth.

I can still hear that sound. For many years I thought I heard the tramp of Alter's feet when at night I pressed my head to my pillow. Of course it was the thump of my own heartbeat, but I believed then that it was Alter and his troops marching through the streets of Pinsk; then I could hear the *Ap la voi . . .* dying in the distance.

We never saw Alter again or heard of him except to learn that he had died somewhere in battle.

Of what avail, then, was your agony, Henye? Where was your promise of life, Reb Arele? And you died an outcast Jew anyway, Mayshe, even if your precious Alter's blood stained the battlefield for Russia. Poor Henye . . . Mayshe . . . Alter . . .

THREE

Dinneh

I APOLOGIZE to the memory of my father for giving him what seems to be a subsidiary role in the story of my mother—Dinneh. I feel, however, that were he, the "Great Shomer," alive today, to read what I have written, he would not consider himself slighted. I think the tears would gather in his eyes, and he would brush them away with the back of his hand—in a gesture truly his.

After Rochel-Leah, who died on the eve of her marriage, my mother, Dinneh, was the first of Reb Michel's girls to survive. Being a girl, in her infancy and childhood Dinneh was considered one of those "empty nutshells" Yentel presented to Michel in such abundance. Eight girls followed the birth of Mayshe before another boy put in an appearance. It was the tradition that inspired the adage:

> *Az men hot techter,*   *If you have daughters*
> *Fargeht der gelechter*   *You have no use for laughter.*

In contrast to what Reb Michel did for his sons, his daughters were sadly neglected. According to the custom of the time, all the education a girl needed was enough Hebrew to enable her to stumble through her prayers; enough Yiddish to enable her to write a letter and to somehow read the *Ze'enah-U-Re'enah* (a translation into Yiddish of the five books of Moses); a rudimentary idea of arithmetic; and instruction in the three special duties of a Jewish woman: *licht benchen*—the blessing of the Sabbath candles; *mikva*—ritual bathing before marital cohabitation; *challe nehmen*—the giving of a portion of the bread she was baking to the priesthood of the temple. The last duty was really nonexistent, since after the destruction of the temple there was no longer any priesthood. The rite was reduced to a symbolic gesture, which demanded that a bit of the dough prepared for the baking of bread be cast into the fire.

My mother in all the days of her long life bitterly resented the meagerness of her youthful education and cordially despised the three special duties, even if she did, in a manner of speaking, observe them. She was a person of extraordinary mentality, imagination and temperament. But these attributes were given no consideration by her parents. Was she like Mayshe to be instructed in Torah and the Talmud? Sheer nonsense! Even the unconventional Michel Bercinsky would not yield to such things. According to my mother, he spent thousands of rubles on every cause and every charity in the town but denied her a ruble with which to pay for instruction in the Russian or Hebrew she had desired so much.

So Dinneh was raised as girls generally were; she received no special attention; her temperamental nature was allowed not the slightest outlet; she had no way of giving play to either her physical or mental energies or to her active imagination. The result was a volcanic energy ready to explode in the narrow confines of her environment.

Dinneh struggled through childhood valiantly. According to all accounts, at seventeen my mother was a vivid girl, powerfully built and beautiful, with a personality that could not be subdued. She was a little above medium height; her skin was tawny, her cheeks red. Her eyes were brown and fiery like her father's, her nose slightly beaked and proud, her mouth rather large and strong, her hair silken brown. Her physical strength was prodigious. When any of Pinsk's wooden sidewalks caved in, the townfolk said:

"Dinneh Michel's must have passed here."

It was when she was seventeen that her father began thinking of arranging a match for her. The young men of Pinsk were far below his desired standard. Reb Michel was then at the height of his power, and he wanted an extraordinary husband for his daughter.

It seems that Reb Michel did not profit much by his experience with Mayshe. In fact, he continued to think that he had made a brilliant match for his son. Oblivious to the misery the young people had endured, he called in the matchmakers and the marriage brokers, and the search for a *chossen* for Dinneh was on.

In all fairness to your great-grandfather, however, it must be said that at the time there was no way other than through the medium of the matchmaker or marriage broker by which a girl of the Jewish middle classes might obtain a husband. No one ever thought of love. To be sure, a man loved his wife and a wife her husband, but that was after the two were married. And even then, they were not supposed to love each other for physical reasons. Physical attraction had no great place (openly, at least) in the decorum of the day. Jewish sons and daughters married according to the laws of

Moses and according to the wishes of their parents, so that the will of God might be done and the nation of Israel increase and multiply.

Since Reb Michel was proud of his caste, and since one could not go about offering his daughter to people, there was no other way of finding a husband for Dinneh except through the marriage broker. It is no wonder, then, that he resorted to these time-honored professionals and laymen.

One day Laybele the marriage broker came to Reb Michel with the announcement that he had found "just the right article" for Dinneh. The red-headed, red-bearded, grizzled old matchmaker grew ecstatic. Far away in the city of Nesvizh there was a young man by the name of Nochim-Mayer Shaikevitsch, who was just what Reb Michel was looking for: "A find!" "An ornament!" "A savant!" "A scholar who did not know the face of a coin!"

Critics of the Jewish people who accuse them of avariciousness should pay heed to the last qualification. Here was a tribe who considered ignorance of wealth, even to the extent of not knowing the face of a coin, a virtue in the men they sought as husbands for their daughters. The instance of Reb Michel and Nochim-Mayer was by no means an isolated one. The high regard for learning and its preference to all other qualifications in a *chossen,* was, as I pointed out in my story of Mayshe, common. So common, indeed, that it found its way into a lullaby with which mothers rocked their babies to sleep:

> *Unter Yonkele's vigele*
> *Shtayt a klor veis zigele*
> *Di zigele is geforen handlen*
> *Rosinkes mit mandlen.*
> *Vas is di beste zach?*
> *As Yonkele zol lerrnen Tanach*

Vas is die beste schayreh
As Yonkele zol lerrnen Tayreh.

Under little Jacob's crib
Stands a snow-white little kid
The little kid atravelling went
On trading nuts and raisins bent
What's desirable more?
That Jacob learn the prophet's lore.
What's better than the merchant's quest?
That Jacob learn the Torah blessed.

The lullaby expresses the necessity of earning a living
through trade, and the far more desirable occupation of
learning. It is one of the most popular lullabies among Jewish mothers and, incidentally, shows the sharp discrimina-
tion against the education of girls. If the child rocked to sleep
happened to be a girl, by the name of *Soreh* (Sarah), for
example, instead of using *her* name in connection with the
study of the prophets and the Torah, the word *chossen*
(groom) was added to it:

Sorele's chossen zol lerrnen Tanach
Sorele's chossen zol lerrnen Tayreh

Sarah's *chossen* know the prophet's lore.
Sarah's *chossen* learn the Torah blessed.

The proposed *chossen* for Dinneh, this "ornament" and
"savant" who "knew not the face of a coin," would surely
have to be given consideration. Reb Michel was greatly in-
trigued. As in the case of Henye and Reb Shlaymke Reb
Nochimke's, Reb Michel sent emissaries to Nesvizh to inquire into the young man's antecedents. But this time the
inquiry was fixed much more closely upon the young man
himself. Just how much did he know? How great was his
learning? The reports that came back were exciting.

Reb Michel quickly acquiesced to the terms set by the
chossen's family, and, failing to profit by what happened to

Mayshe six years earlier, he concluded the agreement without seeing the man who was to marry his daughter. Since Reb Michel was now wealthier than he had been at the time of Mayshe's engagement, he decided to have a brilliant celebration in honor of his great catch for Dinneh. He arranged with the emissaries of the *chossen's* family to have the betrothal take place at an inn somewhere between Pinsk and Nesvizh and instructed them to immediately engage at his expense the very best place they could find. This done, he announced triumphantly to Dinneh that she had become affianced and that in a few weeks the formal celebration of the event would take place.

Then Reb Michel had the surprise of his life. A tempest exploded about his head. The house shook and the windows rattled. Dinneh did what no one else had heretofore dared. She opposed Reb Michel violently. She forgot, however, that she had inherited her furious temper from Reb Michel, who was something of a fiery volcano himself. Reb Michel's surprise may have been great, but Dinneh's was even greater. She encountered more of a conflict than she bargained for.

"Silence, you!" the despot roared after his initial outburst had left her speechless. It was not so much his stamping foot or his upraised hand that frightened the girl, as the fire in his eyes. She fled from him.

Breathlessly, Dinneh ran all the way to the house of Reb Abbe Rosenthal, her father's closest friend. She fell at his feet, and, weeping bitterly, implored him to intercede on her behalf. Now Reb Abbe was a good and wise man. Besides, he had been present at Mayshe's wedding. He considered Mayshe's present state deplorable. Reb Abbe soothed Dinneh as best he could, but she would not be consoled. Finally he promised her that he would go and see this Nochim-

Mayer. If there was anything undesirable about the young man, Reb Abbe pledged his word that he would do his utmost to prevent the engagement from taking place. It was a solemn promise. A good and true friend, Reb Abbe journeyed secretly to Nesvizh.

While elaborate preparations for the betrothal ceremony were taking place, Dinneh anxiously waited for Reb Abbe's return. My mother describes her feelings at the time as those Isaac might have had if he had known that his father Abraham was taking him to the altar to be sacrificed.

At last Reb Abbe came back. His face was shining. He had seen the young man and he was indeed an ornament! Dinneh waited breathlessly for some description. But Reb Abbe only stroked his beard with pleasure and said: "You shall see for yourself." The poor girl was frantic. Though pacified to some extent, she could not bear the thought of being plighted to a man she had never seen.

At last the day arrived. As at Mayshe's wedding, cooks, bakers and musicians had arrived several days before the event. Covered wagons full of people filled the road to the wayside inn between Pinsk and Nesvizh. In one of the last carts, dressed in all her finery, Dinneh sat and wept. She still felt as though she were being led to slaughter. The non-Jewish doctor Dumbrofsky and Llubetsky the marshal sympathized with her as the procession passed their door. Dinneh caught their remarks:

"Bidna Dinneh," they said to each other in Polish. "Poor Dinneh!" And poor Dinneh wept harder than ever. The train of wagons moved steadily forward, however, and reached their destination at sundown.

By that time the *chossen's tzad* (the bridegroom's people) had already arrived. Although they stayed in a house quite apart from the *kalleh's tzad* and although, according to custom, the men and women occupied different quarters of the buildings, there was much running of messengers to and from these various quarters, and there was an impression of some untoward commotion going on. As a matter of fact, a serious dispute was in progress in the *chossen*'s camp.

Dinneh paid no attention to what was going on or to what was being said. The women had just stopped fussing over her: braiding her hair, tying her bodice and fixing the hoops of her crinoline. Night had fallen. In the main house where the ceremony would take place and where the festivities had been prepared with a lavish hand, the musicians were playing. Dinneh glanced about and saw that all the women were now busy primping themselves for their entrances. Suddenly she stole out of the room. Sheltered by the night, she ran across the yard, right to the house where the men of the *chossen*'s party were assembled. The yard was dark, but inside the house the lights were many. She crept up to one of the windows. She lifted her skirts and knelt low beneath the window sill. Stealthily she peeped into the room. It was full of men, dozens of them. To which one of these was she to be pledged? Anxiously she scanned the bearded faces. None of them could possibly belong to the man chosen for her. They were all too old. Far away in a corner of the room she spied a young man. He was surrounded by a group of his elders who talked to him excitedly. That must certainly be the "ornament" they had picked for her.

What she saw made her heart leap. The young man was tall, slender, handsome! She could not get a very clear view of his face, but she caught sight of his black hair combed back over a high, white forehead, his small blonde beard, and his straight, short nose. Dinneh rose to her feet and ran back to the house.

She opened the door in confusion, only to be met with a

chorus of reprimands. Where in the world had she been? Everybody had been looking for her, because—guess what? —here all kinds of pent-up emotions found exuberant expression—the *chossen* had flatly declared that he would enter into no agreement whatsoever before he had seen the *kalleh,* the girl chosen for him! Had anybody ever heard of such a thing! The crowd was hard put to find the right word of indignation for Nochim-Mayer's stubbornness.

Dinneh now knew what caused all the running to and from the various quarters of all the houses, and she guessed that this was the subject discussed so excitedly by the elders who surrounded the young man in the corner of the room. So he was as anxious about her as she had been about him! It was somehow insulting, but she would indeed let him see her before anything was agreed upon. He need not take her like a cat in a bag.

The elders of both parties were nervous. It was such an unusual situation. But Nochim-Mayer had taken a firm stand and there was nothing to do but to let him have his way. It was arranged that Dinneh, guarded by her parents, would wait in the main room to meet Nochim-Mayer.

Accordingly, the three waited in the appointed place. The door opened and in came the man she had hoped would come. But he was not alone. He was flanked on one side by a tall, handsome, rather severe-faced woman—his mother, Hodes—and on the other side by a gentle-mannered, kindly man, with light brown hair and beard—his father, Isaak. Hodes' mother, *die Bobbe* Sorke—grandmother Sorke—a clever-looking woman, followed immediately behind them. As the four came nearer, Dinneh had eyes only for the young man who was to be her husband. She now saw that he was about five feet ten inches tall, that his eyes were gentle and blue gray, that his straight little nose was slightly tilted upward, that his black hair was long and silken, that his beard was soft as down, and that the fingers of his white hands were long and pointed.

The two young people were not allowed to say a word to each other. The older folk talked for a while and then No-chim-Mayer's mother, Hodes, said to him rather petulantly: "Well, you have had your way! We can now go on with the ceremony."

While the sense of what Hodes said was entirely in keeping with what Dinneh wished for, she nevertheless started to dislike Hodes at that moment. My mother says it was the older woman's tone and manner that offended her.

My father was an unusually silent man, and he died before we were old enough to be very much interested in his youth, so that we had no definite idea just what he thought of Dinneh when he first saw her. The fact that he cheerfully went through with the betrothal ceremony was one indication that he was pleased, however; and there was another.

At the betrothal, the wedding day was set eight months ahead. During this period Dinneh and Nochim-Mayer were of course separated, living in their respective home towns. During the engagement period it was not customary for the betrothed to communicate with each other. But, much to Reb Michel's surprise, one day he received a letter for Dinneh from her husband-to-be! And later more letters arrived.

You see, Nochim-Mayer's letters were unusual not only because they were written at all, in a perfect hand, but more particularly because of their amazing substance. Reb Michel, with exceeding pride, carried these epistles to *shul* and read them aloud to gasping groups of listeners. The letters were of a nature quite startling to Pinsk and its people. To begin with, Nochim-Mayer addressed his letters to his *broit*—which Henye said was the German for the word *kalleh*. And then, instead of limiting himself to learned discourse, as a scholar should, the young man spoke of the sun and the moon, and called upon the clouds to convey on airy wings tender words of greeting to his "beloved." It was this more than anything else that startled the listeners. A respectable young man was talking of love to a young woman before they were married! The people looked at one another incredulously. They did not know just what to make of it. There was something so romantic in the way Nochim-Mayer put things, something so lofty in the sentiments expressed, that no man could find it in his heart to take offense. People listened open-mouthed.

As for Dinneh, never in her wildest dreams did she think that what was happening could ever come to pass. Unsatisfied with what she could get out of life, because she could never be or do anything like the men, she suddenly found herself in the center of the stage of her world. She was the object about which a remarkable young man wove a strange web of thought and emotion. I believe Dinneh was the first girl in Jewish Pinsk who walked on air. Thus it happened that Nochim-Mayer Shaikevitsch brought the romantic conception of love into a pious Jewish house. Later he made millions of people thrill to it as, with breathless eagerness they devoured *Shomer's Romanen*—"Shomer's Romances," as his novels were called.

Who was this Nochim-Mayer Shaikevitsch? And where in the world did he get his curious romantic ideas? That is an interesting story.

2

Long ago in the city of Nesvizh there lived a man rever-
ently known as Reb Gavriel Goldberg. In his day he was
considered fabulously wealthy. He acquired his fortune by
means of his freight boats, which plied the Niemen River
and carried the raw and manufactured materials of the native provinces far out to the shores of the Baltic Sea.

At the age of about sixty-five, Reb Gavriel was a hearty
man, but, because he had no children, he had nothing in
particular to live for.

At that time, being childless was considered a calamitous
condition; it meant that a man would die without leaving a
kaddish behind him. *Kaddish* is the prayer said for the dead;
it is devoted not to one's body or soul, but to Israel and its
faith. Because the privilege of saying *kaddish* is given the sons
and not the daughters of a family, the word son and *kaddish*
had in a sense become synonymous. When a man said he
had a *kaddish,* he meant that he had a son. Dying without a
kaddish carried an implication that not only would a man's
house, name and tradition be obliterated, but that a branch
in Israel would be destroyed.

Reb Gavriel was a rich and virile man, and the thought
that his seed would never bloom plagued him severely. Nor
did he relish the thought that his wealth would one day be
distributed among strangers. He brooded over his condition.
His wife was almost as old as he was. They had been married
for nearly fifty years. Never in all that time had she given
him a child, but he had not put her aside because they were
genuinely fond of each other. But now his life was reaching
the allotted biblical span of seventy and he had nothing to
show for it in the way of the desired offspring.

Gravely Reb Gavriel turned to his friends for advice, and immediately there was a division of opinion. There were those who referred to Reb Gavriel's age and spoke with pity of the old wife. Others, however, contended that the house of Israel transcended in importance the fate of any woman, no matter how loyal and honored. The contenders for Israel's cause pointed out to Reb Gavriel the vigor of his state, and voiced their opinion that a healthy young virgin could profit by it for the benefit of his people. This viewpoint strongly appealed to Reb Gavriel. So, after a mighty struggle with himself and against the old lady's protest, he reached a decision. He would put away his wife. Accordingly he set about to obtain a bill of divorcement. But Reb Gavriel had not counted upon the staunchness of the old Jewish law which held that a man could divorce his wife if, after ten years of married life, she remained barren; but that after ten years he could not divorce her for reasons of barrenness. Reb Gavriel had waited almost fifty years, and it was too late.

Now Reb Gavriel was a rich and powerful man who was not accustomed to being opposed. But wealth or no wealth, *kaddish* or no *kaddish*, the rabbis of Nesvizh could find no way of freeing him.

Reb Gavriel's anger was aroused. For decades he had been a benefactor of the town, aiding its every cause and institution, giving much to charity, living a just and righteous life. Surely one could find a *hetter* in the law, a legal precedent, which would permit the fulfillment of his desire. He pleaded his cause eloquently, offering magnanimous provision for the woman he sought to divorce. But no excuse could be found. In great wrath Reb Gavriel took his cause to the rabbis of other towns—and the fight was on!

The story of Reb Gavriel's fight for freedom was of such importance that it was recorded in the official chronicles of the city of Nesvizh. In its day and in the life with which it was concerned, it was an epoch-making affair, involving many Jewish communities and many famous rabbis of the day. Reb Gavriel carried his case from one court to another. The question at issue was the interpretation of the law under extenuating circumstances. While several rabbis saw the justice of some of Reb Gavriel's arguments, none would accept the responsibility of freeing him. When at last a pivotal point in the discussions was reached, up rose the eminent Reb Nochim-Mayer in support of Reb Gavriel's claim. Of all the judges he alone stood out for the man's rights. Just what the exact contentions were I cannot tell you, but Reb Nochim-Mayer took upon himself the responsibility for his action. He granted Reb Gavriel the divorce he sought and gave him the right to marry again.

It was a sensational verdict, accepted in a sensational manner by the Jews of Nesvizh. But that did not end the matter, for Reb Gavriel's wife refused to receive the bill of divorcement into her hands and so make the document legally binding. Nor would she accept the many thousands of rubles that came with it for her care and comfort. She recognized neither the decree nor her husband's freedom and proclaimed herself in the face of all as the loyal and law-abiding wife of the man who rejected her.

Reb Gavriel followed up his hard-won victory with immediate action. Within the space of a few months he married again. His bride was the sixteen-year-old girl Sorke, the orphaned daughter of a good family of the town.

By this time Reb Gavriel was nearly sixty-nine. The marriage ceremony was a solemn affair with only the bride's and groom's closest friends attending. The officiating rabbi was Reb Nochim-Mayer himself, the man upon whose shoulders rested the responsibility and legality of both the divorce and forthcoming marriage. That he felt his position acutely is attested by the manner in which he conducted the marriage ceremony and startled the bride, the groom, and every attending guest at the wedding. Just as he pronounced the old man and young girl man and wife, Reb Nochim-Mayer raised his hands to heaven and exclaimed: "If this union has come about against the will and law of God, may it prove barren as the sands of the desert! If, however, I have acted according to the teachings of our lawgivers and the will of the Almighty, may it be blessed with many children and may even you, Reb Gavriel, together with your wife, live to marry off the youngest of your offspring!" Then he turned to the wide-eyed wedding guests. "Say Amen!" he commanded.

"Amen!" they whispered in secret foreboding.

It was a dramatic moment. Reb Nochim-Mayer's oath, thus publicly taken, gave it a certain solemnity. When the guests dispersed, the young bride sat still and silent, as if petrified by its fearful import.

Many are the tales regarding the manner in which the good citizens of Nesvizh watched Sorke for the next few months. The young bride, who had been so shocked by Reb Nochim-Mayer's oath, soon regained her composure. Sorke was a keen, bright girl of fine appearance. Her marriage to Reb Gavriel did not displease her. She felt herself to be an important figure in a great issue. She placed her faith in the righteousness of Reb Nochim-Mayer's decision. She accepted his oath and had faith in his prophecy. She reasoned that if she was destined to be Reb Gavriel's wife and the mother of a generation that would otherwise be denied him, she had cause to be proud of her fate. It was therefore with a great sense of dignity that she allowed the town to watch her.

Soon it was whispered about that *Sorke krimt zich* ("Sorke was making faces")—that she did not feel well. It was also rumored that she no longer appeared at the ritual bath. This state of affairs could mean one of two things: either that the bride was not living with her husband, or that she was pregnant. The watching grew keener. Sorke proved to be pregnant.

The news spread about the town quickly: "Sorke Gavriel's is going to have a child!"

It was only then that the old wife took the bill of divorcement within her hands, thus recognizing Reb Nochim-Mayer's contention that it was the will of God that it be so. The poor old woman collected her belongings, took the money that was provided for her, and went away to Palestine to die. She could not give one child to her people; she would give her bones to mix with the dust of their land.

The chief concern of Sorke's watchers now was whether her child would be a boy or a girl. Would Reb Gavriel indeed have the *kaddish* he had wanted for nearly a half-century, or would he get a girl? It was a girl he got—my grandmother Hodes. Hodes' first child was my father, your grandfather, Nochim-Mayer Shaikevitsch. He was named for the famed rabbi who had granted Reb Gavriel's divorce and wedded him to Sorke.

Sorke gave her husband many children, sons and daughters. I believe they were ten in number. He lived to be one hundred and ten and saw his very youngest child, a son, married. My mother tells of how she heard *Bobbe* Sorke (grandmother Sorke) reproving herself for marrying off her youngest child at the time she did. Had she not done so, she argued, her Gavriel would have lived on! He could not die, you see, until his youngest child was married! Such was the faith Sorke had in Reb Nochim-Mayer's oath.

3

When Reb Gavriel died, Sorke was fifty-six years old. She had been married to him about forty years. During this time she made herself not only mistress of her husband's house, but also of his freight boats, which sailed down the river and into foreign seas. She traded cleverly with all the foreigners she met, learning their languages and their ways of life. Because of her husband's advanced age, the task of raising their family fell to her. She did so fearlessly and ruled with a firm hand. She established a sort of matriarchate, bringing in her sons as well as her daughters to help her in business transactions, allowing them every opportunity for self-development. Under her direction Gavriel's barges multiplied, and their cargoes increased, and Sorke Gavriel's, as she was called, became the dominant figure in her locality, unsurpassed even by Reb Gavriel.

When Gavriel's and Sorke's first child, Hodes, came of age, she was a girl of signal beauty and attainments remarkable for that time. Dealing with merchants of many lands she, like her mother, spoke, read and wrote their languages. Yet she remained strictly pious and orthodox in her religion. Most conspicuous, however, of all her qualities was her amazing business sense. There was no doubt in her mother's mind that Hodes, like herself, could be the head of an important business establishment. So when Sorke sought a mate for her daughter, she had two things in mind: wealth, with which to establish her daughter in business; and a spiritual quality which would keep him interested in learning and the hereafter so he would leave his temporal affairs to his wife.

Sorke's choice was Isaak Shaikevitsch, one of the three sons of a wealthy house of timber merchants. In Sorke's estimation Isaak was just the sort of husband Hodes needed —a gentle youth, given to study and daydreaming, impractical in worldly matters, yet the heir to a substantial fortune. The match was made. Hodes in fact became the head of a thriving import establishment, and in time the mother of five children: Nochim-Mayer, Yoshe, Lazare, Mielke and Gavriel.

It seems, however, that Isaak did not develop according to the pattern outlined for him by his wife and his mother-in-law, Sorke. He had no desire to become the profound Hebrew scholar they wanted but inclined rather to a human idealism. His position would not have been so intolerable to the matriarchate that governed him had he not been so thoroughly unworldly and impractical. But he was both. He naively trusted everybody and gave away practically everything he owned. The climax came when, upon the death of his father, he allowed his three brothers to trick him out of his inheritance. This was a terrible shock to Hodes. To her businesslike mind, no greater dishonor could befall a man than to be so betrayed—to permit himself to be deprived of a fortune simply through the lack of ordinary business acumen.

Isaak lost grace in the eyes of his wife, the heir-apparent to the matriarchate. Thereafter there was dissension between the two. Hodes' resentment was so bitter that in time it forced Isaak out of his home to wander alone in a Russia unknown to him.

Dinneh Bercinsky Shaikevitsch Shomer, 1904. (Mandelkern Studio, New York)

Shomer (Nochim-Mayer Shaikevitsch)

Joshua Bercinsky (Feldman &
Goldman, New York)

David Bercinsky. This was a
New Year's greeting card.

Fraydel Bercinsky

Menye and Fraydel Bercinsky

Shaikevitsch family group, Pinsk, 1889. Left to right: Dinneh, Rose, Miriam, Abe, Anna. Girls' hair was clipped because of a typhus epidemic.

Miriam Shomer
Zunser and her
sister Rose Shomer.

Miriam Shomer, 1903.

Wedding supper, marriage of Miriam Shomer and Charles Zunser, New York, December 26, 1905. (1) Miriam Shomer Zunser, (2) Charles Zunser, (3) Elyakum Zunser, (4) Dinneh Bercinsky Shaikevitsch Shomer, (5) Abraham Shomer, (6) Rose Shomer, (7) Anna Shomer, (8) Johann Paley, (9) Abraham Goldfaden, (10) Rose Pastor Stokes, (11) Haiye Bercinsky Rosenberg, (12) Abraham Chaim Rosenberg, (13) photograph of Shomer (Nochim-Mayer Shaikevitsch) who had died a month before. Avrom, Dvayreh, Fraydel and Menye Bercinsky are present but unidentified.

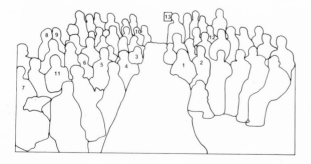

Circa 1940. Miriam and Charles Zunser, their children, children's spouses, and grandchildren in a Brooklyn home. Left to right, seated on floor, Helen Zunser Wortis with Avi Wortis, Miriam Zunser, Florence Zunser Saltz, Frances (Mrs. Shomer) Zunser, Joseph Wortis, Charles Zunser with Henry Wortis, Shomer Zunser with dog and Emily Wortis.

4

What I have told you of Reb Gavriel and Sorke, of Hodes and Isaak will give you an idea of the curious web that formed the background of Nochim-Mayer Shaikevitsch—Dinneh's *chossen.*

I have already noted that the record of Gavriel's landmark divorce and remarriage were entered into the official chronicle of Nesvizh. Legends were woven about the pair, tales of wonder and delight. And these legends, with all their romantic flavor, were handed down to their children and their children's children, of whom Nochim-Mayer was the first.

Little Nochim-Mayer, first grandchild of the legendary couple, had much to stir his imagination. The very name he bore carried with it vision and prophecy! for was he not named for the daring rabbi Nochim-Mayer, who sanctioned Gavriel's divorce and married him to Sorke? Then there was the fantastic tragedy of his own father's life; and there was still another factor that gave flight to his fancy and helped carry the lad to an imaginary world. This factor was a prosaic thing indeed: the contents of his grandmother Sorke's attic.

You will remember that people of many lands and many tongues dealt with Sorke in the lading of her freight boats. It often happened that these foreign merchants carelessly left behind personal articles of some value: hats, coats, knick-knacks, papers, books and all manner of luggage. Waiting for the day when the merchants would return and claim their belongings, Sorke had them stored away for safe-keeping in the attic of the house. In time the collection grew to a prodigious size.

You know what it is to rummage in the cellar or the attic, with what excitement one comes upon a garment that be-

longed to mother when she was a girl or what it means to
find papers and letters not meant for your eyes. Think, then,
of the boy Nochim-Mayer's delight when he came upon
garments worn by people in lands he had never seen, and
what he felt when he picked up books printed in foreign
tongues. And he could read these tongues, too, for he had
learned them from his mother and his amazing grandmother. There were Russian, Polish and German books, and
they did not, as every Hebrew book he had to study, deal
with Torah and Talmud and their abstruse commentaries,
but with life and adventure and romance! If you will remember that everything outside of religious reading was forbidden in Nochim-Mayer's youth, you may have an idea of the
excitement he felt at the discovery he made in the attic.

The boy spent every free moment with his hidden treasure. Every day from dawn till night he had to be in *chayder*
—Hebrew school—to devote himself to the grueling studies
assigned to him by his teacher; and again there were the long
periods which one had to spend in *shul*. But on Sabbath
afternoons, when, after the heavy meal of *tscholent* and *kugel*
the family dropped away in peaceful slumber, one could call
one's time one's own. It was then that the lad stole up to
Bobbe Sorke's attic to bury himself in his secret treasure.

All went well until one Sabbath day when Hodes quietly
followed her son to his hiding place. When she discovered
that he was reading "profane" literature, Hodes' wrath was
so great that, forgetting the holiness of the Sabbath, she
desecrated it by tearing to pieces the volume he was reading.
Thereafter the boy was zealously watched. But no one could
prevent him from smuggling the forbidden pages among
those of his sacred books—a trick Nochim-Mayer learned in
his early youth and curiously enough, his own readers later
practiced on a large scale, when, behind the locked doors of

private homes or the cloistered walls of their synagogues, they eagerly devoured his little books.

The years of his teens Nochim-Mayer spent away from home. I do not know whether it was the dissension between his parents or their high hopes for him that caused the youth to be sent out as a wanderer among the *yeshivahs*—the talmudic colleges of Lithuania. In the great schools of Volozhin and Mir, he received, in its best form, the traditional education given to the young men of Israel. There, too, he came under the influence of that new movement in Russian Jewish life which was making its way by stealth among the intellectual classes. It was the movement for "enlightenment," popularly known by its Hebrew name—*Haskalah.*

Haskalah drew its inspiration from Germany's Moses Mendelssohn, who nearly a century earlier preached the doctrine of European culture for the Jews of the ghetto. The movement for "enlightenment" made its way slowly but surely into Russia. But there was a great difference between the German-Jewish and Russian-Jewish practices; while Mendelssohn's doctrine was accompanied by a drift toward assimilation and the rejection of a national Jewish language, the *Haskalah* movement, though exalting European culture and demanding secular education, at the same time urged the use of Hebrew in the attainment of both, thus laying the foundation for a national Hebrew renaissance. Remember that prior to the *Haskalah* movement, religion was considered the only intellectual pursuit worthy of a Jew, and Hebrew a sacred tongue to be used mainly for religious expression.

We in America may look at the unoffending program of reading and secular studies advanced by the leaders of "enlightenment" and be surprised to learn with what bitter hostility it was regarded. Yet in the early days of the movement, the promulgation of any ideas concerning secular edu-

cation, European culture, or the free use of Hebrew was at
once condemned as "Russification" on the part of the government or the work of dangerous radicals and heretics. The
persecution and trickery practiced for centuries upon the
Jews of Russia by its government had developed in them a
deep distrust of its motives and a tremendous power of
resistance to any proposed change. Every previous project
for "enlightenment" or "Russification" had been a ruse for
the eventual destruction of Jewish life. So now, at any mention of these familiar words, panic seized this unhappy people. They had become a fanatical superstitious mass fighting
behind the reinforced religious and traditional barriers they
had erected for the preservation of their existence.

This was particularly true of the *Chassidim*, who had to a
great extent wandered away from the Book and had become
fetish worshippers with wonder-working *tzaddikim*—saints
—as objects of adoration. The *tzaddikim* and their followers,
steeped in fanaticism, looked aghast at the new movement
and fought desperately against any intellectual intrusion
into their realm of power.

To the greatest part of the Russian-Jewish masses, then,
the doctrine of "enlightenment" was heresy aimed at the
destruction of a people; the standard-bearers of the movement had to fear the fate of heretics. A small advanced
element of the masses, however, received the movement for
"enlightenment" as a new gospel which would bring about
the rebirth of Jewish life. Cautiously the *Haskalah* movement
made its way through the fear and gloom of fanaticism, its
influence spreading, its doctrines filtering by degrees into
the very *yeshivahs,* the great schools and colleges of religious
learning, where it obtained a secret though glamorous following among the keen-witted students.

By the time my father, Nochim-Mayer, had reached the

yeshivah of Volozhin, the new movement had already arrived there. In Vilna it had advanced so far as to boast openly of two monthly Hebrew journals and several published volumes of secular learning and *belles-lettres* in that tongue. Nevertheless an adherent of "enlightenment" was still regarded as a dangerous radical and had to advance his faith through secret and subterranean channels. This, however, was no detriment to radicals who were proud of their faith and gloried in their own secret heroism.

Nochim-Mayer was now such a hero. He devoured the new Hebrew literature, steeped himself in its spirit and participated in its activity by secretly writing Hebrew verse. In spite of his heroism, however, this very young man was world weary. He had been rooming from one *yeshivah* to another. Because of the disagreement between his parents, he had no real home to return to, and he truly longed for one.

This was his state of mind when Hodes arranged for his marriage with the eldest daughter of a certain Reb Michel Bercinsky of the town of Pinsk.

Weary Nochim-Mayer readily fell in with her plans. But how could he, advanced student of "enlightenment" that he was, consent to bind himself to a girl he had never seen? The spirit of revolt was upon him; so, defying the edict of the double matriarchate on the very eve of his betrothal, he demanded his rights. His father, though entirely in agreement with his son, had to remain mute in the presence of the ruling women of the tribe.

That Sorke and Hodes had to concede to the young man's wishes you have already seen. And you have also seen how he and Dinneh met and how their betrothal was celebrated.

When after his betrothal he returned to his native Nesvizh, Nochim-Mayer remembered the vital presence of the girl he was to marry and poured out his hungry heart in the letters he wrote her. He spiced these with the rich Hebrew and German of the "enlightenment" he knew so well, and he colored them with the fervor of his longing, thus bringing a startling conception of romance to his *kalleh* in Pinsk. No wonder his letters created a sensation.

5

Early in the month of March, in 1866, at a wayside inn in the hamlet of Ploskin, my mother, Dinneh Bercinsky, and my father, Nochim-Mayer Shaikevitsch, were married.

At three in the afternoon the *kalleh* was dressed in her veil and wedding gown of black moiré silk with its long train. She sat and watched her girlfriends making merry about her. She herself was a little faint, because, following the traditional custom, *chossen* and *kalleh* had to fast on the day of their wedding. But the fiddlers, drummers and clarinetists struck up a merry tune, and away went her gaily-dressed girlfriends in a merry dance. My mother says that they danced the quadrille and the lancers, which were the fashionable dances of the day. But that was before they really warmed up, before they broke into the traditional Jewish dances. Then they plunged into the *brayges tanz*, the *patch tanz* and many other Jewish folk dances. The girls gleefully put on a dance of mock distress, illustrated by necessary gestures of despair. They sang:

Vosshe vell ich ton	What will I do
Vosshe vell ich ton	What will I do
As der Baal Choiv	When the creditor
Vet kummen monen?	Comes for his money?
Az der Baal Choiv	When the creditor
Vet kommen monen?	Comes for his money?

Vell ich hoben	If I have it,
Vell ich geben,	I will give it,
Vell ich nit hoben	If I haven't,
Vell ich nit geben.	I won't give it,
Ain vort ich hob nit!	In a word—I haven't
Ain vort ich hob nit!	In a word—I haven't.

But right here the *marshaloch,* the wedding bard, appeared ready to remind the *kalleh* in rhyme of the importance of the step she was taking. He placed her in the middle of the room while all the women gathered around her with their handkerchiefs in hand, ready for the weeping that would follow. The wedding bard then began to harangue the poor bride as only a man paid for the service could. He reminded her of her youth, her happy life with her father and mother; he warned her that these days of happiness were now at an end and tormented her with horrible speculations on what might be in store for her. He wailed over her as one bewails the dead, except that it was done in rhyme. The women and girls, hearing his cries and the heartrending fate that might befall the fair young bride, broke out into loud weeping. Fortunately, Dinneh was a strong girl and did not go faint, as many another young bride would and did. She was dissolved in a flood of tears, however.

But now, in through the door to the merry tune of the *klezmer* (a band of lowly musicians) came the wedding procession, led by Nochim-Mayer escorted by his father, mother, grandmother and friends. A hail of rice, sugar and oats were thrown upon the young man by the gathered throng. Rice and oats were for fertility, sugar for the sweetness of life. The gay, yet solemn, procession, all except Nochim-Mayer, advanced to the *kalleh*'s chair with lit candles woven of many colored strands. Dinneh was surrounded by her kinfolk, also bearing flaming candles. The *chossen* and his party arrived and halted in front of her chair. Nochim-Mayer looked at the radiant girl to whom he had written his fervent letters and dropped the veil over her face.

To the accompaniment of gay music he and his party then made their way to the open field where the marriage ceremony would take place, and where now the *chuppe*—the wedding canopy—was held high by four men. There Nochim-Mayer was stationed to await the *kalleh* and her train.

Up across the field they came, Dinneh in the forefront escorted by her father and mother. The music played. Eagerly the throng pressed forward, their lighted tapers held aloft. At last the *kalleh* too was under the *chuppe*. Slowly she circled about Nochim-Mayer, seven times.

Now it was the officiating rabbi's turn to perform his duty. He greeted and blessed *chossen* and *kalleh* and their kin. Then he said a prayer in memory of the dear departed whose presence was missed at the union of these two. Naturally everybody wept at the mention of the beloved dead. The rabbi then placed a little glass under the *chossen*'s heel for him to smash. There are two popular interpretations of this part of the ceremony: it reminds the celebrants of the destruction of Jerusalem, or proves that the bridegroom is a virile man. The wine was then sipped from a common cup by bride and groom, the ring was placed on Dinneh's finger and the two were pronounced man and wife according to the "law of Moses and Israel."

From the time it began until this juncture, the marriage ceremony had been a solemn affair for the principals and wedding guests alike. But now, upon the pronouncement of the union, a new, joyous note was sounded, and people cried, *"Mazeltov! Mazeltov!"* Then there was a burst of music, while the bride was kissed by the women, the bridegroom by the men. The women then kissed each other and the men did likewise and everybody started to dance.

A word about the dancing at a Jewish wedding: you dance not because you know how, but because the spirit moves you. Outside of the prohibition of men dancing with women there are no restrictions, or prearranged or practiced steps or forms. Women may dance with women and men with men if they so choose, but that, too, is not necessary. There is no order about the dance. Each person, as the impulse moves him, gets up and dances. Old and young, great and small dance separately or opposite each other. When the fiddles strike up a merry strain, and the cornet blows, when the drums boom and the tambourines jingle, all stamp their feet, clap their hands, lift their skirts and make steps—any kind of steps! If you are a man, you lift your coat tails and hop around. If you are a woman you grab a neighbor, whirl about with her, or go backward and forward in front of her, improvising as you dance. A group of people form a ring and dance in a circle, each one creating his own steps, just so long as he keeps time with the music. If somebody of any importance is at the wedding, the dancing ring will probably form around him. Dancing at a Jewish wedding (not a modern American one, of course) means a bodily expression of joy. And, indeed, if one cannot or will not for some reason move one's body or feet, one can certainly carry on with one's hands. Waving arms and snapping fingers are very acceptable substitutes for dancing.

There were also special dances, such as the *kosher tanz, mitzvah tanz, heidim deidim,* the *brayges tanz* and *patch tanz*, which I have already mentioned. Even for these one needed no special instruction. All you needed was to get the idea of what the dance was about, and then you joined it.

In a *brayges tanz*—a "sulky dance"—two women pretend that they have had a quarrel, that one is sulky in consequence and that the other is very eager to make up with her. The offended one dances about, keeping her face averted from her anxious friend. In vain the suppliant does everything possible to get the sulky girl's attention and to look into her eyes. In pantomime she offers the offended one gifts: her earrings, her ring, her bracelet or any other treasure. At each refusal the suppliant wrings her hands and makes gestures of despair. Finally, the offended girl relents; the two then throw their arms about each other, the music screams with joy, and the women dance happily together.

The *patch tanz,* or "clap dance," is one in which no dignified person indulges. The crowd dances in a jolly ring, stopping at intervals to clap their hands and stamp their feet in a given measure. The ring is then resumed, to be broken up again and again by the stamping and clapping.

A *heidim deidim* is danced by men. It consists simply of two men whirling about after entwining their right arms so that each man's hand rests on the other man's shoulder. Many such couples, with their arms so entwined, dance about the room, lifting their legs as high as possible, while the music plays traditional melodies and everybody, including the dancers, sings *"heidim deidim"*—which means nothing in particular. The dancers then change to their left arms and spin about again, their heads thrown back, their free hands up in the air, their fingers snapping in ecstasy. In variation the free hand holds aloft the flying skirt of the *caftan,* or gabardine.

A *kosher tanz* is a wedding dance for two, generally confined to the principals of the occasion and those very close to them. It is, I believe, the only dance in which a man and woman were allowed to dance together. Thus, the bride's mother will dance a *"kosher tanz"* with the bridegroom's father, or the bride's father with the bridegroom's mother. Grandmothers or grandfathers, too, may have the honor of this dance, and the bride may be the partner of any one of the dignitaries mentioned. On rare occasions the rabbi himself will participate in its dignified steps. Since the *kosher tanz* is a dance of honor, all other dancing ceases when this one is in progress. The assembled guests gather about the dancing pair. The man and woman step out gravely into the middle of the room; since holding hands by men and women is strictly avoided, each takes hold of one corner of a large handkerchief and the two move slowly around in a circle, keeping step with the music.

A *mitzvah tanz,* a dance of "good deed," is one in which the bride dances with all the guests and even with beggars who have come to the wedding. It is also the dance performed by one woman, who trots backward before the bride and groom as they emerge from under the *chuppe.*

But, to return to Dinneh's and Nochim-Mayer's wedding out in the field in the hamlet of Ploskin. . . .

After the spontaneous outbursts of merriment, the crowd made its way to the main house of the inn where the wedding feast was waiting. Across the field the dancing procession moved, headed by Nochim-Mayer and Dinneh, who were now man and wife.

All went well until they reached the door of the inn. There a sudden commotion arose. Hodes was defending her Nochim-Mayer's right to be the first to enter the house by trying to push him through the door. But Dinneh's friends were claiming the right for her by urging her forward at the same time. It was generally believed that whichever one of a newly married couple was the first to cross the threshold would be dominant in the life they were beginning together. The pushing argument at the door was therefore real and earnest, but it did not last very long, for the young husband gallantly stepped aside and allowed his wife to be the first.

The wedding feast was a sumptuous one, both for wedding guests and beggars. The latter, numbering several score, were fed plentifully at tables set out for them in the open field.

But no matter how gay the atmosphere, how bright and brilliant the gathering, how grand the banquet, the young couple were uneasy. They well knew that following the feast they would have to endure a most embarrassing ceremony: that of being escorted to their nuptial bed, as indeed they were. Whispered advice was given to the bridegroom by Berel, Reb Michel's brother, while Dinneh received instructions from Sprintze, the respected old woman who had charge of the wedding. The two young people were horribly uncomfortable and utterly helpless, but they had to submit to the traditional custom and make the best of it.

I have noted before that Dinneh's dislike for Hodes was engendered at the time of the betrothal when the older woman showed her impatience at Nochim-Mayer's request to see his bride-to-be. That dislike was deepened when Hodes disputed Dinneh's right to cross the threshold, but it grew into positive hatred when Hodes, during the week which followed the marriage, would not permit the bride to sit in daylight at her husband's side, warning her that the years of her life would be cut short if she did so.

At the end of the long wedding festivities Nochim-Mayer bade good-bye to his parents, to his *Bobbe* Sorke and to all the good people of Nesvizh who had come to attend his wedding. He was leaving them to go to Pinsk to live at the house of his father-in-law, Reb Michel Bercinsky, where he was to have three years' *kest.* But before he left the wayside inn and its memories, he went out at dawn into the field, and there, upon a lonely tree, carved the name of his bride entwined in that of his own.

6

When Nochim-Mayer arrived in Pinsk, there was much talk among the curious. Here at last was that "ornament" from Nesvizh who "knew not the face of a coin," and who wrote such astonishing letters. Friends, foes and acquaintances of Reb Michel's flocked to his house to see and hear this wonder of a son-in-law. They found there was much more to see than hear. The tall young man with his pitch-black hair, blonde beard, blue gray eyes and Slavic cast of features was a distinct personality, but he did not talk. He sat quietly and listened to what they had to say, holding a cigarette between the long tapering fingers of his white hand. Those of the curious, however, who stayed on and were persistent enough, finally got their reward when the gentle young man showed them his beautiful manuscripts. These were poems written in the classical Hebrew of the Bible. When Nochim-Mayer did talk, his hearers were surprised at his store of Talmudic learning, at his knowledge of the new Hebrew literature and finally at his genial sense of humor.

Nochim-Mayer was a great success. Reb Michel swelled with pride as he watched the best young men of the town gather about his son-in-law. No wonder Reb Michel developed a genuine affection for Nochim-Mayer, and that he never lorded over him as he did every other member of the family.

A new life began in the Bercinsky household. Mayshe and Henye somehow receded into the background. Nochim-Mayer took the place of honor. The learned of the younger generation crowded about him to discuss the new "enlightenment," to read its literature and, in a lighter mood, to play chess. Within a short time Nochim-Mayer's and Dinneh's room became, in a manner of speaking, the intellectual center of the town. This group in later years yielded, besides Shomer, two other men of letters who became famous in Hebrew literature and one orator later to be known as the tribune of his people. These were Avrom Chaim Rosenberg, Dov-Baer Debzevitch, and Zwi-Hirsch Masliansky.

A great day dawned for Nochim-Mayer when an essay of his was published in the highly prized Hebrew journal *Ha-Melitz*. It created something of a sensation not only in Reb Michel's house, but in the whole town. Everyone was proud that one of the town's adopted sons had achieved such distinction. In those days, unlike our own, writers were few, and those who achieved print were extremely rare. The printed word, moreover, was very much respected.

Nochim-Mayer's writing, like that of the *maskilim* (apostles of "enlightenment") of his day, had to be in Hebrew, in spite of the fact that the Jewish masses spoke Yiddish. Yiddish was literally their mother tongue, because the Jewish mother knew no other language. The boys and not the girls were sent to school; hence the men and not the women knew Hebrew. In the vast majority of cases the women did not even understand the Hebrew prayers which they recited every day of their lives. In the women's gallery at every synagogue (men do not sit with women in the orthodox house of prayer), there was a *zogerke,* a speaker or reader, who read the Hebrew service aloud so that the women might repeat the words after her. For their knowledge of the Five Books of Moses, they had the *Ze'enah-U-Re'enah,* the *Teitsch Chumesh.* This, as I have already said, consisted of a translation in a language that was neither Yiddish nor German, but a mixture of the two, with curious idiosyncrasies of its own.

It is easy to see that the new literature of the Hebrew

renaissance was, like classical Hebrew literature, a mystery
to the women of East European Jewry.

Another element of the Jewish population which *Haskalah*
excluded was the workman. Because of poverty his education did not extend far beyond the *chayder* of his early childhood. He certainly was not prepared to follow either the
language of the new "enlightenment" or the theoretical and
controversial subjects with which it was concerned. *Haskalah*
and its achievements, then, had little meaning for women
and the poor, uncultured masses. The new Hebrew literature
reached but a few. Only the *maskilim* and their followers
grew with and profited by the new movement.

In spite of all this, Hebrew—and not Yiddish, the mother
tongue—continued to be the language of the printed word
used for the dissemination of learning. This was perfectly
natural. Throughout the centuries Jewish youth had been
educated in Hebrew and not in the languages adopted or
evolved by these people in their ceaseless wanderings.
Throughout the centuries, too, the Jewish masses had become alienated from a general cultural conception. The only
culture that remained permanent with them was their religious one, and this was carried on in the Hebrew in which
it was conceived. The learned leaders of "enlightenment"
loved the beautiful language of the prophets and despised
the humble Yiddish spoken by the uneducated multitude.
They regarded Yiddish as jargon, the expression of the ignorant. How could they possibly bring forth a cultural movement in the tongue of the unschooled? The idea was un-
thinkable. Of course, every one of the leaders of
"enlightenment" knew Yiddish; they had been brought up
in that tongue, but they held it in contempt, nevertheless.
Hebrew, Polish, Russian and German were now very much
in vogue among the intelligentsia. Yiddish, poor thing, was

undergoing a metamorphosis in the hands of a throng who sought to dignify it by burdening it heavily with German. But since the German so used was not quite German, and the Yiddish so mixed was not exactly Yiddish, the result was an illegitimate composite. Later, when Yiddish began to be used in a purer form and for its own sake, the German mixture was called in derision *Deutschmarish.* However, at the time it held sway it was highly respected. In fact, *Deutschmarish* is still used by many not-too-well-informed Yiddish-speaking Jews who would assume a superior attitude.

Years later a small group of writers tried to reach down to the uneducated by recreating Jewish life in the Yiddish vernacular. Their readers came not from the unschooled, but from among those elements of "enlightenment" which saw the justice of Yiddish expression. At best, however, and even at the zenith of this period, the literary works of these writers reached but a comparative few. They nowhere touched the large masses who were, you must remember, not an illiterate but a decidedly nonreading people. The great Yiddish-speaking public continued to remain but distantly aware of the world, its culture and literature. It continued to look on at a respectful distance and in a rather awesome mood upon those who could follow the old and now the new Hebrew learning.

You now see why Nochim-Mayer, an ardent adherent of *Haskalah,* had of necessity to write in Hebrew and why he seemed to have reached the pinnacle of his career when his essay appeared in *Ha-Melitz.* The fact that only the initiated could read him gave him a place of preeminence in the community.

Although a *Chassid,* Reb Michel looked with sympathetic eyes upon *Haskalah.* Something in it reminded him of his own early struggles for knowledge. True, the new movement went far afield, but its breadth and scope responded to something in his own heart. It was therefore with a sense of pride that he thrust out his chest at Nochim-Mayer's accomplishment. This was indeed a son-in-law after his own heart.

For Dinneh here was exactly the thing for which her own heart had longed. Something important was occurring in her life. The great movement for enlightenment which she had heard so much about was beating about her. It throbbed in the very confines of her room. Certainly she was thrilled and elated. But she had her secret hours of bitterness. If only she could follow this thing she was so proud of. If only she had had the preparation. Here she was in the midst of plenty, and she could receive only the crumbs that fell from the table. For once her resentment against her father became bitter; this man had done so much for his sons and so little for his daughters.

Dinneh could do nothing to relieve her bitterness. It was all too late. Now more than ever it was impossible to get the education she so much wanted. Her babies were coming. And there were other formidable obstacles to contend with. More than ever her father's house was full of people. The educated Henye was there, elbowing her way to obtain what she needed for her Mayshe, for her children, and their nurses. The old servant Sosche was there with her many helpers, cooking and baking for the large family, for the *orchim* (the strangers at the table) and for the visiting *chazzan* (cantor) and his singers. But above all, her mother, Yentel, was there with her everlasting poor and her distribution of loaves, with the many separate little pots for her Michel.

Yentel was thoroughly out of patience with the crowd of children she had brought into the world. Heaven knows, she never had too much love for any of them; but they had to be abided. Now there was the new array of grandchildren. The situation was simply out of hand. Yentel did not refrain from making things unpleasant for all concerned. She controlled the household with the keys to the cupboards; these she held very securely, while the great house with all its children, in-laws, servants, wet nurses and grandchildren, was kept waiting.

As if this were not enough, there was another element to complicate Dinneh's situation. This was her younger sister, Haiye, a fascinating girl with nothing in particular to do but watch Nochim-Mayer. Haiye, like Dinneh, was hungry for knowledge. Her father gave her no better chance to obtain it than he did his older daughter, but Haiye had the advantage of having her romantic brother-in-law in the house. Everybody who was intellectually interesting gathered about the beloved young man; why then should she be excluded from the circle? She made up her mind she would not be. So Haiye was forever in Dinneh's and Nochim-Mayer's room, forever listening to the discussions and somehow comprehending them. At least such was her pretense. And now, of all things, Nochim-Mayer was teaching Haiye to play chess, while she, Dinneh, had no time or patience to look at the game. I don't think my mother ever forgave my father for teaching, and Haiye for learning, it.

According to my mother, both Henye and Mayshe were envious of Nochim-Mayer's position in the house and consequently of hers. It seems that the Bercinsky household was not a very tranquil abode at that time.

The turmoil among the females was further increased by each married one's yearly bearing of a baby. During the Succoth holidays (the Feast of Tabernacles) when the *ethrog,* a citrus fruit brought from Palestine, received its daily blessing, there was a contest among the women for the secret biting off of the *ethrog*'s stem. The belief was that the woman who succeeded in doing so would give birth to a boy. As Yentel, Henye, Dinneh and the younger servants in the house were pregnant at all times, the contest was a serious one.

Dinneh held her head high and was proud before her little world. Her husband was indeed extraordinary; but behind closed doors she was exasperated with him. The promised three years of *kest* were coming to a close, and there he was sitting in his room clad in his dressing robe, reading, thinking, daydreaming! Hebrew verse and Hebrew essays were fine things; still, one had to make a living, especially when one's family was increasing.

Reb Michel had been carrying the vast expense of the household alone. The day arrived when his funds suddenly ebbed. Mayshe had again lost several thousand of his father's rubles; this time in the cloth business. Now he, as well as Nochim-Mayer, would have to find something profitable to do.

While Mayshe was worrying over his own affairs, Dinneh's dowry was brought out of hiding and her learned young husband was launched in the lumber business.

To this day my mother grows red with vexation when she recalls his business activities. Suddenly the great courtyard in Reb Michel's house was loaded with lumber. Rain or shine, wagonloads of logs were delivered to young Nochim-Mayer Shaikevitsch of Nesvizh. Men were set to work cutting the logs into various shapes and sizes. But did these boards or beams or what you will ever leave the yard? That is why my mother grows red with vexation.

"Nochim-Mayer! Nochim-Mayer! Simon the contractor is out in the yard. He needs beams for the new house he is building!"

"Eh? . . . What?" came from the young man as he roused himself from his dreams. "Where? Who?"

"Out in the yard! Simon the contractor!"

Nochim-Mayer drew the girdle of his dressing robe a bit tighter and stepped out of the house. As he went, my mother says with a chagrin that still rankles, he twirled the silken cord of his girdle until the tassels spun in the air. After a long time he returned with his client, both deeply involved in a discussion about Nochim-Mayer's latest article in the *Ha-Melitz*. The contractor happened to be a sort of *maskil* himself, so the two of them had completely forgotten the little matter of beams, and their talk centered entirely on "enlightenment."

That, my mother says, is how her husband did business with all the men of learning. But if his clients happened to be simple working men who did not know *Haskalah,* then Nochim-Mayer's business transactions resulted in sales by which he sold the lumber for less than it cost him!

While Dinneh lay in childbed with her second child, her mother, Yentel, lay in childbirth with her twenty-fourth. Dinneh had a girl whom they called Shayndele, and Yentel had a boy who was named Joshua.

Of course it was Yentel and not Dinneh who had to be fussed over. What was Dinneh in comparison to her mother! But then Dinneh's first child, the golden-haired boy Gavriel, suddenly became ill with diphtheria. Before anything could be done for the child, he died in his father's arms.

Powerful young Dinneh bent for a moment beneath her sorrows. Then suddenly one of her problems solved itself. Haiye fell in love.

Haiye's was the first love affair in your great-grandfather's house, and it swayed the lives of the people it concerned like trees in a gale. The struggle it developed among father, daughter, suitor and others involved gave rise to a curious situation in the city itself, and, incidentally, pushed Nochim-Mayer out upon an unknown and untrodden path which was destined to influence the lives of thousands of people.

7

While Haiye was struggling with her father, the man she loved and still another man who sought above all things to win her for himself, Nochim-Mayer sat by helplessly in Reb Michel's house. There was nothing Nochim-Mayer could do to help the poor girl. He was himself in a pitiful state. In this very house, at the very time Haiye's passionate romance was being broken, Nochim-Mayer saw his children arrive and die.

The first to go was little Gavriel. Then two little daughters died. There was only five-year-old Shayndele left now—Shayndele, who was born at the same time that Yentel gave birth to Joshua. She was a bright, pretty child endowed with a sweet singing voice. Similarly gifted was little Joshua. The entire household delighted when the two babies put their heads together and sang in perfect unison the little Hebrew song:

Eliyohu Hanovi	*Elijah the Prophet*
Eliyohu Hatishbi	*Elijah the Tishbite*
Eliyohu, Eliyohu	*Elijah, Elijah*
Eliyohu Hagilodi	*Elijah the Gileadite*
Bemehayroh	*Speedily in our day*
Yovo aylaynu	*Oh may he come to us*
Im Moshiach	*With Messiah*
Ben David	*David's son.*

But now, during the first *seder* (feast of Passover), Shayn-dele coughed a great croupy cough. The next day she died. Dinneh took the passing of her favorite child dreadfully to heart. To spare her the sight of seeing her baby's grave, no one would tell her where the child was buried. One day she stole away to the cemetery and in a casual way asked the sexton, who did not recognize her, to point out to her the place where the last of Reb Michel's dead grandchildren was buried. On that little grave Dinneh was found unconscious by her searching family. She was carried home and lay ill with a fever for many weeks. But her powerful constitution served her well. The crisis came and went; she recovered.

She was well again, but her economic plight was in no way relieved. Nochim-Mayer had no money with which to bury his dead children, nor to welcome the newcomer that was on its way. He tried teaching in Pinsk and in other towns, but he had no talent for that art. He simply did not know which way to turn and he could no longer appeal to his father-in-law for help. The promised three years' *kest* had already been extended to three times that number and still the man who knew not the face of a coin was leaning heavily upon his father-in-law, whose choice he had been. Reb Michel was now staggering under the load imposed upon him by the innumerable members of his household.

A neighbor of Reb Michel's, a clever woman who was known as Dvayreh-Tzippe's, happened at this time to be traveling on a train bound for Vilna. There she got into conversation with a fellow traveler, a woman of that city.

"Oh, you are from Pinsk?" the latter asked. "I have a nephew there who is the son-in-law of a certain Michel Bercinsky."

This woman was Nochim-Mayer's aunt, Ronye, the sister of Hodes, the second child of the ancient Reb Gavriel and

Bobbe Sorke. She had married into the rich Vigodsky family of Vilna and was now playing an important role in the Jewish community of that city.

Dvayreh-Tzippe's raised her head and tilted it to one side, as was her wont, and gave Ronye a picture of her charming nephew's plight.

"A splendid young man," she concluded, "and a splendid young wife; but how they suffer! It is a pity that some of Nochim-Mayer's relatives do not bestir themselves in his behalf; especially when there are such clever and important people among them." There the sly old woman looked hard, accusingly and admiringly at her fellow traveler. Ronye Vigodsky broke under that look. She promised that immediately upon her arrival in Vilna she would see that something was done for her nephew in Pinsk.

And so it happened that Nochim-Mayer Shaikevitsch received a letter from his Aunt Ronye asking him to come to Vilna, where his influential uncle would try to obtain a position for him. Nochim-Mayer bade good-bye to Pinsk, his wife and the children who lay in the ancient cemetery. A new life was to begin for him and a new era for the Yiddish-speaking masses.

8

Poor Dinneh was in bed with her fifth child. The turbaned midwife bent low over her:

"It is a boy," she said.

But the words brought no cheer to the sick woman. Another child was entering the world, perhaps only to leave it for an early grave. She was sick in body and soul. How dark the world was about her.

Her husband had been away a few months now. He was

sitting around at his Uncle Vigodsky's house waiting, Micawber-like, for something to turn up. He was not at her side when this child came. She had no money with which to call in the doctor. She had no money with which to buy the medicine she needed. Her father was away in Minsk bothering about his business. She could not turn to her sorely-tried and impatient mother for everything she needed. She borrowed a few *kopecks* from the old servant Sosche for a bottle of ergot. She begged the aged woman to secretly draw off a little extra soup for her from the family pot. The faithful servant did as she was bid and tried to cheer up the weary patient.

"What will you call your little boy?" she asked.

"Avrom," Dinneh said indifferently.

Dinneh lay in bed thinking what to do for her newborn son. How was she to buy him the swaddling clothes he needed? How was she to keep him alive in the house where her four other children had died? How was she to pay the wet nurse when she had not a *groschen* to her name? (In her most dire extremity the thought of nursing her own baby never even occurred to Dinneh.) In the thick of her misery Sosche brought her a letter from Vilna. Dinneh took it hopelessly. She had stopped expecting anything from her husband. She tore open the envelope. Two new Polish rubles fluttered to the floor. The patient almost jumped out of bed with excitement. Two new Polish rubles from Nochim-Mayer! Overcome, she sat up and wept great tears of joy. The little sum seemed a vast fortune to her. In her ecstasy Dinneh did not notice that her husband had failed to tell her how he had earned the money. Nor did she just now care to know. It was enough that he had actually sent it to her. A new hope rose on her horizon. Perhaps she had been mistaken about her husband after all. Perhaps he could and would yet make a living for her and her new infant son. She clasped the boy close to her heart and allowed her tears to fall upon his tiny face.

A few days later two more rubles came from Vilna and then five rubles at one time! Then more and more rubles! Reb Michel's household was in an uproar. Something had happened to Nochim-Mayer! He was earning money!

"But what was he about?" Reb Michel wondered.

On a Sabbath afternoon, just when the family had finished the Sabbath meal, Zelik *the melamed,* the Hebrew teacher, came bounding into the room in a strange state of excitement.

"Reb Michel!" he cried in a voice that was hardly his own, *"men hot eich beshribben!"*

It is too bad I must translate these words for you. Any explanation of them, no matter how good, must fall short of their quality and significance.

In translation the sentence means: "Reb Michel, you have been written about!" But that's not at all what Zelik meant. What he conveyed was: "Reb Michel, someone has exposed you all—you and your household, and the things that happen in it."

You must understand that Zelik spoke not only with his lips. His hands, his eyes, his nose, his beard—all were part and parcel of his speech. His exclamation had something of the effect of a thunderbolt. The family jumped to its feet; its many eyes were fastened upon the disheveled pedagogue. Panting for breath, the man kept waving about his head something which looked like a booklet.

Surely he had gone crazy, for it was impossible that anybody be actually written about. Still, the man kept up his frantic waving. He had to be subdued, which indeed he was,

by Reb Michel himself. The booklet was torn from his hand
and placed upon the table. There Reb Michel gazed at its
unbound and coverless title page. His amazed eyes saw this
Yiddish legend: *Mechautonim fun Sonim. A kurzer roman fun
Shomer* ("Kinsmen out of Enemies; a short novel by
Shomer"). But that doesn't give the exact idiomatic meaning
of the words; the English title would not be as appealing as
the original. There is no swing or rhyme to the words as
there is in the Yiddish; finally, there is no implied contradiction of terms. Perhaps a title like "Friendly Enemies" would
be more in keeping with the original, but then it would fall
foul of its meaning.

The Yiddish booklet was in the hands of the Bercinsky
family, and the frantic, disheveled Hebrew teacher was in-
sisting that in it Reb Michel and his household had been
described. There was nothing to do but to prove or disprove
the crazy man's notion. Let him read the thing aloud that
very moment. The family held its breath. A place was made
for Zelik the *melamed,* right in the middle of the room. A
circle of agitated people drew their chairs close. Zelik picked
up *Mechautonim fun Sonim* and began to read, and the story he
read was an exciting one. It dealt with a romance of two
young people, of a fight between contending forces for a
high office, and finally of a marriage whereby the erstwhile
enemies became kinsmen. It was Haiye's story. In the description of the characters Reb Michel and his family easily
recognized themselves. Zelik was right. Reb Michel and his
household had certainly been written about.

Now the reader was through. Eyes widened in amazement. Who could have done this! No one was maligned, but
who knew all the details described in the story? And who
could have told the thing in this exciting manner?

Again the title page was consulted. It said that the story

was written by one "Shomer." No one had ever heard such a name. No given name, no initial, nothing whatever but just one word consisting of three letters: a *shin,* pronounced as *sh,* a *mem* meaning M, and a *raish,* R. *Shin, mem, raish:* Sh M R. True to Hebrew form, no vowels. These are supplied by the reader. The word then read "Shomer." But what sort cf a name was that?

While everybody looked questioningly at everybody else, Reb Michel took to pacing the floor. Suddenly he stopped.

"I know who wrote this," he said. "This is Nochim-Mayer's work! Nobody else could do it."

Of course he was right.

Within the next few days every obtainable copy of *Mechautonim fun Sonim* was seized upon by the people of Pinsk. Those who could not read gathered about those who could. Everywhere in large and small circles men and women, learned and unlearned, scholars and working men were listening intently not only to a story of a family they knew but to an exciting tale they could easily grasp and follow with great excitement.

9

Aunt Ronye and Uncle Vigodsky received Nochim-Mayer kindly when he came to Vilna. Vigodsky was a rich and influential man much in the public eye. He had no doubt at all but that he could place his nephew somewhere in business where he could make a living for himself. He was therefore somewhat appalled when he got to know Nochim-Mayer.

"What a curious fellow!" Vigodsky said. *"A Yid mit a bord* (a Jew with a beard) and yet as naïve as a child." The man trusted everybody. Took people at their word. Had implicit confidence in the things they told him. He romanticized everything and everybody. That was his big trouble.

Uncle Vigodsky was considerably disturbed. How could he put an utterly unworldly man into business? He couldn't! Let Nochim-Mayer sit around a while. Perhaps something would turn up for him.

So it happened that the Vigodsky household underwent the very experience which had so exasperated Dinneh: Nochim-Mayer read or wrote or sat in his lounging robe gazing with dreamy eyes into unseen distances, and twirled the cord of his girdle until the tassels spun in the air.

Aunt Ronye gasped. Why didn't this man go out and hustle for himself? What was the use of his sitting there daydreaming? And what good was it even if he did shut himself up for hours to read or write? What was he writing about, anyway?

It was now Vigodsky's turn to calm his wife as she had calmed him after his first vigorous observations concerning Nochim-Mayer's behavior. Let her wait. The Russian-Turkish War was just about to erupt. Vigodsky was expecting a government contract in army supplies. Nochim-Mayer might be found useful in the execution of its details.

Since, as a matter of fact, Aunt Ronye was fond of her nephew and found fault only with his unbusinesslike conduct, the expectation of his being usefully employed quickly restored her patience. So now the two waited in amicable anticipation of great things to happen, while Nochim-Mayer secretly plotted his own salvation.

One morning he dressed himself in his best clothes, tucked a sheaf of papers under his arm and went forth into the city. Briskly he wound his way among Vilna's crooked little streets. But his stride lost a good deal of its vigor as he approached the object of his destination—the editorial office

of the Hebrew monthly *Ha-Karmel.* By the time he reached
its doors the young man's courage was nowhere in sight. He
stood at the door, his hand on its knob, but with no courage
to turn, to push, to enter.

The Vigodskys did not know and would have been very
much surprised had they been told that this scheming
nephew had made up his mind to see the renowned Samuel
Joseph Fuenn, savant, author, publisher and editor of *Ha-Karmel.*

When, tremulously, Nochim-Mayer asked to see Herr
Fuenn, he was told to wait, which he did with a deep sense
of gratitude. It gave him a chance to regain his breath and
to admonish himself inwardly for being so nervous.

Fuenn received the young man graciously. Yes, yes, he
had seen his contributions to *Ha-Melitz.* Yes, yes, Shaikevitsch had a very charming style and a fine, fluent command
of biblical Hebrew. The two men talked of many things and
people. But all talk must end sometime, and theirs now drew
to a close. Fuenn rose to his feet. He was certainly pleased
to meet the young author. He was certainly glad to know
that he, too, like all aspirants of Hebrew writing, had been
drawn to Vilna. Shaikevitsch must by all means call on him
again. He shook the pale young man's hand and bade him
good-bye, but still the fellow lingered.

Fuenn smiled indulgently: What was it? Did Herr Shaikevitsch have something else to say to him? Hesitatingly Nochim-Mayer drew a manuscript from his pocket.

"I would very much like you to see this," he heard himself
saying.

Again Fuenn smiled indulgently. "Ah, so! Another Hebrew essay." Why hadn't he said so?

"It is not an essay," Nochim-Mayer faltered. "And it is
not in Hebrew. It is a story in Yiddish."

The great editor looked at him quickly and not altogether pleasantly. But Nochim-Mayer had now found his tongue. Anxiety drove him on. He begged Fuenn to take a look.

"But, really, I have no time," the editor protested. "You realize that I am a very busy man. There are people right there now waiting for me."

"But just a glance," Nochim-Mayer pleaded.

Fuenn yielded to the pale man's plea. He took the manuscript and gave it a hasty glance.

Then something happened that was to happen thousands of times to those who looked at my father's pages. In Vilna, it occurred for the first time to the first man who saw Shomer's first Yiddish book in manuscript. In a few moments Samuel Joseph Fuenn had forgotten everything else about him, his attention riveted upon the page before him.

Fuenn did not put down the manuscript until he had read the last word of its very last line.

I do not know exactly what happened between the author and editor immediately after the reading, but when everything was said and done and the publication of the book assured, the beaming editor turned to the elated author and said: "How much shall we give you for your story, young man?"

"Three rubles," said he who knew not the face of a coin.

Triumphant, Nochim-Mayer received the munificent sum he had asked for.

Two of these rubles were the ones that fluttered out of an envelope and fell at the foot of Dinneh's sickbed. The other ruble Nochim-Mayer kept for his own extravagant needs.

Before leaving Fuenn, Nochim-Mayer explained his curious pseudonym, "Shomer." Fearing to reveal his identity to the home folk whom he described, he used just the last letters of his name. These he then reversed in order. (Sh-*shin,* the last letter in the Yiddish of Shaikevitsch; *mem-M*, the last letter of Nochim; and *raish-R,* the last letter in Mayer.) Of course, everybody understood about the vowels.

Fuenn laughed at the complexity of "Shomer's" achievement. He patted the young man on the back and asked him by all means to bring him his next story. The two parted joyfully.

The next day Shomer again called at Fuenn's office. The editor greeted him warmly.

"You have some corrections to make in your manuscript?"

"Oh, no," said the author, "I brought you the other story you asked for."

The editor looked at him incredulously. But Shomer drew the manuscript from his pocket. He had written it during the night.

Fuenn read the second story from beginning to end. He bought it at the same price he had paid for the first one. On the following eight nights (the Sabbath excepted) Shomer repeated his feat. In as many days the publishing house purchased his output, though they did not pay at once for all of it. Then they called a halt. The firm had bought plenty for its twenty-seven rubles. It would have to stop to consider which of the stories was to be published first.

So Shomer went back to Vigodsky's to twirl the tassels of his girdle, and the publishing house of Shriftzezer & Rosenkranz prepared to issue the stories, which were destined to bring them a fortune.

But fate had not neglected Nochim-Mayer. At the critical moment, when he had sent his last ruble to Dinneh, in came his uncle with the glad tidings that he had a job. Vigodsky had received the contract he had been waiting for. He was to supply hay and oats for the army's cavalry horses. Nochim-Mayer would be a *podradchik*—a commission merchant, one of the many whom his uncle engaged to go out among the peasants and buy up their crops. For his trouble he would receive the really magnificent sum of twenty rubles a month!

Dinneh received the first postal money order for this amount while she was at table with the great Bercinsky family during the Purim feast. (No matter what Reb Michel's financial difficulties were, the celebration was carried on in great splendor.) Dinneh's exaltation was so great that she felt vastly more important than the Persian Queen Esther about whom the celebration was centered.

Soon she took her infant son, Avrom, and moved out of her father's house, where she had lived the thirteen years of her wedded life. At last she had a home of her own.

10

With the fate of his stories in the hands of his publisher, Nochim-Mayer went to work at his job. Just what effect his work, or, for that matter, the war itself had upon my father I cannot say. I have never heard him make any reference to it except one, and that concerned neither Russian nor Turk, nor even the hay and oats he gathered for the Czar's horses.

During his feed-gathering activities, Nochim-Mayer once stayed at a Jewish wayside inn. For a little while he used it as a center from which to inspect the fields of the neighboring peasants before buying their crops. Days at a time he tramped about the vicinity, returning to the inn when his inspections were over.

Upon one such return he found the inn quite transformed. It had been prepared for a wedding. The place had been scrubbed from top to bottom, curtains and linen washed, furniture polished, clean yellow sand scattered over clean white floors. At one end of the largest room in the house improvised tables had been set up for the men, at the other end of the room similar tables were arranged for the women. (At a wedding feast, as in the synagogue, men and women do not sit together.) The place was fragrant with the odor of fish and roasts and many delicacies in the making. The wedding ceremony was to take place the next day, but the *mechautonim* (in-laws) had already arrived, and now, many more wagonloads of guests were stopping at the door.

The innkeeper quickly assigned these to their various chambers, each according to his rank and standing in the families to be united. All rooms were full now, but still more people kept coming.

The innkeeper was quite beside himself. Where was he to put so many people? He jammed the rooms to twice their capacity, he filled every nook and corner of the house, but still the celebrants came. Finally the haylofts in the barns were turned into sleeping quarters and peace prevailed. But another difficulty arose. The *chossen* insisted that he must have a quiet place for the night. He had to prepare the dissertation he was to deliver the next day, and it was impossible for him to write (and rehearse) in crowded quarters. He had to have seclusion.

The *chossen* was in the nervous, excited frame of mind quite natural to one in his position, and he could not be reasoned with. Arguments were of no avail. The innkeeper finally thought of something. There was a young man, a *podradchik,* in the house who had a little room all to himself. He was a quiet sort and away most of the time. Perhaps he could be induced to share his room with the *chossen.* Since the *chossen* agreed to the proposition, Nochim-Mayer was sought out anxiously and his consent obtained.

The *chossen* immediately took himself to Nochim-Mayer's room while the crop gatherer, in kind consideration, wandered about the fields in the moonlight. But bedtime had of necessity to come. After a good long while the dew-drenched *podradchik* stole silently into his room to find the *chossen* sweating over his labors.

Without daring to breathe, Nochim-Mayer slipped off his clothes and got into bed. But he could not sleep because of the lamplight by which the *chossen* was writing. So he lay wide-eyed, watching the man in his agony. The more he wrote, the more he destroyed.

Nochim-Mayer turned his face to the wall; perhaps now he could get some sleep. But it was of no use. The *chossen* had taken to pacing the floor, mopping his brow and gesticulating. By and by he glared at himself in the mirror and uttered strange sounds and sentences between his teeth. But God was merciful. The oil in the lamp had burned dry. The room was dark now. In sheer exhaustion, without even stopping to undress, the poor young man flung himself across the bed and sank into troubled sleep.

Nochim-Mayer rose early the next morning. He had far to go. This time his journey would take him far afield. He would not be back before a fortnight. As he stood at the door he looked with compassion at the prostrate figure across the bed. Nearby on the table lay a tortured manuscript. Nochim-Mayer picked it up and read it. It was unspeakably bad. He sat down, took a few clean sheets of paper, and wrote a brand new dissertation on the theme indicated by the *chossen*. He placed his neat pages over the tortured ones and quietly left the room.

When he returned two weeks later he found an innkeeper who looked at him with awe.

"Who are you?" the man demanded.

Immediately the incident of the dissertation flashed through Nochim-Mayer's mind. But he looked at the man with innocent eyes and reminded him that he was the *podradchik* who was gathering hay and oats for the Czar's horses. But the innkeeper continued to stare. Whereupon Nochim-Mayer begged for an explanation of his host's strange behavior. He got it.

It seems that the morning of Nochim-Mayer's departure, the *chossen* came running to the innkeeper in something like a panic. He demanded to know who had been in his room. No matter how assured, he would not accept the explanation that no one had been in it besides himself and the *podradchik*.

"But he looked like an ordinary human being," the *chossen* said.

"What else would you have him be?" the innkeeper tried to reason with him.

It was no use. The fellow looked as if he were possessed. He could not be calmed. He asked ridiculous questions, searched about for some unseen presence, and made a general nuisance of himself. Finally convinced that there really was no one except the *mechautonim* in the house, and that the *podradchik* would not return for many a day, the man ceased his curious antics and slumped into stony silence. Thus he continued until the great moment came when he had to deliver his dissertation. Then he gave such a magnificent reading that even his own people were astonished at the young man's brilliance. Not until that moment had they realized what a prize they had in him. It was even whispered about that his family regretted having made the match they did for him.

The only one who had any suspicions was the innkeeper. He had reason to believe that the *chossen*'s excitement on his wedding morning, his search for some mystic presence, as

well as the excellence of his address, had a profound relationship to the *podradchik.*

But my father never gave the *chossen* away. To this day his
family must be wondering what has become of his brilliance
after the delivery of his memorable dissertation.

11

You surmise, of course, that Nochim-Mayer did not stay
with his Uncle Vigodsky for any length of time. When the
war was over, the nephew went back to whence he came.
How well he did for himself during the Russian-Turkish
conflict may be deduced from the fact that he came home as
penniless as he went, though every other *podradchik* returned
from the war wealthy. My mother never ceased chiding my
father for that scrupulous honesty of his. Still, upon his
return to Pinsk, Nochim-Mayer was not quite the man who
left it. He had gone away as So-and-So, Reb Michel's son-
in-law. He came back as "Shomer." His stories had been
published.

Shomer's name was buzzed about everywhere. In a few
years that name became a household word in every Jewish
town and hamlet in Russia.

What happened to Shomer and the readers of Yiddish
during this period is so strange that it has something of the
nature of a fairy tale. You see, while there is nothing new
in a writer's sudden rise to fame and influence, there is a
unique element in Shomer's case. His was not an instance of
a writer striking the reading public's fancy and so becoming
a popular favorite. He became the idol of a reading public
which did not *exist* before the advent of his writing; there
had been no great Yiddish-reading masses before Shomer.
He created them. It is not my intention to discuss the literary

merits of my father's writings, but his work had a great
effect on hundreds of thousands of people. Everywhere the
stories were greedily devoured and passed on to neighbors.
Neighbors read them in similar fashion and pressed them
upon people who as a rule never read Yiddish. Soon everywhere in Russian, Polish and Lithuanian towns with Jewish
inhabitants there were repetitions of the scenes we witnessed in Pinsk: the common people—women and working
men, who could not or did not read—gathered about someone who could, to hear "Shomer."

In the days I speak of there were not only no books,
newspapers or periodicals for the common people, but there
were no theaters, no lectures, no movies, no concerts, no
entertainment whatsoever outside of home celebrations, the
synagogue and the occasional visits of itinerant cantors. The
world was limited to a little circle in the locality in which the
people happened to be living. Shomer, who held his listeners
spellbound by the glamour of his tales, opened their eyes to
new strange worlds, to wide horizons, which spread in many
directions.

The reading circles multiplied. Soon Shomer's booklets
became books, his stories grew into "romances"—novels.
(The publishing house of Romm had by this time called my
father to Vilna and kept him writing at a pace of which he
alone was capable.) Now he lashed out with courage and
flayed the religious bigots who obstructed the advance of
culture. (Behold the standard bearer of *Haskalah*.) He wrote
novels with Jewish historical backgrounds. (Behold the student of the *yeshivah*.) Most exciting of all, he created unreal
dukes and princesses, in fantastic love episodes with his
heroes and heroines. (Behold the influence of his reading in
Bobbe Sorke's attic.) In these fantastic tales he broke away
from the old Yiddish of his realistic stories and set the dia-

logue of his characters in the affected German-Yiddish speech of the "cultured" classes.

But his readers were offended neither by his speech nor his people. On the contrary, that German-Yiddish (which only later came to be despised as *Deutschmarish*) and the unreal people he created lifted them, for the moment, out of the drabness of their lives. They seemed to touch the unreachable, to secure the unattainable. Shomer's sensational writings with their extravagant incidents, with their reward for the good and punishment for the wicked, affected uninformed, unsophisticated readers as fairy tales affect children.

It is only fifty-odd years since my father began to write. Thousands of people living today remember the thrill of their first contact with Shomer. Mention his name to any one of these and a magic picture rises in their mind's eye:

Saturday afternoon after the Sabbath meal. In the best room of the house the members of the household are assembled. Friends and neighbors join them. Old and young, employers and servants are gathered in a friendly circle to listen to the reading of Shomer's latest story or to a continuation of a *roman*—novel—that had been started the week or several weeks before. The continued episodes of the *roman* hold the listeners spellbound. When of necessity the book is finally laid away with the promise of a continued reading for the following Sabbath, the people disband reluctantly. Their minds are full of the tales they have heard. Together with the characters depicted in the book, they have laughed and wept. And now the illiterate women who cannot and the working men who do not read have to wait for the next Sabbath before they can find out just what has happened to the much-loved or much-hated people in the book.

Because hundreds of thousands of listeners could not bear this suspense, they took to reading Yiddish. They simply would not be dependent upon others to learn the fate of their and Shomer's heroes. Thus it happened that within the period of a few short years a great Yiddish-reading multitude was created.

Though a good deal of the reading of Shomer was done publicly in the manner just described, a great part of it had to be done privately and in secret. This was because in hundreds of homes Yiddish-reading as well as novel-reading was still prohibited. Each was considered disgraceful. Candles were secreted in bedrooms and barns, to be lit by stealth in the dead of the night for reading Shomer. And many of his followers tell of their watch by night as the candles sank in their sockets, hoping that they might not burn away before the end of the chapter had been reached.

It was Shomer who brought the first knowledge of a great world beyond the Jewish Pale to many thousands of young men who had spent their lives in the confines of the synagogues. It was Shomer who caused them to emerge later to become physicians, writers, lawyers, artists and men of the world.

For all this it makes me sad to look back at my father's life. Sweet, gentle, imaginative, aspiring and trusting, he poured his abundant talent upon his people, transforming their lives. He wrote by day and night until he himself could not count the volumes he had penned. Scholars and librarians say that he has produced some three hundred novels and long short stories, some fifty plays and an endless number of poems, essays and articles of every description. Publishers grew rich on his output, booksellers amassed fortunes, theaters grew up around him, while actors and managers flourished in the wealth he made for them. Yet he himself received only a pittance for his trouble. He never copyrighted anything; never demanded anything for himself or his family. He was as naive as a child in worldly matters and cared nothing at all for wealth and pomp. He was a natural writer and rejoiced in his task. He beamed over his accomplishment, delighting in the effect it produced upon his people. Like a romantic, aspiring parent he was proud when the children he had taught to read clamored for books and knowledge and foreign lands.

But my father did not observe that many of his children were outgrowing fairy tales, that they were catching up with the writers whom before his day they could not read, let alone understand. Nor did he see that a new school of writers had sprung up, to cater to the vast reading public he had created.

One day he woke up to find that these younger men had risen against him. Without comprehending the miracle he had wrought they cut him down from his high position. Bitterly they criticized the extravagance of his tales, the unreality of his characterizations, the Germanized Yiddish of his speech. In their zeal to destroy him for the sake of the finer literature for the new Yiddish reading public, they pointed only to his highblown romances and entirely ignored his homely Yiddish tales with their honest pictures of true people. They denied him rank or credit of any kind.

The naive man looked in bewilderment at the assailants about him and could not defend himself. They had forgotten the time, the place, the conditions in which he rose. They disregarded the favor with which the Germanized Yiddish of his day had been looked upon; they did not consider the disfavor in which the writing of Yiddish had been held. Like the young radicals of all new movements, they were violent and intolerant.

The Yiddish literary men, following upon the heels of Shomer, were brilliant young writers—keen minds, with glittering talents. It was easy for them to destroy the teller of fairy tales. The best way to do so was to hold him up to ridicule before his worshipful public. This they did with zeal.

It became the fashion to deride Shomer. And so it happened that those who only yesterday spoke with ecstasy of his writings and the good influence he had exercised over their lives, suddenly turned away from him. And so, too, it happened that a multitude of young writers who timidly stood at his threshold seeking his approbation, quickly turned about and flung mud at him. It became the amusement of the hour among the undiscriminating, as well as among those who really had the cause of literature at heart, to abuse Shomer.

My father was overwhelmed. Feebly he struggled against this abuse, quickly to sink into silence. But he never for one moment deserted his pen. He could no more live without writing than he could without breathing.

Many hard years followed. He died here in America at the age of fifty-nine. When his death was announced, something akin to a shock went through the Yiddish-reading world. What! Shomer has died? Shomer! Why the name is like a legend! . . . He seemed to have lived so long ago. And was he only fifty-nine? So much had transpired between his day and this! So Shomer has died! Shomer! . . . our teacher, our leader—the man who awakened us from our slumber! Shomer! Do you remember those days back in the old home when Shomer's stories were read? how his stories were smuggled into the synagogue? how anxiously we watched the sinking candle? how we wept when the lovers were parted? how we got our first glimpse of a world beyond the *shul* through Shomer? how I first learned to read because of Shomer? how my thirst for education was first awakened by

Shomer? how I got my first start in writing because Shomer inspired me? . . . You remember? . . . Well, Shomer is dead!

Yes, Shomer was dead. He died in a New York hospital, on the eve of my wedding to your father.

He died full of sorrow and regret, full of disappointment. The work of his life, the great thing he had done for his people, had been belittled by people who did not know how to evaluate it. And for all his labors and all the wealth he made for others, he died a poor man. And not a single personal hope of his had been realized. Not a child of his settled or provided for. Not a single one married. He died in the midst of things . . . just so. All ended.

Nochim-Mayer of the remote little Russian town of Nesvizh, died in New York, and a hundred thousand Jews turned out to follow him to his grave. Apparently, then, his people had not forgotten him even in America. And in modern Russia where Yiddish is fostered, there is a slogan, "Back to Shomer," which means, give us once more a man who could rouse a lethargic mass, a man who could by the magic of his pen inspire the multitude and lead them in wonder to dare and to achieve.

See what I have done. I have stalled time in its course and anticipated it by some fifty-odd years! We must go back over the rocky road of years and stop again at the city of Pinsk when Nochim-Mayer returned as Shomer.

In the course of a few years, *Bidna Dinneh* (poor Dinneh) became the feared and respected Madame Shaikevitsch. A little later she was a telling influence in the Yiddish theater of Odessa, and her home in that city was a salon for the Jewish literary lights of the day.

It was in Odessa, by the way, that my brother Isaac (who died at the age of two), Rose, Anna and I were born. To illustrate to you how much my mother's position in the theater meant to her, let me say that she remembers our birthdays only by their relationship to the things that happened in father's playhouse at that time. Thus, one was born about the time when the Yiddish theater was closed by governmental decree after Alexander II was assassinated, and another, myself, was born on the occasion of the premiere of a certain play. It was inconsiderate of me to come into the world at such an exciting moment. My only defense is that perhaps the excitement brought me on.

FOUR

Haiye

YOU KNOW A GOOD BIT about Haiye from what was said of her in the story of my mother. She was the girl who lingered in mother's room during the first year of her marriage, much to mother's distress. It was Haiye who listened to the learned conversation of my father and his circle of friends who aspired to "enlightenment," and it was she who learned to play chess and so aroused the envy of her harassed older sister. Haiye, too, was the one who actually brought a love affair, the first of its kind, into Reb Michel's house. The incident outraged her father and became the substance of the story Shomer used in his *Mechautonim fun Sonim.*

When you glimpsed Haiye in the lobby of the theater at the time Bertha Kalich appeared in Rose's and my play, *Eine fun Folk,* she was stumpy, palsied, an old woman with tangled hair and a weird light in her eyes. But in her day, as I have said, she was beautiful. Small and well made, she had white skin, a fine high forehead, a perfect nose, lustrous brown eyes, full lips and a mass of soft brown curls. Her hands and feet were small and extremely dainty.

My mother says that Haiye was a year younger than she.

Haiye insisted upon at least six or seven years. What the truth is, I am not sure, but I know that my mother adds a few extra years to the ages of people she does not like.

"You know," she once said to me rather solemnly, when I happened to displease her, "that you are almost fifty years old?" She had slapped on six years.

I took the statement seriously and said, "You don't say! Then how old is Abe?"

Mother loves Abe. She knew that Abe is about seven years older than I; if I were fifty, Abe would have to be fifty-seven, and that wouldn't do.

Mother thought a while. "Abe?" she asked and fell silent for a moment. I would give her no help.

"Abe?" she asked again, looking me straight in the eye. "Well, maybe I made a mistake about your age."

But Haiye, too, was unreliable in the matter of dates. She had a way of romanticizing. Even at a late day she attributed to herself qualities of youth and brilliance which had long ceased to be hers. So there was no telling just what really was the difference in age between the two sisters. For that matter everybody in the Bercinsky family was a little mixed up about his or her years. Since neither grandfather nor anybody else took the trouble of writing down a birthday when it occurred, and since there were so many children in the family, all they had when they grew up was a general idea of when they came into the world. Certain events in the history of the town helped. Thus, my mother knew that she was born in the year when the Cossacks passed through Pinsk and set fire to the city, and that happened in 1848. Another daughter dated her birth from the year and approximate month in which a windstorm uprooted the *Listcher Vald,* the nearby forest of Listch; and a third knew that she was born in the same year, and about the same time the cow gave birth to two freak calves. The boys were set right in a

way by the military records. But these, too, were undepend-
able; the entry of a boy's birth in the city register may have
been delayed for a year or two without anyone being wiser.

Since there is really no way of telling how old Haiye was,
let us say that she was eighteen years old when the great
moment of her life came and she fell in love. I begin at this
point in Haiye's life because there is nothing I can say of her
before that. None of the girls of your great-grandfather's
house attained any notice or importance until they were
ready to be married. At that point, you see, they became
important because they could bring more glory to the family
in the form of a man, and they were in a position to extend
the life of the tribe.

Haiye, however, did not follow the custom and wait
until she was spoken for by the matchmaker on behalf of
some family or other. She fell in love. The object of this
scandalous emotion was Elia Baillin, an intelligent young
man, one of those who crowded into Nochim-Mayer's
room to discuss *Haskalah*. He was a member of the Lurie
family, the richest in Pinsk, and a student at the government rabbinical school at Zhytomir. He was slight, blond,
blue eyed and curly headed. His chief fault, as far as
Haiye was concerned, was that his family employed as
their legal adviser Reb Michel's foremost rival, the
learned lawyer Getzel Tsichovsky.

But Elia Baillin was a fine young fellow who did not
involve himself in family squabbles. Besides, Reb Michel
and *Gospodin* Tsichovsky were now on very good terms.
Young Baillin had come to Pinsk to visit his relatives; but
hearing of Nochim-Mayer, he, like all the other young intel-
lectuals of Pinsk, came to Reb Michel's house to pay his
respects to the *Nesvizher* or *maskil* (citizen of Nesvizh or follower of the enlightenment). In Nochim-Mayer's room Bail-

lin saw Haiye. My mother, who was present at the time, says that the minute these two set eyes upon each other, it was as if a flame enveloped them. At that moment the two young people plunged into a passion which, though it gave meaning to their lives, marked them forever.

Today it is hardly possible to grasp the enormous difficulties confronting a person who happened to fall in love at a house like Reb Michel's in a community like Pinsk some sixty years ago. The government of the house, was, as you know, an absolute despotism. The community was strictly orthodox and forbidding, and "being in love" was a shameful state to find oneself in. Poor Haiye! What was she to do? What, indeed, if not turn to her romantic brother-in-law, Dinneh's husband, the man who wrote Hebrew verse and essays for periodicals, the man whose fantastic letters to his *kalleh* had set Pinsk on its ear? Nochim-Mayer sympathized with the young girl's troubles. Innocent as a lamb, he wiped his eyes with the back of his hand, smiled into his beard, and asked Baillin again and again to come to see him. Of course, Baillin came and of course Haiye was there to meet him.

Finally Dinneh grew rebellious. What was this? Was she going to harbor a romance in her room behind her father's back? And was her little corner in the house never to be rid of her pestiferous sister? At last she gained a whip hand over the ambitious young woman who made her life miserable. If Haiye wanted secrecy, if she wanted peace, she would have to keep out of Dinneh's room. Haiye agreed at once. But where was she to see Baillin?

Baillin had a new idea. He was an expert mathematician. Haiye was a girl most eager to learn. Why not teach her mathematics? At once he arranged with legal adviser Getzel Tsichovsky to permit Reb Michel's daughter to come to his house for lessons.

Now, Tsichovsky knew better than anyone else that
Haiye Bercinsky had a very fine home of her own in which
to take lessons in mathematics; but it pleased him to think
that Reb Michel's daughter was coming to his house more
or less secretly. This was one way of getting even with the
rival who had so often outwitted him. If the intrigue were
discovered, Getzel Tsichovsky could argue innocently, "Indeed, it was only a case of mathematics!"

The arrangements were completed and Haiye entered
upon an elaborate course of study which necessitated her
presence in Tsichovsky's house several times a week. As it
happened, Baillin was really a good teacher and Haiye a
good student. Soon the girl mastered algebra and the course
of true love ran bright and warm.

At about this time Jewish Pinsk was preparing for the
election of a government or crown rabbi. The election and
one of the candidates for office became vitally connected
with Haiye's story.

Up to the time of Alexander II (1855) there was no such
thing as a government rabbi in Russia. Every large Jewish
community had its own *Rov*, or rabbi, who was the spiritual
mentor of his people and their temporal tribunal on civic and
legal matters where Jewish law was involved. These latter
dealt with *kashruth* (the dietary laws), with marriage and
divorce, with right and wrong according to Jewish precepts,
with debt settlements, inheritance and many other matters
of human difference. It was only on rare occasion that the
Jews disputed the *Rov*'s decision or took their troubles to the
government court of law.

A government rabbi or *Rabbiner* had none of the sanctity
of the office held by the *Rov*. But he was a government
representative and so a person of importance. It was his

business to keep the record of the births and deaths in the Jewish community, present to the government the names of those reaching military age, and transact other matters for the government relating to Jewish life. The *Rabbiner* was required to be a man of modern, secular learning, to know Russian and Hebrew, and to be familiar with the ways and customs of his own people. In short the *Rabbiner* was the city's Jewish registrar and the government intermediary in the Jewish affairs of the community.

In many cities the crown rabbi was appointed by the leaders of the community. In Pinsk this office was elective. For years the man chosen for the post had been one Berel Fialkow, Reb Michel's brother-in-law, the husband of one of Yentel's sisters. He was not a particularly learned man, nor was he very conversant in Russian. But he was as good a man as could be found at the time the office was inaugurated. Now, however, there were many graduates of the *Rabbiner-schulen* (rabbinical crown schools) which had been especially established to train men for the office. There was therefore no longer any sense in keeping unqualified people at such posts. The government, moreover, urged that the old-fashioned officials were to go as soon as possible.

But Berel Fialkow was Michel Bercinsky's brother-in-law, and Reb Michel Bercinsky was a power in the community; in fact, he was its virtual ruler. His will among his followers was tantamount to law, and he willed that Berel Fialkow should remain in office. But our friend Getzel Tsichovsky opposed him. Once again a fight was on between the rivals.

It seems that Reb Michel had built up some sort of a political machine. When he put forth a candidate, that candidate won. Once or twice he had espoused Berel Fialkow's cause and the man got in. Now he again put Fialkow up as his candidate. He argued that the man's long years of experience, service and devotion to his office entitled him to keep his place. Naturally, a hue and cry arose from the opposing camp. Because Reb Michel would not brook contradiction, because he was intent upon keeping Fialkow in office, and because he well knew that the people opposing him were his bitterest rivals in every walk of life, he regarded them one and all as his personal enemies.

Machine or no machine, one could not come before the public and say, "This is the man I want for the *Rabbiner* post and you need mention no other." One had to be politic. If anyone presented himself as a qualified candidate for office, one had to question him, think profoundly, tell him he would be considered; nevertheless, one had to resist him and class him as one of the enemy's camp.

Into the turmoil of this election walked one Avrom Chaim Rosenberg, a native son of Pinsk, who had just returned from the *Rabbiner-schule* in Zhytomir where he was graduated with high honors. Many years before, when Avrom Chaim was a little boy, he had been the wonder of Pinsk because of his great capacity for learning. His father, Reb Uziel, was one of the most scholarly as well as one of the poorest men in the town. Avrom Chaim's mother died when he was still a little child. Reb Uziel raised the boy not so much on food and drink as on Talmud and scripture. At the age of thirteen, the tall, gaunt lad was a prodigy. He knew the Talmud to an astonishing extent, to say nothing of *Chumesh* and *Rashi* (the Pentateuch and its principal commentary). But even a prodigy must eat, and his father had not enough bread to feed even a starved stomach. Not knowing how else to provide for his son, Reb Uziel considered marriage for him.

There was a rich *rayfeh* in Pinsk who had an oldish and unattractive daughter. (A *rayfeh*, or *feldsher*, was a barber-surgeon, a sort of a cross between a doctor and orderly. He was in fact an unlicensed medical practitioner who picked up his knowledge by working with a physician or in a hospital. A *rayfeh* was a much-needed but not much respected member of the community, often referred to contemptuously as the "enema maker.")

The *rayfeh* of this story had amassed a fortune through his skillful medical practice, and now he was ambitious for his daughter. He knew Reb Uziel's plight and he realized the advantage of having the scholarly boy for a son-in-law. By such an alliance his daughter's as well as his own standing in the community would be raised.

But the boy was only thirteen, and his daughter was . . . !

The *rayfeh* calculated, and easily overcame his own natural objection. Was there any law anywhere stipulating just what the ages of a husband and wife should be? No. A few years one way or another. What did it matter?

So the ambitious man came to Reb Uziel with a proposal for his learned and hungry son: if the boy would become engaged to his unprepossessing daughter, he could come at once to live in his house, where there was food aplenty. Avrom Chaim could then go on with his studies unmolested until he reached the marriageable age of—say, sixteen. Then he, the *rayfeh,* would give his daughter a handsome dowry, the two youngsters would get married and everything would be splendid.

Reb Uziel looked out of the sunken sockets of his eyes at the *rayfeh*'s full round face and thought it was a good idea. Since Avrom Chaim was too young and too much of a scholar to be bothered with such matters, the transaction was concluded without him. Accordingly, the prodigy went to live at the *rayfeh*'s house and at the end of the stipulated time he married the now older and still more unprepossessing daughter.

Fourteen years later the unloved wife died, leaving her husband of thirty with four children. At about the same time, because of Polish unrest, money had greatly depreciated and Rosenberg lost the thousand rubles his wife had brought him. He was left with nothing but trouble. The poor young man was quite beside himself. How was he to look after his brood? Though he was much in demand as a teacher, he considered this mode of earning a living a precarious one. Besides, now he was in the prime of his early manhood and very ambitious. Why should he waste his time in Pinsk doing nothing in particular to better himself? So, leaving his two boys and two girls in the care of his erstwhile father-in-law, he took himself to the *Rabbiner-schule* in Zhytomir, there to qualify for the official post of crown rabbi. After graduating with high honors, he returned to his native city to stand for office in the coming election.

And so it happened that Avrom Chaim Rosenberg entered the election contest at the time when Michel Bercinsky was preparing to hold out for Berel Fialkow; and so, too, it happened that he entered Haiye's romance, tangling it hopelessly.

2

When Avrom Chaim Rosenberg arrived in town, he was quickly told by the initiated that if he wanted office he would first have to get into the good graces of Reb Michel. Rosenberg was abashed. How could he break in on a person he did not know and ask for his support? But he was quickly reassured: this Reb Michel had a son-in-law who was something of a curiosity; every *maskil* who came to town sought him out. Why should not Rosenberg do so, too? Reb Michel then could be seen and, well, perhaps the rest would somehow work out.

So one fine day a striking personality presented itself at Bercinsky's door and asked to see Nochim-Mayer Shaikevitsch. Rosenberg was over six feet tall, straight, with a carriage that was proud and dignified. His shiny black hair was combed back in orderly fashion; his short black beard was trim. His cold, gray eyes looked straight ahead of him through gold-rimmed spectacles. He spoke Russian fluently and he was now not only a great scholar of Talmudic literature, but an ardent champion of *Haskalah.*

Avrom Chaim Rosenberg and Nochim-Mayer Shaikevitsch had much in common and found much to say to each other. Together they sought the good offices of the man of iron will who ruled Pinsk.

Reb Michel looked and listened critically to Reb Uziel's son, whose mental faculties had been acclaimed practically since his infancy. And this man wanted to be the *Rabbiner* in Pinsk instead of his faithful brother-in-law Berel Fialkow. A formidable candidate. A dangerous enemy! Far more so than any other man in the field.

While the three men talked, Haiye came into the room with a message for her father. Haiye came into the room— and suddenly everything in Avrom Chaim that had been denied him, all beauty and love, seemed to spring to life. The learned man forgot the rabbinate and whatever else he came for. All the coldness and lack of sentiment that Rosenberg was accused of by the *rayfeh*'s family, had, at the sight of the girl, vanished. All his aroused emotions seemed to concentrate themselves on one object: Haiye.

Rosenberg became a constant visitor at Reb Michel's house. Looking at Haiye with hungry eyes, it did not take him long to discern the girl's secret: her love affair with Baillin, her visits to Tsichovsky, her lessons in mathematics. So, the slight young man with the blonde curls was luring Haiye with algebra! Not bad. But if that was the case, he, Rosenberg, had a bag of tricks all his own. He, too, would take to educating her. He would teach her Russian; and he would do it right in her father's house, under Baillin's very nose.

Soon Rosenberg's big overshoes found their place in the main hall instead of near Nochim-Mayer's door.

"Ah!" Yentel would say caustically, observing those enormous overshoes, "the long one is here again!" His six feet two looked gigantic to her four feet nothing.

During the days when he could not get to see his pupil, he sent her messages—Russian messages—many of them by his twelve-year-old son, Uziel. The boy, a clever child, was much impressed by the household of his father's pupil, and particularly by her little sister Fraydel. But that is another episode in the Bercinsky family drama.

Now Baillin was quite aghast with apprehension. What was going on? What was he to do? He certainly could not raise any objections to Haiye's learning Russian. He certainly could not criticize Rosenberg's method. He taught her in the open where everybody could see them. But did Rosenberg put any special meaning into the . . . "I love—you love—we love" of the conjugations? Baillin ached and wondered and waited patiently for the hours of algebra when he might balance his equations and determine unknown quantities.

But not all of his problems could be solved to his entire satisfaction. Assured of Haiye's love, he still had to leave her unprotected in the hands of that teacher of Russian while he himself had to return to the *Rabbiner-schule* from which his rival had already been graduated. It was a distressing situation.

What Baillin and Haiye said to each other in their secret hour of parting nobody knows, but it is certain that they vowed eternal love until "the sun grows cold and the stars grow old and the leaves of the judgment books unfold!"

Baillin went away to Zhytomir and left Rosenberg in possession. How well the Russian lessons proceeded or for how long I cannot tell you, but a day came when the erstwhile distinguished rabbinical candidate again presented himself to Reb Michel, this time to ask for his daughter's hand.

Reb Michel looked at Avrom Chaim Rosenberg and wondered how such a keen and intelligent man could ask for the impossible. Here he was, a widower of over thirty-five, the father of four big children, the former son-in-law of a *rayfeh*, asking nothing less than the hand of the lovely young daughter of Reb Michel Bercinsky.

Reb Michel told him plainly what he thought of his proposition, but Rosenberg was by no means defeated. He swallowed hard. Never mind his humble past, the *rayfeh*'s daughter or his four children. He would reach a station even so lovely a creature as Haiye would be honored to share.

Rosenberg opened a private school for the study of Russian, Hebrew and secular subjects. And he resolved that, come what might, he would be the crown rabbi of Pinsk and Haiye would be his wife. He enlisted the help of Getzel Tsichovsky.

Now Haiye was frightened. In haste she wrote to Baillin urging his immediate return. Something would have to be done, for Rosenberg was giving her no peace. Now, she argued, was Baillin's chance to step in and ask her father for her hand. At this moment, to ward off Rosenberg, Reb Michel might overlook the young man's boldness.

Slight, blond, impetuous young Baillin came rushing back to Pinsk to appear before his beloved one's temperamental father. Modest though the youth was, he proclaimed his advantages: his age, his education, his family, his connections. But Reb Michel gazed at him in wonder.

"Elia Baillin," he said to the agitated young man, "but you forget . . ."

"Forget what?" Elia stammered, thoughts of Tsichovsky running through his mind.

"Must I speak?" Reb Michel's trembling hand revealed his agitation. But Baillin insisted.

"Your aunt," Reb Michel said gravely, "has left the Jewish faith. She has gone over to another religion. An apostate!"

There is no word that has a more frightful ring than *meshummad* (apostate) when uttered by a religious Jew. It sullies the name of one's family for generations.

"But," poor Baillin stammered, "she is so far away; in another town—in another country—I have never spoken to her. I have never even seen her."

Reb Michel shook his head. "Forget that you have ever met Haiye," he said. "Never speak of this again."

This was the end. Baillin knew it, and felt it, though his thoughts ran back to Haiye and vowed that come what might, they would never leave each other. Baillin never again spoke to Reb Michel of his daughter; but he followed her everywhere, by day and by night. He loved her, and he knew that his love was returned.

One night Reb Michel came home from a late meeting at the town hall. He entered the courtyard and was about to fasten the gate when he saw someone leap from a window of the house.

"A burglar," Reb Michel thought.

With his usual courage he made straight for the intruder.

He caught Baillin. The trembling youth explained that, through the closed window, he had been watching Haiye in her sleep. But Reb Michel raged. Upon pain of bodily punishment he forbade Baillin to come anywhere within view of his house. Baillin disappeared.

The next morning Reb Michel sent for Rosenberg. He had reconsidered his proposal, he told him; also, he would support his candidacy for the rabbinate.

Haiye put up a desperate fight. She loved Baillin; but she could not hold out against the combined forces of the father she loved and feared, the mother she hated, and the determination of the man for whom she had become a consuming flame.

This was the story my father used in his *Mechautonim fun Sonim,* the tale which so fascinated the editor Samuel Joseph Fuenn, and which later was read with such avidity by Reb Michel's household and the people of the city of Pinsk. Rosenberg, you see, who had been considered an enemy, had now become a kinsman by marriage. Hence the title of the tale.

Rosenberg was of course elected to the crown rabbinate, but he did not marry Haiye without trouble, for the girl put every possible obstacle in his way. She insisted that she would not marry him while his daughter Shayne-Channe, a girl of seventeen, remained unmarried at his home. When the father hastily made a match for her, Haiye declared that she would not undertake to mother his other three children, of whom the youngest was the boy Uziel. The three then had to be provided for and placed in the care of their maternal grandfather, the *rayfeh.* Then only could the scholarly crown rabbi of Pinsk establish the woman he loved in an environment he thought fitting for her. He furnished a fine home, engaged servants, and catered to his wife's ambition for culture by buying a piano and obtaining the best available teacher for her. This was no mean accomplishment, for pianos and instructors were rare in the Pinsk of that day. The pampered young wife had become the envy of all the young women of the town.

While all this was going on, Baillin was distraught. The young man beat his breast, tore his hair, swore eternal vengeance against the man who had robbed him of his love, and against the woman who, from his point of view, had betrayed him.

One day he burst into Dinneh's and Nochim-Mayer's room, where other members of the Bercinsky household were present.

"She wanted to be the wife of the crown rabbi, did she?" he screamed. "Well, she shall not be that for any length of time! You see the palm of this hand?" he continued, thrusting forward that trembling member. "When hair grows upon it, Rosenberg will be reelected to his office!"

And, strange as it may seem, when Baillin came back from Zhytomir a full-fledged candidate for the rabbinate, he, with his relatives the Luries, gave Rosenberg such a battle at the polls, that, despite Rosenberg's strength and Reb Michel's influence, he drove the man from his post. Then, at the proper time, he strode into Rosenberg's house demanding the books and the keys of the office. Even as he did so he looked about eagerly for Haiye, but she was nowhere to be seen. She had hidden herself in a clothes closet where she almost suffocated her baby boy Mayshe to prevent him from crying loud enough for Baillin to hear.

For a time Rosenberg remained in Pinsk teaching at his private school, but, when a call came from Nikolayiev offering the crown rabbinate for that city, he gladly accepted. At last he could put distance between Haiye and the man she

. . . well, I don't think that Rosenberg would have cared to name the emotion his wife had for the man she was leaving behind.

I don't know much about Haiye's and Rosenberg's life during their long stay in Nikolayiev. All I know is that they lived in state, that they had three more children, all of whom bore biblical names, that Rosenberg became widely known as a Hebrew scholar and writer, that Haiye, with the air of a grand dame, considered herself the symbol of lost love. As a child I had only one glimpse of the great lady, when she came to Pinsk on a visit; I knew her only when, some years later, she, with her husband and children, came to America.

3

Rosenberg and Haiye were heartsick on being transplanted to a foreign land at middle age. Everything they were proud of, everything that was important to them and adorned them was lopped off, and nothing was left but a bare little stump of existence. That is what happened to thousands like them, of the most respected Jewish families of Russia, who were forced to leave their country by the terror of Alexander III's reign. When I think of proud, romantic Haiye cooped up in an ugly little New York flat, without means or help, of scholarly Rosenberg slaving in the dark cellar that held his printing shop, of his doing chores for his wife by day and sitting through the nights over the manuscripts he was writing, I cannot help grieving for their tragedy.

Like all the immigrants who came to America in the last decade of the last century, Rosenberg and Haiye were quickly lost in the hubbub of the new world. They and their children were just so many "greenhorns" among tens of

thousands more. They were of no significance, and nobody
paid any attention to them. A tall white-haired scholarly
man toiling in a dingy shop? Well, what of it? There were
many more like him. A short, round little woman struggling
along in a miserable tenement? Who cared? Their children
forced into the cellar printing shop with their father? Well,
why not? Were they the only children in New York's cellars? Station, life, position, all had vanished when the crown
rabbi left the country in which he was born and came with
a horde of other immigrants to start life over again in the
land of promise. Values had changed. Things that seemed
important in Nikolayiev took on a comic aspect in New
York. Haiye considered herself a woman of quality and education. But there were tens of thousands of women in New
York with whom she could not compare. She thought herself too good for the common drudgery of life? Well, she
needn't be ridiculous. At her age she was romanticizing.

Haiye shut herself up in her ramshackle home and associated with nobody. Behind the locked doors of her flat
she wore the old velvet wraps she had brought from Nikolayiev and maintained her dignity. Her aged husband eked
out a living for his family as best he could, and when the
children emerged from his cellar, became students and
finally attained their chosen professions, he, Rosenberg,
the great scholar, at seventy began a new Hebrew work,
his monumental *Ozar ha-Shemot,* an encyclopedia of the
Bible. It was a task that would take a young man a lifetime
to complete. When questioned on the scope of the project,
Rosenberg swallowed hard, as was his wont, and said
coolly that he would work on it as long as he happened to
live. If he died before completing his work, well, at least
some of it would be done. As a matter of fact, he finished
the project, published it in ten parts and lived to see it

hailed as an invaluable contribution to Hebrew literature.

But his wife gave him no attention. All his grand accomplishments, which he dedicated to her, did not impress her. To Haiye, Rosenberg remained the man who had blasted her romance and deprived her of her heart's desire. Perhaps it was her longing for the irretrievable past that caused her to identify it with Baillin, the man she had loved, and to make him the symbol of all things worthwhile in the past. Rosenberg represented the grueling present, and he had no defense against his wife's unreasonable attitude.

"The late lamented Baillin," he would begin, with the slightest shade of satisfaction that he could speak of his rival as one who had passed, as indeed, Baillin had. But Rosenberg could not get very much further, for Haiye would fly at him in a fury.

Thus the lives of these two people passed in a confused mixture of misery and passion. Their four children grew up. Then three of them cast off the Rosenberg name, which their father had made famous. They found it too Jewish and a hindrance to their advancement. They adopted a Russian name and married Gentiles. And these were the children whose mother, Haiye, was sacrificed because the man she loved had an aunt—unknown to him—who went over to another faith!

In the last days of her life Haiye was cared for by the stepdaughter she would not have in the house when she married Rosenberg. That daughter was another old woman transplanted to America. Had it not been for her care Haiye's last days would have been miserable indeed.

Avrom Chaim Rosenberg died when he was nearly ninety years old. Haiye survived him by a few months. He was buried in a cemetery in Brooklyn; she was cremated in a western city where one of her sons had finally taken her to be cared for. The tombstone that marks Rosenberg's grave carries the legend that the remains of the husband and wife rest together in the sod. This is not true, for in death even as in life they were apart. Perhaps their children had placed a handful of Haiye's ashes in their father's grave. If so, the ashes would be symbolic, for it was ashes—both of love and life—that Haiye gave to her remarkable husband.

FIVE

Dvayreh

DVAYREH WAS THE ONLY ONE of Reb Michel's children who hated both her father and mother with a bitterness that never abated. I do not know whether or not they deserved this hatred. All I can do is to give you both her story and my childhood impressions of her.

Dvayreh was the last of the many girls who preceded Reb Michel's and Yentel's second son, Avrom. Her birth was, as we may imagine, no event of great moment.

"Another *muchinetze* has arrived," Yentel remarked. *Muchinetze* is an improvised word derived from Russian and means a female sufferer.

With the coming of Avrom the entire pack of girls, Dvayreh included, faded into the background. They had been born; very well, let them live. But Avrom was there now—another *kaddish*—and a new light was shed upon the house.

When Dvayreh was about five years old she was the prettiest and merriest of all the children in the great house. She hopped about like an elf. Her favorite playmate was Darel-Derel, the little daughter of one of the servants in the house. This child was so called to denote the manner in which she mixed up all the words and phrases that came into her mouth.

One day the family was much concerned with little Avrom, who had fallen sick. Beautiful little Dvayreh and Darel-Derel were left to themselves in the yard where they danced about. Great was their joy when the huge gates opened and into the courtyard rode the equipage of a Polish nobleman who had come to consult *Pani* Bercinsky on legal matters. While the nobleman was thus engaged, his servant, the driver, had an argument with his horses. The two little girls were much amused to see the man talking to the beasts and so came close to listen. At the peak of the argument, the driver raised his hand and hit one of the horses on the head. There was an immediate stampede. Horses and coach ran wild about the yard, the driver in angry pursuit, the two little girls running about in fright. When the animals were finally brought under control, Darel-Derel was nowhere to be seen (she had dropped into the cellar) but little Dvayreh lay in the courtyard with a great ugly wound over her left eye, where the horse's hoof had trampled her.

The doctor who was hurriedly called had a hard time bringing the little girl to life. When she drew breath again, her face was marked forever. There was a deep scar on her forehead over her left eye, and the eye itself was thrown out of focus. Her neck, too, was scarred.

I do not know whether Dvayreh's mind was affected because of the slight indentation of the skull or whether she became a backward child because she was conscious of her disfigurement. Perhaps, too, being marred, she was considered a damaged article.

It is easy to understand that, in such a light, her position in the house was not an enviable one. People in those days did not indulge in psychology. Neither did they know of complexes. If a child—or, for that matter, a grown-up person —was not up to the mark, so much the worse for him. He was a numbskull, an idiot, a fool, and that was that.

So Dvayreh grew to maidenhood a marked creature. Her education was even less than that given the other Bercinsky daughters. Her talk, always uncouth because of its self-consciousness, was made ridiculous by the look of her crossed eyes and the jerkiness of her gestures. Dvayreh became not only the black sheep of the family, but the butt of general amusement. Still, a daughter of an old Jewish home had to be married off no matter what she was—especially when there were other children close behind her growing into manhood and womanhood. No younger member of a family was eligible for marriage while an older brother or sister remained single. Only on rare occasions would an older brother step aside to permit the marriage of a younger sister. The sidetracking of an older daughter for the marriage of a younger one was a deed most solemnly avoided since it would openly imply the undesirability of the older one. So it happened that one unattractive daughter would for years block the marriages of a long line of younger girls.

Dvayreh was followed by the adored second son, Avrom, and behind him, among a host of girls who did not survive, were Fraydel and Menye, bright and blooming. Though these girls were considerably younger than Dvayreh, there was no doubt in Reb Michel's mind that his extremely unattractive daughter would form a stumbling block for the rest of the children. For her own sake as well as for theirs she had to be safely guided into marriage.

Reb Michel, as you know, was a resourceful man. He took himself to a distant town, where he visited the *klois* (synagogue) and mingled with its poverty-stricken students. He

came upon one who was much to his liking for the object
he had in mind. This young man, Shmuel by name, had been
orphaned since early childhood. He came from a good family, was fairly handsome, a good student and honest. Reb
Michel talked to Shmuel and made clear what was on his
mind. He, Reb Michel, had a rather unattractive daughter,
one getting on in years. She was no great catch, but her
father was willing and ready to make life-long provision for
her and the man she married. Food, shelter and every opportunity to study would be given in abundance to Dvayreh's
husband. He would never have need to worry, never have
a care to heed. Besides, Reb Michel said, such a man would
gain a most devoted wife; for his daughter, being what she
was, would greatly cherish the man who made her his wife.
Reb Michel talked and Shmuel yielded.

So it happened that Reb Michel came home in triumph
with a *chossen* for Dvayreh, and the poor creature was raised
to an ecstasy of joy. She, like all the pretty girls of the town,
had become a *kalleh.*

We suppose logically that to secure his find, Reb Michel
should have arranged for an immediate marriage between
Dvayreh and Shmuel. But there was custom to observe and
there was such a thing as decorum. Rushing a marriage was
decidedly in bad taste. Besides, both *chossen* and *kalleh* had to
be prepared for their marriage. So Shmuel was lodged in Reb
Michel's house while tailors and dressmakers were called in
to fit out the pair.

In Pinsk the making of a garment was not a matter of a
couple of days' work. The tailors and their apprentices sat
on their work tables, their legs crossed beneath them, their
measuring tapes about their necks, their skullcaps perched
on the backs of their heads, their singing voices raised
blithely in their special little tailor ditties, while shears

flashed, and needles stitched the fine materials of the wedding garments.

Dvayreh, whose sweet singing voice had not been impaired by the horse's trampling hoofs, kept up a merry refrain from morn till night. Her chief concern now was the goose-down she had gathered for many years in anticipation of the great event which was now actually to occur. From many hidden cupboards of the house she brought forth great sacks of white down and proceeded to divide it into pillows and featherbeds. Since in those days felt or hair mattresses were hardly known to Pinsk, and since woolen blankets were but rarely used, featherbeds were held in the highest possible esteem. Indeed, such bedclothes were so highly regarded that they were the first thing to think of for a bride's wedding outfit. If they were of good quality, feather beds were passed on from generation to generation. I myself still have a couple of pillows given to me by my mother who brought them from Pinsk where she probably received them from her mother.

So there Dvayreh sat in the yard, singing at the top of her voice and stuffing the tickings full of down. What did she care if it formed a snowlike flurry about her and covered her hair with an unbecoming whiteness? What did she care if she wore an old shabby dress while she was thus happily engaged? What did she care if she looked her very worst! Soon enough these would be things of magnificent comfort. Feathers could then be brushed away and the fine new clothes which the tailors were making could then be worn. Happy days were in sight of Dvayreh's deep-set eyes.

But curious things were happening inside the house, where Dvayreh's *chossen* sat swaying over his books. Two magnificent blooming young girls were running circles about him, teasing him and driving him to distraction. These were Fraydel and Menye. From their infancy they had laughed at Dvayreh. She was that grotesque older sister who had always been the amusement of the family. Now that queer sister was—of all things—going to get married. And here was the fellow who was going to take her. The girls rocked with laughter. They pictured Dvayreh in tender moments when she would look at her husband with her crossed eyes. They had visions of her saying words of affection in her abrupt manner while her hands fluttered and her voice broke in the most unexpected places. The girls held their sides with laughter, and Shmuel, through the corner of his eye, saw them do it.

Shmuel rocked over his books harder than ever. The girls continued to giggle, and they asked him impertinent questions. They were young and very bold. Shmuel grew red but he would not answer. A religious man does not speak to women unless he has to, and he never looks at them even if they are blooming and beautiful. He kept to his books and his studies, but nobody knew what went on inside of him.

In the intervals when Reb Michel was home all was well. Then there was talk of *Chumesh* (Pentateuch) and *Rashi* (eleventh-century commentator on Torah and Talmud), and many points of Talmudic lore were discussed. But no sooner was the Czar out of his kingdom than mischief was at work again, and Yentel paid no attention at all.

The featherbeds were done at last and the tailors were bringing in the finished garments for inspection. One by one these were now being tried on, and the battles that were waged in Dvayreh's room at these fittings were disgraceful. The queer older sister's tongue lashed the younger ones, and they either answered back in anger or mocked her pitilessly —until she drove them out of her sight.

Shmuel, in his room, was also trying on his clothes. When he put on the fine black suit in which he was to be married, he also placed the gold watch which Reb Michel had given him in his pocket and fastened it securely with its golden chain. Things might be well if only—

Shmuel and the tailors came out into the *salle* to get the family's opinion of the garment. Everybody gathered about him in admiration. Fraydel and Menye were quite in ecstasy. The tailors, of course, could not stop praising his figure and the fit of the costume they had created. Just then in through the door came Dvayreh in her wedding dress. She, too, wanted an opinion. Poor, unfortunate Dvayreh! With no one but the dressmakers to help her, and they unable to cope with her, her gown was not at all what it should have been. The figure she presented was more like a scarecrow's than a woman's. The gathering in the *salle* took a quick look and was dumbfounded.

Finally Fraydel and Menye stepped out. They must have rehearsed their greeting for together they said:

"Killeh Mizeltov!"

They used the word *killeh* instead of *kalleh. Kalleh* means bride-to-be. *Killeh* means a rupture. The two words sound very much alike. They said *mizeltov* for *mazeltov.* The latter word means good luck; the former has no meaning. It was just a distortion of the kindly greeting.

In her anger Dvayreh caught up a stick and ran after her pretty sisters. Shmuel looked on in anguish. When the excitement had subsided he complained of a headache. He must go for a walk, he said. He slipped on his coat, got his hat, went out and never returned.

2

It was not only a matter of a bride being deserted on the eve of her marriage. Dvayreh was a marked woman, losing her chance for life. In those days, deserting a bride was a matter of even greater significance than it is today, and it left an indelible stain on the woman's name. Dvayreh was now marked not only in face but in name. Forevermore she would be known as the deserted one, the undesirable, the creature whom no man would have either for home, comfort or opportunity.

I cannot tell you of the suffering Dvayreh must have endured. All this happened long before my time. But I know that she became a cursing, disturbing element in grandfather's house. She kept to her room whenever possible, there to sing in a strain of deep melancholy, to weep or to pray to God for the destruction of her family.

It was certain now that Dvayreh would remain unmarried. What was to become of Avrom? Of Fraydel and Menye? True, these two girls had by their youthful heedlessness brought this evil upon Dvayreh; but it was up to Reb Michel to solve the almost insoluble problem. Should he let Dvayreh remain an old maid? Should he marry off the younger children before her? Should he at all hazards try to get a husband for her?

Resourceful Reb Michel finally arrived at a satisfactory conclusion. He knew exactly the man who would marry Dvayreh in spite of everything.

Reb Michel had a brother by the name of Berel, whom I have already mentioned. He was that slow, phlegmatic man who would do nothing but pray and beget children. This was the brother for whom Reb Michel bought the "city scales"—that is, the privilege of weighing for a price per pound the produce that came or went as freight on the boats which plied the Pina River.

Though he was known as Berel the Master of the Scales, it was really his wife, Gittle, who carried on his business. Besides this she managed his house and bore him many children.

There is an unusual Yiddish folk song which must have been created by women like Gittle. It goes:

> *Loift er in Beth'medresh*
> *Un laihent alle sedres*
> *Er loift shin, aher*
> *Un burtshet vi a ber*
> *Di veib zizt in her haim*
> *Ferumert zich dos leben*
> *Oi vai zu ihr*
> *Vos far a man men hot ihr gegeben*
> *In mark darf zi loifen*
> *Holz darf zi kaifen*
>
> *Brait darf zi baken*
> *Holz darf zi haken*
> *Nashen darf zi di kinder*
> *Yederen bazinder*
> *Dem shlofen laigen*
> *Dem zumachen di aigen*
> *Dem di kop shmiren*
> *Dem in droisen fihren*
> *Un dos is noch nit gor*
> *A brith oif alle yor*

> He runs to the synagogue
> And reads all the laws,
> He runs here and there
> Growling like a bear.
>
> The wife stays at home
> Crying up to heaven,
> Oh, woe unto her,
> What a husband she was given!

To market she must hurry
Wood to buy and worry,
Bread she must bake,
Kindling she must break;

The children she must care for,
That's what she was there for,
Put this one to bed,
Smear up that one's head;

Soothe this one's ache,
To the out-house that one take,
And for measure full or near,
A baby every year.

Gittle's was the lot of the woman described in the song. She hustled, cared for the home and bore many children. She wheezed with asthma until she could wheeze no longer. She died young and left Berel with a family of five children, three of whom were asthmatic.

When she was buried, Berel raised his eyes to the high heavens for help; he himself could do nothing whatsoever. Soon he lost the "scales" and the income on which to subsist. Then he turned not to heaven but directly to his brother Michel for help. And that already burdened man shouldered the responsibility.

In the depth of his anxiety for Dvayreh, Reb Michel thought of Berel. Here was a man with a helpless brood without a woman to aid them. And here was forlorn, unwanted Dvayreh without a hope in the world for a husband. Why not unite them?

The Jewish law, while forbidding the marriage of aunt and nephew, permits the marriage of uncle and niece. Such matches are by no means uncommon. So Michel came home one day and told Dvayreh that she was going to be married after all—that is, if she wanted to be. He named the man he proposed as her husband. Dvayreh looked at her father in her own queer way, nodded consent, and went off muttering.

What Berel thought of the match it is hard to say, but he quickly acquiesced in his brother's plans. I am afraid he had no choice in the matter. He was not only supported by his brother, but he knew that as a pious Jew he was living in a state of sin if he lived without a wife. (It is obligatory for a pious Jew of eighteen or over to marry and have a wife so that he may live in peace with himself and not look with offending eyes upon the women who come within his ken.) What other chance did Berel have of getting a woman to share his life?

So Reb Michel and Berel concluded the match and set the day for the wedding.

Many people gathered at Reb Michel's house for the wedding. All who wished the family well and were sorry for Dvayreh now came to bid her *mazeltov.* She would be a respected married woman.

Wearing the dress she had so joyously put on and so ruefully taken off in preparation for her union with Shmuel, Dvayreh allowed herself to be married to Berel. The wedding feast was as gay as it was ample. If there were titters among the young folk as they regarded the bride and groom, these were quickly suppressed. Dvayreh's marriage meant peace at home and the clearance of the matrimonial path for the rest of the Bercinsky family.

When at last the ceremonies were over, the feast board deserted and the last of the company departed, Berel made ready to take his bride home.

But at that moment Dvayreh looked at her father and her husband with a fierce, sardonic expression. Never would she go to Berel's home, she screamed. Never would she share his bed or board. All she wanted was to clear her name of the stigma her family had forced upon her. She was no longer to be known as the unwanted but rather as the unwanting. Did they think they could get rid of her by palming her off on a doddering old man? Well, they had been mistaken. She was a married woman now, but she would divorce her husband for many good reasons that she knew of, her father would have to help her go through with it all, and he would have to keep her in his own house and provide for her until such time as he could find the proper man for her to marry.

Consternation fell upon the family. They well knew what Dvayreh's determination meant. There would be no peace from her.

No amount of talk could budge Dvayreh from her decision. She held her family up to ridicule, she cursed each member of it bitterly and she went back to her room and locked the door behind her.

You may have guessed that Dvayreh did not state her case as clearly as I tell it to you here; she was not exactly articulate. But there was no mistaking the things she meant, and there was no uncertainty of what she would do.

And so Dvayreh brought down the anger of her tribe upon her. She gained a new name for herself: *die meshugeneh* —the lunatic—and by that name she was thereafter known.

That of all Reb Michel's children Dvayreh should have been the only one to resist his will, that of all the women in the world this poor marked creature should have remained for many years and through her own choice "a wife in name only" seems a bit preposterous. But it is true. Dvayreh never crossed the threshold of her husband's house.

3

I first saw Dvayreh when I was a small child. She was then about thirty. Of course she lived at her father's, that is, my grandfather's house. Childhood colors everything that comes within its vision, and when I look back at my grandfather's house it is as if I were gazing upon a place of enchantment. I see those vast rooms with their corner mirrors in the *salle* reaching from floor to ceiling. I see the great sofas, the chairs, the silver closet, the paintings, the immense clock, the table with its many lit Sabbath candles as so many charmed objects in a dream. I see the gaiety of its festivals, I hear the singing of the *chazzan* and his choir, the singing in which the large family joins—singing which, alas, has long ceased. It is all very far away, yet very clear and real to me. Grandfather's house, that place of my childhood's desire, seems now a place of turmoil and force as well as gaiety. Over all its beauty looms one dark shadow—Dvayreh. She is gloomy, alone, dressed in black. Her hair is tightly drawn back from her forehead to reveal the ugly scar on the temple over her left eye. Her eyes are deeply sunk in her head and give her an evil look. No one has a kind word for her. No one pays any attention to her. Her room is the only dark one in the house.

I remember: Dvayreh goes about the house muttering, muttering. What is she saying? I steal up to her and listen. She is uttering the most frightful imprecations. She is imploring the high heavens to bring down the most awful punishments upon her father and mother! She pours unbelievable curses upon the heads of her sisters Fraydel and Menye! These two young women burst into the room. Both are gaily dressed, Fraydel in red, for she is a gypsy type—

a brunette with black bangs and flashing dark eyes. Menye is in white. Her cheeks are flushed and she prefers pale colors and wears innumerable strings of beads about her neck. They rush into the room together chattering gaily. Dvayreh meets them with curses. She calls them vile names. They laugh at her and call her *meshugeneh*. Everyone in the house calls her that. *"Avek meshugeneh!"* "Go away, you lunatic!" Dvayreh hears that wherever she turns. Lunatic! Go away, you lunatic! And off she goes to her dark room muttering, cursing.

Once my mother had to go to a spa. She took Anna along, and left Rose and me to be cared for at grandfather's house. Fraydel and Menye were supposed to take care of us, but actually Dvayreh did. The pretty girls only took us out for a little lark or two, but Dvayreh kept us clean and played games with us. Yes, indeed, she played, singing all the while. I distinctly remember one of our games—"cat and mouse": Dvayreh placed two chairs between her and Rose or me. We were the mice, she the cat. We hid behind the back of the chair, peeping out every little while to see if the coast was clear. Dvayreh, behind her chair, did similar peeping to see when the mouse would start running. So there we stood, each behind a chair, spying upon each other and singing slyly as we did so:

> *Eh—ku, ku*
> *Ku-e ku-e ku ku,*
> *Eh—ku, ku,*
> *Ku-e, ku-e, ku.*

This we repeated until the mouse ventured forth and started to run around the chairs pursued by the cat. Of course, in the end Dvayreh always caught us; she then folded us close in her arms in her own awkward way and said kind things to us. We liked her very much.

At night Dvayreh put us to sleep in her bed. After we undressed and were safe under the feather comforters, she would come into the room with a mouthful of water which she emptied into our hands. This was to make sure that we were clean before we uttered the name of God when we mentioned Him in our prayers. It was she who taught us the bedtime prayer. We said it in Hebrew, of course, which neither we nor Dvayreh, for that matter, understood. Sometimes Dvayreh did not leave us in the darkness at once. She would sit at the foot of the bed singing all sorts of little songs to us. Most of them were folksongs, or the songs of Elyakum Zunser, the man who was to be your paternal grandfather. How poor Dvayreh sang those songs, shedding tears as she sang! Then she would rise in her curiously abrupt way, wipe her crossed eyes and her nose with her hands, say a sort of comical "good night" in a rather raucous voice and leave us in the dark. No matter how sorry we were for Dvayreh we could not help laughing a little at her when she left.

In the morning before we got out of bed Dvayreh again brought a mouthful of water which she emptied into our hands. (Pious Jews must not, on rising, walk more than a few feet without washing their hands.) Later she washed and dressed us and taught us to say the morning prayer, also in the unfamiliar Hebrew. If in the broad daylight Dvayreh tried to engage us closely in any task, she was not very successful. We were too busy watching her odd ways and her manner of speech. Her movements were so clumsy and abrupt! Her speech, even in kindness, was so curiously harsh!

Once we heard Dvayreh quarreling with her sister Menye. She concluded her argument by saying, *"A shed in dein taten's tatarein."* "May the devil enter into your father's father."

Since Menye was her own sister, Dvayreh was cursing her own grandfather. Even we children could not help laughing at Dvayreh. Poor thing.

4

When her parents died Dvayreh was about fifty. She was still unmarried. The make-believe wedding with Berel did not count. She had divorced him as she had threatened.

When the Bercinsky houses were sold and the money received and distributed, some of it was allotted to Dvayreh. It was then that she went to Homel where Menye lived and finally made the long trip to join her kin in America. This queer middle-aged woman, who had never seen anything of the world beyond the few streets surrounding her father's house, suddenly found herself traveling across the countries of Europe and across the great Atlantic in company with Avrom, Menye and the latter's husband, Boruch.

She landed in New York about twenty-nine years ago. She had no affection for anyone here but Nochim-Mayer, who had been kind to her in Pinsk. But he, poor man, was living out his last few weeks at the hospital. He would not, out of pride, let any of the new arrivals see him in his agony. Dvayreh, like the others, did not see him again alive. She followed his funeral procession in tearful reverence.

When the newcomers were assigned to the homes of their different relatives, Dvayreh's lot fell in with Haiye. Out of mercy to both these women, I will not record this period of bondage. But you will be interested to hear that Dvayreh was married.

As luck would have it, Dvayreh was again to be the laughing-stock of a new generation of youngsters who did not even know her. Her new husband's name was "Elephant," and that was enough to make her the object of their endless mirth. This was heightened to a great degree when the "Elephant" showed up one day and turned out to be a dwarfish man with long, dangling arms and disheveled hair.

This was the man Dvayreh married in America. The marriage was arranged by a matchmaker. I don't know how it all came about. It was an adjustment of mercy, I think, made by Haiye and Rosenberg, for which poor Dvayreh was extremely grateful. She certainly could not hope to pick or choose again, and she ached to have a corner in the world she could call her own, so she took whatever man would have her. "Elephant" was a widower who wanted a wife to cook and wash and sew for him so that he could live cheaply on the few dollars a week he earned polishing new toilet seats. The man considered himself worthy of a dowry, and members of the family pooled their contributions and presented it (several hundred dollars) to Dvayreh when she was married at my mother's house.

The two were established in a little Harlem apartment, and there they stayed for twenty-five years until "Elephant" died. I had a curious experience when I went to see Dvayreh after her husband's demise. Two or three times I knocked at her door before I heard her well-remembered voice call out in a queer Russian: *"K'toh tam?"* "Who is there?"

Why in Russian? Because Dvayreh in her mind still lived in Pinsk. Anyone who knocks at the door must surely be a *goy*—a Gentile; and a Gentile, of course, speaks Russian. Hearing my answer and being assured that it was a relative, Dvayreh opened the door. In I walked and the queer woman clicked her heels together, put her hand to her forehead in a military salute, and indeed gave that salute in Russian. My heart sank, but I bade her good morning and sat down to what I expected to be a conversation. It turned out to be a

monologue, with Dvayreh doing the talking. Her hearing
was impaired, and her deeply sunken eyes seemed not to see
me. But she knew who I was and felt at ease. I was a friend
to whom she could open her heart, and so she did. I listened
attentively and did my best not to laugh and not to cry,
although I wanted very much to do both. Dvayreh talked
on. She had been buried in this dark hole every minute of
the time since she married, but she pointed to the wretched
dwelling with pride.

"Do you see? Do you see?" she asked. "All this is mine.
Do you know of many people who have three rooms all to
themselves? And all this furniture! It's mine. And all the
pillows and all the featherbeds! And this stove, you see? I
am going to start a fire soon, and the house will be warm and
comfortable like a paradise. And I have plenty to eat—and
I go to *shul.* I am a person, the equal of all."

All this she said in a Yiddish dialect I did not know still
existed. It contained quaint Russian and Polish words that
I had not heard since my childhood in Pinsk. Then Dvayreh
told me of her husband.

It seemed that for a moment she had forgotten he was
dead. She praised the man's words and deeds, but the things
she unwittingly revealed were so appalling that a picture of
a monster grew before my eyes. Yet this woman tried to
convert every cruelty he visited upon her into an act of
affection. Poor Dvayreh.

She would wipe her bad eye with the back of her hand
saying:

"If only things do not get worse. I am so happy! So
happy!"

Finally we got around to her husband's death. She grew
very still. Yes, of course, she knew he was gone. She started
to tell me how the end came.

She began with an illness from which he had suffered twenty-four years ago, and which had nothing whatsoever to do with his death. But she went right through, down the years, in her queer way. Finally she admitted the man was dead and wept for the beast. I tried to comfort her and pointed out that her loss was not so grave as she imagined it to be. But she said with great dignity:

"We shall not speak evil of the dead. God will judge us all, each in his turn." Then she continued softly, "I do not wish to leave this place, where I was, so to speak" (here she laughed) "the head of the house."

As I was leaving she stopped me: "You have a little boy, haven't you?" she asked. I told her that my son was a young man now with a golden mustache.

"But a little boy," she whispered, "a little boy. It is so nice to have a little boy." She held out her thin empty old arms to a vision she must have nursed during her many bitter years at grandfather's house.

Dvayreh saluted me again in military fashion as I passed through her door and down the stairs. I wondered how much of that salute was real and how much feigned, to hide the curious vanity and depth of emotion she had so unexpectedly revealed. I had a sudden memory of my childhood days when she said a comical "good night" after weeping through her melancholy songs. I wondered again—could it be possible that she had been feigning all her life?

SIX

Avrom

UNTIL HE WAS TWENTY-ONE Avrom was the heart and soul of his father's house, the apple, so to speak, of its eye. Yet in my own day, whenever anyone asked about Avrom there was a queer lull in the conversation followed by a heavy-hearted "Ah" and "Oh" and a "Hush" and "Shush," until one felt it had been indiscreet to raise the subject. The strangeness of all this was enhanced by the fact that normally the Bercinskys were a talkative clan with vivid imaginations, who loved nothing better than to dramatize the events in their lives. But there was something about Avrom's life they could not talk about, let alone dramatize. They kept it in the bottom of their hearts, forcing themselves to be silent. Those few of the Bercinskys who still live, when asked about the matter, shake their aged heads and with feeble gestures brush it away into the limbo of failing consciousness: let the dead past bury the dead!

But how bright was Avrom's beginning! Although he was Reb Michel's and Yentel's eleventh child, he was only their second son. The other nine children were girls, and his birth quite naturally created a sensation. Avrom entered life at the time when his father had returned from Minsk, where, as you will remember, he had been held in prison on the false accusation of Simche, the man who had sought to destroy him. Avrom, then, coming when he did, was regarded as the harbinger of joy and was jubilantly received as such. The rejoicing that marked the occasion of his circumcision reached the proportions of a town festival. It lasted for two weeks, during which the beggars of the city and the strangers within its gates were feasted in Reb Michel's courtyard. At the end of this period the glad father presented to his own old *shul* of Pinsk a *porocheth* (the ornamental curtain that hangs in front of the holy Ark of the Law), upon which was embroidered in threads of pure gold *Zaycher ha-Brith Avrom*— "In commemoration of the Covenant of Abraham [Avrom]."

To convey the father's love for his newborn boy, I must note that his first son, Mayshe, was already a young man of marriageable age when this second son arrived. Reb Michel now felt that with two sons to carry on his name and tradition, it was the destiny of his house to live on for ages. I emphasize the father's belief in destiny, for it was this which guided him in the affairs of his son and led the youth into the web of mystery that surrounded his life.

When Reb Michel looked upon his son in the cradle, he resolved that the child should know the greater things in life. Nothing was to interfere with his intellectual development or stunt his growth. What worried the father was not the present or the immediate days to come, but the future, when his son would be called upon to serve in the dreaded army of the Czars—the army, with its knouts and floggings, its forced marches and coarse fare, its life away from Jews and Jewishness. To insure his son against the remotest possibility of these harmful things, Reb Michel bought Avrom a *kvitantzie.*

A *kvitantzie* was a certificate issued for a price in the days
of Nicholas I, which exempted its holder from military service. Since at the time of Avrom's birth such certificates were
no longer issued, those which were still in circulation commanded a great price. For a large amount (about two thousand rubles, I am told) Reb Michel bought such a document
from a Polish nobleman whose son had died before reaching
military age. So the infant boy slept soundly in his cradle,
while hidden away in a secret chest a piece of paper once
issued by a greedy Czar protected the years of his life to
come.

The boy grew older, but he did not reveal any signs of the
great things which were expected of him. He ate well and
slept well, he was charming and agreeable, but he had nothing of that hunger for knowledge which Mayshe had possessed in such abundance, and with which Dinneh and
Haiye were consumed. The boy studied and knew his lessons, but that was all. He was not particularly sharp, did not
concentrate and penetrate as would a real *Gemoreh keppel* (literally, a Talmud head—a mind that displays aptitude for
Talmudic and rabbinical lore). If Reb Michel was disappointed, he did not show it, for Avrom was by all means a
lad to be proud of. He was tall and handsome, good and
kind, and like so many of the Bercinskys, endowed with a
sweet singing voice.

Avrom, or Avremel, as he was affectionately called, grew
to manhood. Now he had reached the military age of
twenty-one, and he was wonderful to behold—almost six
feet tall, slender, straight, with soft wavy black hair and
dark velvet eyes. But these eyes were nearsighted, a fact that
changed the course of his life and gave the destiny Reb
Michel believed in a chance to work her curious tricks.

Reb Michel thought solemnly: if Avremel was nearsighted, he would probably be rejected by the military authorities for service in the army. Why then waste the precious *kvitantzie?* After twenty-one years of safekeeping, it was worth three times the price he had paid for it. It could be saved for either of his two younger sons or it could be sold. The boys, David and Joshua, Reb Michel's twenty-third and twenty-fourth children, were still quite young. The burdened father needed money, and the *kvitantzie* at this moment would be a lifesaver. The aging man decided that he would wait to see what would happen when Avremel came up for the *prisive* (examination by the military authorities).

The day arrived. Avrom, among a host of other young men, was ordered to report for examination. The marketplace was crowded. The town hall where the prospective soldiers were interrogated was surrounded by hundreds of anxious parents. Inside the house the young men were subjected to much questioning and rigid physical examinations. This was the day of glory for the maimed and the halt, the crippled and the marred. With secret joy they exhibited their deformities, knowing that by these they would be saved from years of privation and pain. At last Avrom's turn came. He was a perfect specimen—except for his eyes. *Gebrakevet!* —came a cry from the crowd of anxious watchers as Avrom Bercinsky came smilingly out the door. (*Gebrakevet* is a Yiddish corruption of the Russian word meaning rejected.) But the crowd was wrong. Avrom had not been rejected. He would be sent up to Minsk to the government military hospital, for further examination.

Well, then! The matter was not as simple as one could have wished. Avrom had to go to Minsk, and of course, his uneasy father armed with the *kvitantzie* had to go along. Avrom was entered into the army hospital where the seri-

ousness of his handicap would be ascertained. Reb Michel
really did not have to be so anxious about the matter, for his
son wore glasses and really could not see, let alone shoot,
without them. There was no doubt about his being finally
rejected. But the father could neither sleep nor be at ease.
Who could tell but that complications might arise? An impatient doctor might in a fit of irritation pass the young man
along. You can imagine Reb Michel's joy, then, when at the
hospital he heard the doctor report "bad." His elation over
that word was such that upon leaving he put a hundred-
ruble bill into the doctor's hand. But the sagacious official
mistook the nature of the gift. He had an idea that, having
received money, he was called upon to do something to earn
it. He blinded Avrom so badly that the young man had to
stay in Minsk for weeks to regain his nearsighted vision.

While Reb Michel was waiting for his son to recover from
the effects of the doctor's unexpected and exuberant gratitude, his many friends gathered about him. Among them
were those of many years ago who had witnessed his incar-
ceration and had brought cheer to his prison cell by discuss-
ing with him matters of the Law or Talmud. These good
people now recalled the far-off days of tribulation and rejoiced again at the happy manner of their termination. They
recalled Yentel's visit to the governor, and together they
remembered that she was at that time big with child—with
Avrom. It was a curious coincidence, they pointed out, that
Minsk should twice have been the place for a turning point
in Avrom's existence. At the threshold of his life he was
hastened into birth by his mother's experience in that city,
and now he was freed from military bondage. Clearly his
fate was bound up with Minsk. Nothing then would be
more fitting than that he should choose one of its daughters
to be his wife.

So the talk went, and so the idea of a *Minsker shudduch*—a match made in Minsk—was dangled before Reb Michel's eyes. Soon there was more than talk, and the father was besieged with offers for his son.

Among them was a suit of exceptional merit, involving one of the leading families of the city, and, as report had it, a young, charming, pious, educated girl. By this time, you see, not only the families, but the personalities of the principals involved in a marriage were freely discussed. Avrom was called in to hear what the characteristically eloquent matchmaker had to say:

There was a family that ranked among the wealthiest in the city; it had been steeped for generations in holy learning. There were only two children in it, the daughter who was proposed for Avrom and just one little brother; so that when, in a hundred years, the parents passed away, the entire wealth of the house would be divided between these two children. This was a match of *yiches* (prestige) and wealth such as Reb Michel might expect for such a son as his; a son who now, by reason of his freedom from military service, was worth twice his weight in gold. Yes, indeed, who did not know Reb Michel's worth! And who did not realize the pricelessness of his son! But, if you were to search through all the worlds, you could not find a better match than the one proposed, a better family than the one presented.

Avrom interposed. The family was all right, but how about the girl? The girl? The *shadchen* (matchmaker) was off again. The girl! Why had they not heard? Well! Well! Well! She was—well, how could the matchmaker describe a person like this girl when he was but a poor mortal with a limited number of words for speech? The girl was a *tzaztke* (a toy or doll), a pearl, a diamond, and a *tzimmes* (pudding) rolled into one. But what was the use of talking? Why couldn't father and son arrange to see both the family and the girl and convince themselves of how inadequate words were to describe them?

Needless to say, the matchmaker had his way. So one fine day, after the proper exchange of courtesies, father and son met mother and daughter. I am told there was a father, but somehow he did not seem to matter very much in the proceedings. It was the mother who made decisions.

It seems that what Reb Michel and Avrom saw made their hearts leap, each along the lines of his own desire. The matchmaker for once had much to recommend his talk. The older man was much impressed by the grace and learning of the family, but he did not forget its wealth. Time had taught him a lesson. He knew how Mayshe and Nochim-Mayer had struggled for a living, and he hoped that his beloved Avrom would be spared their plight. Surely this family of Minsk would know how to value his son. Surely here he would be protected from the world's coarse hands, for obviously Avrom was highly desirable.

If Reb Michel was impressed by his possible *mechautonim,* Avrom was held spellbound by the daughter. She was attractive and possessed of charm and beauty. But the strange thing about her was her behavior. There she sat, fine of form, lovely of face, graceful in manner, but seemingly uninterested in the proceedings. Her mother cast anxious glances upon her, but the girl only lowered her eyes, sealed her lips, and would not say a word. Didn't she want to be married? Didn't she see what a fine young man had come to view her? But there she sat, silent and demure, sad if you will, without a word for anybody, without a look at father, mother, suitor or friend. Upon leaving, the mother laughed off her daughter's silence. Simple modesty, no more! Just the shyness of a well-bred girl. Oh yes, she was modern and had received a fine modern secular education and all that, but she was still her mother's daughter—a true Jewish maiden. Avrom was greatly impressed. That girl, Soreh-Minye, was truly remarkable. His heart beat fast with hope.

Negotiations were pressed, but they did not go on at the pace Reb Michel expected. There was something, somewhere, that prevented matters from being finalized. Just what it was, neither father, son nor matchmaker really knew.

Reb Michel grew impatient. But when he met the mother again, she was more desirous of the match than ever. She was in fact rather excited about it. She promised more, much more than was expected of her. Dowry, *kest,* presents—all in great abundance. She even undertook to pay all the costs of the marriage celebration should it indeed take place. She laughed a little. So did Reb Michel. Well, why shouldn't it take place? Of course, it was only a matter of a few days now when all would be settled.

While Reb Michel waited, he made sure to inquire into every detail about the family to see what was holding things up, but everything was exactly as it should be.

The Bercinskys grew impatient. They were getting ready to leave the city. But still the final word was missing. Whose word? Nobody seemed exactly to know. Was it Soreh-Minye's?

At last the matchmaker appeared with a shining face. Everything was settled. Reb Michel and his son had swept everything before them. The betrothal would take place at once. The marriage would follow soon after. And so it came to pass that Reb Michel's and Yentel's dearly beloved, handsome, but not-too-brilliant son Avrom became plighted to the educated, pensive, mysterious Soreh-Minye of Minsk, the only daughter of her indulgent parents.

When some little time later the marriage celebration was being prepared, Reb Michel sold his precious *kvitantzie* for six thousand rubles. But he did not use the money to ease his financial needs. He spent it royally to outfit his son in a manner commensurate with his new station in life.

The wedding took place in Minsk, and it was there that, amid tears and sighs, Reb Michel and Yentel took leave of their darling son. For the pain they felt at parting, they consoled themselves with the thought that, with his lovely wife in his rich new home, he would be happier than they could ever make him in Pinsk. It was fate, said Reb Michel, which had brought Avrom to the capital of the province, there to meet Soreh-Minye, the woman destined to be his wife.

2

I do not know just how long after his marriage Avrom became part of the mystery that surrounded Soreh-Minye. But it was soon enough, I believe, though in Pinsk the "Ahs" and the "Ohs" did not start for years to come. It took a long time for Soreh-Minye's and now Avrom's secret to reach that city. And even then all was as vague as a rumor. What was there in Avrom's life that provoked all that whispered talk? Hush. Silence!

All my life I have heard conflicting reports about Avrom. He was engaged in a big flour business. He was not "doing much." He had a fine family of children. Avrom and his children were rather distant from each other. Avrom and his children were very close. With all he had Avrom should be a very happy man. With all he didn't have Avrom had nothing to be happy about. But what was it he lacked? Silence!

Then the rumor was that Avrom had come to blows with someone—a man, an important man. And then finally word was that Avrom had left Minsk. He lived in Warsaw.

In Warsaw? Yes, don't you know he has a fine position there? He is a transport agent for a bank. But what in the world has become of his business? Oh, his wife manages that. Does he come home at all? Of course he does! What a silly question! Don't you know he is desperately in love with his wife? Well then, why is he in Warsaw and she in Minsk? Hush!

That was the story until this curious piece of news arrived: instead of sticking to his transport agency whereby the once pampered son managed to eke out a living for himself, he was now indulging in something that would probably bring him a great fortune. He was reportedly eager to take Soreh-Minye—that is his wife—away from Minsk. You see, he wanted to have her with him in Warsaw. And how was he going to make a great fortune? Well, of course one can't be sure of such things. But Avrom . . . you see . . . Avrom was playing the lottery. Well, of all things! A gambling game. And he such a pious man! He *is* pious, isn't he? Of course he is pious. That's why he sits up nights weeping over the Psalms of David, praying to the Almighty that his lottery ticket may win.

To all of us Avrom's plight was vague and mysterious—and yet we had some inkling, just as you who hear this story have, that Soreh-Minye was behind it and that it involved a romance. Only recently I was told the true, bitter story:

When Soreh-Minye sat silently, with eyes downcast while her betrothal was discussed, she was in love with another man. The man was not of her own faith, and, if you remember how Haiye and Baillin were torn apart because he had an aunt who had left the Jewish faith, you understand that it was impossible for Soreh-Minye's adventure to end in anything but anguish.

That Soreh-Minye and her lover fought for their happiness may be concluded from the delayed negotiations at the time of her betrothal. No wonder her mother laughed nervously and promised more dowry and gifts than were expected of her. Had the reasons for the girl's behavior been suspected, there would have been no talk of marriage for her with anyone at all in the Jewish community. Soreh-Minye as well as her family would have been shunned. Her mother well knew the danger of her position and fought fiercely for her daughter's happiness. She married her off to Reb Michel's cherished son but could not forbid her daughter to love the man of her heart. And her lover never sought another woman in marriage and never left the city. He stayed on where he could be near the woman who could not be his wife, and remained forever a tormenting shadow in Avrom's life.

3

When the boatload of our relatives came to America just before I was married, Avrom was among them. He was well on in his forties. When he walked into our home I was shocked. He looked so much like grandfather Reb Michel, whom I had not seen for many years. But a second glance changed that impression; no, he was not at all like grandfather. He had the same statuesque figure, to be sure, and the same type of handsome face, forehead and beard, but he lacked the glowing, animated personality I remembered so well. Where was the flash of those eyes, the snap, the wisdom of that nimble tongue? Physically Avrom was only a pale shadow of my grandfather. In spirit he resembled him not at all.

Der Fetter Avremel, as we called Uncle Avrom, stayed with us. Often when the family had retired, he sat alone in the dark, gazing out the window onto New York's unfamiliar streets. But I doubt that he ever saw what passed before his eyes, for his gaze was really turned inward, backward, to the home he had left, to his wife and children who were thousands of miles away.

Avrom had come to America to seek his fortune. The lottery had failed him. Perhaps America, the land of promise, would not. True, it was a bit late in life to begin all over again, especially in a new country, in a strange environment, but the Lord is merciful.

One night I surprised my uncle as he sat in the dark by the window. I came into the room quietly and sat beside him. He was a lonely, unhappy man. I too was unhappy at the time, since my poor father was dying at the hospital. We talked together a little. We spoke in whispers in order not to disturb the sleeping family. It was the first and only time Uncle Avrom and I talked together intimately. He asked me about our years in America, about the man I was to marry. Minsk knew Zunser well; it had nurtured him in the heyday of his career. The entire Jewish population sang his songs, and now I was to marry Zunser's son. We talked on and on. After a while I ventured a question about my poor uncle's wife. The unhappy man put a soft hand on mine. *"Freg nit Manyele,"* he said. "Do not ask, Manyele." He used the diminutive of my Russian name. We sat in silence, each absorbed in our thoughts; his of a marriage that had failed; mine of one which I hoped would not.

Finally we discussed his presence in America. What did he mean to do here? Avrom shrugged, helpless, as he passed his hand through his graying hair. "I will turn a big wheel," he said. "Or," he added, with a laugh in which there was a suggestion of terror, "I will have to get a basket and peddle matches on one of the corners of your Hester Street." No doubt he had noticed those aged men with long gray beards who stood humbly about on Hester Street, selling their simple wares to the bedraggled immigrants from many lands who made up New York's crowded ghetto—lost souls in a world they did not know, which knew them not.

But Uncle Avrom was spared the humiliation of these aged Jews in exile. He went back home; at least, as close to his home as possible. He went back to Warsaw. A little later he yielded to his weakness and made a trip to Minsk. But the gentleman of high rank who admired his wife still lived at the house adjoining his mother-in-law's. Humbled, Avrom crept back to the lottery and the Psalms of David. He went back to Warsaw, where he was finally overtaken by the First World War.

When Russia concluded a separate peace with Germany, Poland—and so Warsaw—was cut off from Russia and from Minsk. No communication could pass between these two cities. Avrom, an old man now, was completely cut off from his family. He sent a desperate letter or two to his relatives in America—a cry for help across the seas—and then there was silence.

Many years passed before we learned what had become of him. Then we were told that Avrom, a disheveled, bedraggled old man, stood daily in a Warsaw breadline waiting his turn for a crust of bread. We were also told that one day he collapsed where he stood. The doctor said he had died of starvation.

The *porocheth* Reb Michel had presented to the *shul* in honor of Avrom's birth still hung before its holy Ark at the time the cherished son fell in the breadline. Sometime after that, the ancient building burned to the ground. I often wonder if the new government, which was so badly in need of money, salvaged its precious ornaments together with the pure gold in the embroidered words "In commemoration of the Covenant of Avrom" or whether the curtain, gold and all, was simply mixed with the ashes of the ancient *shul*, for which Reb Michel once waged such a valiant fight.

SEVEN

Fraydel and Menye

I CANNOT TELL YOU of Fraydel without telling you of Menye; and I cannot tell you of Menye without saying something about our home in Pinsk; and I cannot mention Pinsk without telling you why we returned there from Odessa, where Rose, Anna and I were born; and when I mention Odessa I will have to tell you how we were forced to leave that city.

You may remember that after my father became famous as a novelist, he was called to Odessa by a troupe of actors to establish a Yiddish theater there. Odessa was to South Russia what Vilna was to Lithuanian Russia: a center of Jewish culture and learning. Abraham Goldfaden, the father of the Yiddish theater, was playing there with great success and it was felt that the town could sustain a second such venture. The Yiddish theater as such was rather a new thing in Jewish life. While it had its remote beginnings in the *Purim shpiel,* which I described when I talked of Purim at my grandfather's house, the actual Yiddish theater did not come into existence until Goldfaden, a gifted man of European culture, gave it life. He gathered the stray Yiddish entertainers of the wine cellars of Bucharest, where he was living at the time;

he introduced them to ambitious young shoemakers, waiters and barmaids who had no glory to lose and much to gain by their appearance in public. He taught them how to walk, talk, sing, act and dance; he welded them into a theatrical troupe, wrote operettas for them, devised scenery, improvised an orchestra, provided music by robbing every European composer of note, and produced a colorful theater such as the Yiddish world had never seen. The Jewish masses, which by reason of *Haskalah* and a rather benevolent political regime had just emerged from the forbidding restraints of fanaticism, fell upon the new medium of culture and amusement with a ravenous appetite. In no time at all the infant Yiddish theater became a powerful stripling. The operettas Goldfaden wrote were of such quality that they not only have survived to this day, but are still considered the very best of the Yiddish theater repertoire.

My father was called to Odessa not to compete with Goldfaden, but rather to extend the scope of the theater. As Goldfaden put it in a letter to my father, while he, Goldfaden, created farce and operettas, my father wrote drama. But father was successful not only in these *lebensbilder* (pictures of life), as they were called, but also in comedy, especially where he created roles for that genial comedian Sigmund Mogulesco. Mogulesco's roles were so well suited to the man that in the days when Shomer was out of favor Mogulesco continued to perform the plays, but under his own name. At my father's theater in Odessa such actors as Jacob P. Adler and his wife, Sara, then known as Di Hyamovitschke, learned their art.

All went gloriously with my family in Odessa. The theater flourished, their home was a center of its activity, their literary friends were many and the children who were born to them there did not die. Perhaps this was so because mother could now afford to engage nurses who knew how to care for her babies, a matter in which she herself was woefully deficient.

Naturally we children became attached to our nurses, but we had to pay dearly for our show of affection by being punished for it in a manner quite common in Jewish homes of that time: we were called in uncomplimentary fashion by our nurses' names. Thus Rose, the gravest offender, was troubled throughout her childhood by being referred to, when scolded, as Chaiye-Soreh, which was her nurse's name. To some extent I escaped this punishment when my nurse was summarily dismissed after mother had discovered that I had spent much of my young life in the city prison where the nurse's husband had been jailed for theft.

I say all went well; but the day came when all the Yiddish theaters of Russia were closed by government decree. This blow fell upon the Jewish people shortly after Alexander II was assassinated by a group of nihilists.

Alexander II had started his reign as a reformer and liberal ruler. Immediately upon his accession to the throne he had granted certain reforms in the interest of the peasants and had promised wide political liberation. Oppressed Russia lifted its head and waited. But as Alexander's reign wore on, it became increasingly autocratic. There was bitter disappointment among those classes which had hoped for the salvation of the Russian people through a constitutional government. In the struggle that ensued between the government and the underground revolutionists, the radicals developed a group of nihilists who dedicated themselves to terrorism.

On the thirteenth of March, 1881, Alexander was driving in his carriage through one of the principal streets of St. Petersburg when (so the story goes) a woman threw herself in the path of his horses with a gesture of supplication. As the Czar half rose to see who the woman was, a bomb exploded under the vehicle, blowing it to pieces. Alexander died a few hours later. It was said that in a pocket of his coat was found a draft of that long-awaited *ukaz* of political liberation—the constitution.

Alexander III, who succeeded him, was a zealot of the first order. He believed in the sacred prerogatives of autocracy. Of course, the more liberal ruler's proposed constitution never saw the light. The new Czar drew in the reins of government in the manner of his grandfather, Nicholas I. He reestablished the old despotism, promulgated a severe doctrine of Russification and lent himself whole-heartedly to a violent policy of anti-Semitism.

Once more Russia was in the gloom of despotism, and the Jews were again in darkness. It goes without saying that everything Goldfaden and my father had established in Odessa was swept away like so much driftwood. Actors, writers, musicians lingered for a while in dismay, then broke camp and scattered. A group of the Odessa troupe made their way to America, to establish a Yiddish theater there.

For a time my people stayed on in Odessa, not knowing what do to. There they witnessed a pogrom, one of the many that were carefully planned by the government authorities to distract the people's attention from the real political issues. The pogroms broke out simultaneously in various parts of the country.

After the high promise of Alexander II's reign, when Jews were urged to come out into the sunlight, to share in the brotherhood of the Russian people, this plunge back into barbarism brought about a period of the bitterest disillusionment. Out of its self-searching emanated the doctrine of "auto-emancipation" through territorialism and Zionism.

Many an assimilationist joined the *Hoveve Zion* (Lovers of Zion) groups when they journeyed to Palestine to fertilize the arid fields with their blood and to leave their withered bodies in the malarial marshes but nevertheless to establish agricultural colonies which were to become their people's pride.

In the anguish of those days in Odessa, my father sent his family back to Pinsk while he returned to Vilna to write for the publishing house of Madame Romm.

2

Because I was scarcely three years old when we came to Pinsk, I do not remember our first home there. The first picture of home that comes to my mind is associated with a large sunny room with many windows and many, many plants: cactus, oleander, geranium and "bleeding hearts," I think. These were left in my mother's care by a man called *Dotch der Commornik,* who for some reason had to leave the city for a time. The plants clustered in the bay window made an enchanting place to dream of at night and to browse in by day. The parlor also contained an oblong table covered by a long fringed cloth, a grand piano and a huge desk over which hung a picture of my father. Everyone who came into the house wondered at this picture because it was made up of minute script in which the story of his life was told.

This grand parlor opened into my father's and mother's bedroom. Looking in from the large sunny room, one could see nothing but the tapestry that hung between the two beds. It represented a roaring lion in a jungle. Sitting under the parlor table, I would look through the fringes of its cloth at the lion on the opposite wall, fearing that someday it would spring and devour us all. Under the table where I sat

were some wonderful big books with pictures in them. Rose
and I would bend our heads over these together. There were
pictures of Skobeloff, Gambetta and Patti, and many other
illustrations. Anna's favorite picture (she joined us on rare
occasions) was one we called *di grobe stunna.* I don't know
exactly now what we meant by that term, but the print
represented a fat woman sitting on the ground with a stick
in her hand. Rose's favorite was Gambetta. She was very
romantic and loved that name, so soft and regal sounding.
The face of the man himself was no less imposing: great soft
eyes, a soft curly beard, and a lovely nose in profile. When
we played games and had to choose grand names for ourselves, Rose would be "Gambetta." Or she would be "Alexander." When we were female characters, Rose chose to be
"Patti" or "Fradel" or "Rowena." I suspect now that Rose
got her romantic ideas through her secret reading of father's
novels, a practice she began before she was eight years old.
When we would get down to earth and play about people
not quite so remote as her Gambettas, Rose would be *Brilliantenshtayn,* meaning Brilliant Stone. I, emulating her,
would be *Diamantenshtayn*—Diamond Stone—but somehow
my diamonds sounded less glowing and glittering than her
brilliants. We would foist a poor *Goldshtayn,* Gold Stone,
upon Anna, but she was too young to appreciate the difference. Besides, Anna was busy building a castle for herself
out of tins that had contained cocoa from Holland, or em-
ploying those tins in an elaborate display for her grocery
store.

The house we lived in was one of two that belonged to our
landlord. His and our houses were situated in the same
court. They faced the same street, possessed a common fence
and entrance gate and were separated from each other by the
length of a yard which on rainy days took on the appearance

of a swamp. Long wooden planks were laid from the entrance gate to the back door of both houses.

The mud puddles of our yard as well as those of all other
yards belonging to the proud homes of Pinsk were the
happy hunting grounds of the pigs of the city. These animals, I must say, had only a distant resemblance to their
kinsmen in America. There was nothing sleek or fat about
them. The pigs of Pinsk looked like pigs. They were dirty
and ravenous, with filthy snouts and squeaky voices. They
were taller and thinner than their American cousins, and
they were covered with a heavy coat of bristles. The children
of the town would run after the pigs and tear handfuls of
bristles from their backs. Often the pigs, attempting to force
themselves into some yard, would try to crawl under a fence
and become wedged in the mud. On such occasions the
children satisfied their lust for bristles, and the housemaids
had their vengeance upon these pests which were forever
rooting up their yards. Often the pigs invaded the anteroom
of many a house, ate up the stored vegetables, upset the
barrels of drinking water, or turned the slop pails upside
down. They were a great nuisance in any town, but they
were a special nuisance in a Jewish town where the pig stood
for everything that was unclean and unholy. Yet these crea-
tures were in possession of the city. They paraded the
streets, and many a good citizen who did not care to dispute
their right of way had to step down from the sidewalk into
the gutter and allow the pig to pass by in all his filthy
splendor.

The most interesting part of our house was the kitchen,
because of its stove. It did not resemble any of the porcelain
stoves of Europe, and there is nothing in New York, with the
possible exception of the baker's oven, with which I can
compare it. The New York oven of the baker lacks the *pripe-*

chuk, a sort of a grate in front and to one side of the baking oven, under which a wood fire is lit to permit quick cooking. You broke up some faggots, put them on the *pripechuk,* set the pots and kettles upon the grate, struck a match and there you were. Soon the fire was blazing and your broth was boiling. But at the same time the pot and the kettle were both black; soot and smoke, grime and embers were everywhere! It was a pleasure to remove the pots as soon as possible from the *pripechuk* and push them into the deep recesses of the hot oven, where the food could resume its quiet cooking. Water for tea, the national drink of Russia, could not be boiled satisfactorily on the *pripechuk.* There was too much dirt and fuss and no way of bringing the needed amount of water to the table except in soot-covered kettles. Hence the samovar, a special contraption designed for boiling water for tea. A separate little grate for the fire (there was no gas or electricity in Russia), a separate well-covered tank for the water, and the whole thing—a luminous structure of brass—could be set before you. It was a fine device, this samovar, before which you could sit at leisure for hours and drink your two, five, ten, twenty, forty glasses of boiling tea. You gasp: forty? Forty glasses of hot tea in succession? That is what I said, for that was the number my grandfather's friend Shimon consumed as he sat before the samovar, sweat running down his forehead and into his beard, his great fur cap on the back of his head. Of course he was an exceptional tea drinker, but twenty glasses was by no means an unusual record, while five or ten glasses of tea was a matter for no comment at all. In Russia's long and very cold winters, when the blood froze in your veins and vodka was served to warm you up for a little while only to leave you colder than ever, there was nothing to make life quite so tolerable as the friendly samovar. You gathered about it with your friends, you ate herring and onions and black bread with your tea if you were hungry, you flavored the beverage with raspberry, cherry, or wild strawberry preserves if you were entertaining elegant company, or you put slices of lemon or fresh apples into it.

But to get back to the kitchen stove. The most interesting part of it was not the *pripechuk,* or its oven, in which all the bread used by the family was baked, but its commodious top, built like a platform. That was the warmest corner of the house, and as far as we children were concerned, it was the best. But alas we were not allowed to use it. The place was reserved for the servants as their sleeping quarters. I passed many Thursday nights watching the servants through the open door as they prepared the fish, fowl and vegetables for the coming Sabbath. How I envied them the privilege of staying up late, and finally curling up on top of the kitchen stove!

3

It was in the sunlit parlor that we children had our first and only glimpse of father's mother, *die Bobbe* Hodes. My mother always referred to her as *Hodke*—the diminutive and derisive form of her given name.

I don't know what brought *Bobbe* Hodes to Pinsk. Father was not at home. I believe he was in Vilna at the time. *Bobbe* Hodes came in and fairly took our breath away. She was tall and statuesque. Her features, like my father's, were Slavic. Being a pious woman, she wore a wig; but it was small, smooth, glossy and had two long braids which were circled about the back of her head. There she stood, a regal figure, her close black bodice buttoned up to her chin with what seemed to be a hundred little buttons, her voluminous skirts billowing about her, her white jeweled hands folded. She looked at us sharply, not very kindly, I am afraid, and then opened a bag and brought out a box of marmalade, a special confection that has little in common with the American version.

I don't think my mother received her very kindly, or was very warmly regarded by her in return. We never saw grandmother Hodes again. The large photograph of her that hung in our dining room was somehow lost when father was no longer with us.

It was in our sunlit parlor, too, that we got our first glimpse of Haiye when she visited Pinsk from Nikolayiev. Just what brought her to her home town I don't know. Perhaps it was her desire to see her family; perhaps it was her hunger for a look at Baillin. Whatever it was, in she blew one day in pompous fashion, the train of her elegant dress trailing behind her, the blue veil of her little hat fluttering in the breeze as she entered the house. She was short and pleasantly plump, her bosom high, her waistline tiny. She shook the brown, silky ringlets that clustered about her face, and laughed in a rich contralto voice that was at once haughty and uneasy. There was much excitement in the house as in guarded whispers it was related how Rosenberg kept bombarding her with telegrams for her immediate return. The excitement grew when someone ran into the room and said that Baillin was passing the house. There was wild speculation about his dogging her footsteps as my mother and several others rushed to the windows to see if Baillin was actually in sight. I remember crowding in among the many petticoats and mounting a footstool to look out of the window without knocking my nose on the sill.

"There! There!" my mother said.

I saw a slender young man passing swiftly on the opposite

side of the street. He carried his hat in his hand and his soft
light curls fluttered in the wind. He turned the corner and
disappeared. Later, when Haiye was about to enter the carriage that was waiting for her at the door, Baillin again
passed by. Two red spots burned on Haiye's cheeks. She
went back to Nikolayiev the very next day.

4

I wonder if you remember Fraydel? She came to our house
once when I was ill with pneumonia. She came with Aunt
Rose and both of them remained standing at the bedroom
door looking in at me anxiously. They did not know until
that moment that I was really ill. Do you remember the
incident? They sat with your father and you in the dining
room, talking very seriously. I must have been in a delirium
at the time, for it seemed to me I was somewhere on a wide
plain beyond which spread the desert. It was very hot. You
three children were grouped around me. Then you all rose,
joined hands, and with Helen in the middle danced across
the field toward the desert. The sun was high and bright and
the field shone with dazzling whiteness. I was horrified. I
knew that if you kept going in the direction of the desert
you would be lost there, and die of heat and thirst. I tried
to call you back but could not raise my voice; but there you
were—the three of you—dancing along toward death. Making what seemed to me a superhuman effort, I cried out to
you to stop and as I did, your father, Rose, you and Fraydel
rushed into the room to see what was the matter with me.

That was the last time I saw Fraydel. A few months after
that, she, not I, died of pneumonia.

Menye, of course, you know very well. It seems to me that
she retains enough charm to give you an idea of her youthful

attractiveness. Only a year ago she flirted disgracefully with your Uncle Max when they danced together. He was amused and encouraged her; whereupon Menye forgot her age, weight and many ailments; she rose to her feet, assumed a grand manner, and performed a dance she had learned a half-century before. She held her head high, placed Max's hand, Russian fashion, on what should have been her waist, and to the astonishment of all, heaved her two hundred and fifty pounds lightly over our parlor floor. Of course, the dance did not last long, for she was out of breath in no time; but the little we saw opened a window on her past.

No doubt we children saw these two young women, Fraydel and Menye, as soon as we arrived in Pinsk from Odessa, but it seems that they left no definite impression on me. The first time I had a close view of our aunts came when our little brother, Mayshale, became violently ill with a cough. My father was away in Vilna. My mother was frightened. She had lost so many children through croup and diphtheria. At once she sent a message to grandfather to ask that her three little girls be taken to his home.

Early next morning a sleigh drew up in front of our door. Fraydel had come to take us away, and we were greatly impressed by her. She was a slender figure in a long black tight-fitting coat with a collar of fur which had the appearance of being sprinkled with snow. She wore a high round Russian cap of the same material and under that cap flashed her large, lustrous dark eyes. She put Rose and Anna and me into our coats, wrapped and tied warm woolen shawls about our heads, and packed us in among the many blankets in the open sleigh. She tucked us in carefully against the cold, climbed into the vehicle and told the driver to go. The man, also wearing a round Russian cap and many shawls about his neck and shoulders, cracked his whip, cried a loud *Niyaw*

(Giddyap) to his horses, and away we went. Both horses had shaggy yellow manes and heavy feet, but they trotted along nimbly enough, the tinkling bells of their harness making a merry sound.

Soon enough we were in grandfather's house. There we saw Menye. Soft and languorous, she sat in a big chair, smoking a cigarette! As we came in the two sisters seemed to speak sharply to each other. Fraydel then took us out of our many wraps, washed us, fed us and told us how to occupy ourselves in the big house. In the evening she put us to bed. Rose slept with Menye, I with Fraydel, Anna with grandmother Yentel, I think.

Fraydel and Menye shared one room. It was the very chamber once occupied by my father and mother during their long period of *kest* at grandfather's house. It was a large room overlooking a garden.

Fraydel's bed stood on one side of the room; Menye's on the other. Between them stood their separate washstands. Rose and I spent our mornings watching our beautiful but quarreling aunts. What they quarreled about we did not know till later. Every morning we were there, Fraydel would jump out of bed very early. She was grandfather's favorite daughter, and he depended upon her. She had to collect money, pay bills, run important errands and do all manner of things for him. She made her toilet quickly, scrubbed herself clean, brushed her teeth, combed out her magnificent black hair that reached almost to her knees. This she then rolled up in a fine knot at the back of her head, leaving full bangs of cut hair over her low, wide forehead. She was straight and slender, a little above medium height. Her eyes were large and dark, like grandfather's. Her nose was straight and fine, but it had a small brown flat mole on one side. Her mouth was rather large. Her skin was dark, and there was a deep red glow in her cheeks. She was what we would call a beautiful brunette. She did two things that scandalized us as children: she used face powder, and, like Menye, she smoked cigarettes. Having made her toilet, Fraydel would slip on a dark skirt and a Russian blouse with high collar and cuffs elaborately embroidered by her own hand. These things done, she would rush off for a light breakfast and on to her many duties.

Menye lingered in bed. She was in every way different from her older sister. Soft, white and pleasantly plump, her face was round, her nose small and somewhat flat like her mother's. Her eyes were large and brown with curious, soft, warm lights in their depths. Her hair was short and sparse, but silken, brown and curly. Fraydel spoke rapidly, with animation; Menye in a soft, low voice. When she talked to people she had a way of looking into their eyes closely, intimately. Men loved her.

When she was finally out of bed, Menye would sit at the window and look out dreamily. By that time Fraydel had already attended to many, many matters, and grandmother Yentel had long been in *shul.* Before leaving the house Yentel made sure to stow many little delicacies away under Menye's pillow. Menye was Yentel's twenty-second, but favorite child. Dreams dreamed and delicacies eaten, Menye would get down to her toilet. That was when Rose and I were lost in wonderment. First she used one kind of soap, then another. Then there was one kind of toilet water, then a second, a third, and a fourth. Scrubbing her small white teeth was like going through a religious rite. Then the matter of doing things to one's hair. Then powdering oneself all over. Then gazing at oneself in the mirror. Our gaping did not in the least disturb Menye. She went about her business with no concern for us. Finally she got into her clothes. For

us the great moment came when our beautiful aunt put on
a white blouse and opened up her box of beads. She wound
string after string of these bright ornaments about her throat
—red, blue, yellow, green, black.

I don't know what Menye did with herself all day while
Fraydel bustled about; but in the evening she would emerge
rested, radiant, alluring.

We stayed only a few days at grandfather's house. At the
end of our visit the sleigh was at the door again and we were
bundled in for our return home. But when we opened the
door we hardly recognized the place. All the mirrors were
turned to the walls. The pictures were covered. The fringed
tablecloth and the tapestry were gone. Everything pretty
about the house had been removed. My mother sat on a very
low stool so that she looked as if she were sitting on the
floor. About her were other people similarly seated. They
were all swaying and moaning and repeating strange Hebrew prayers. As we came in with a great shout of joy,
Fraydel quieted us quickly. Then someone said solemnly:

"Hush children, Mayshale is dead."

As time went on we children became aware that Fraydel
and Menye were the subjects of constant discussion among
my mother and her many relations. Menye was criticized for
the uneasiness she caused grandfather by surrounding herself with so many admirers; Fraydel for her tenacious adher-
ence to the unhappy Uziel, the man she loved but could not
marry.

You may remember that Uziel was Avron Chaim Rosenberg's youngest boy by his first wife, the *rayfeh*'s daughter.
He was the youth who as a boy had carried his father's
messages to Haiye and fell in love with her little sister Fraydel. He had always been sensitive and keen witted, and he
had received an excellent education. When Haiye became

Rosenberg's wife, Uziel with his brother and sister went to live at the *rayfeh*'s house. But the man was old and widowed and could do little for his deceased daughter's three youngsters, so they were quite unhappy. Uziel found some solace when some time later Reb Michel engaged him to transcribe Russian documents and to help in the preparation of legal papers. Uziel, too, wanted to be a lawyer. He was encouraged in this by Fraydel's lovelit eyes. A great tenderness developed between the two young people, which led them secretly to pledge themselves to each other. All day long, then, Uziel worked in the light of his beloved's presence, but at the end of the day he had to go back to a home where he could find neither peace nor rest. In this unhappy state he walked the streets aimlessly, always ending his wanderings by vainly circling Fraydel's house.

When Rosenberg finally sent him to Vilna to attend a government vocational school, the young man could not remain there because of his longing for the girl. He disappointed his father, deserted his studies and came back to Pinsk to work for Reb Michel. But now he found there a fellow worker, a hearty Russian by the name of Kahl, who, according to Reb Michel, liked nothing so much as the "bitter drop"—vodka. Kahl was a sociable fellow and could not enjoy his pleasures alone. Why then not share them with the lovesick boy at his side? Soon the two were great friends. When work was over they walked, talked and drank together.

For Uziel this last occupation was something of a revelation. It provided an easy way to escape his misery. And because Uziel had much misery to escape from, he drank often. But as time wore on, he found it increasingly hard to forget his pain. The worst of it all was that one had to pay for this elixir of oblivion, so that every *groschen* the young man owned was left at the tavern. With his pockets empty, Uziel took to pawning things for cash.

Throughout all this, Fraydel stood by unflinchingly. Her plighted troth with Uziel, though secret, was a bond not to be broken. Yet what was she to do! In secret the two met, remonstrated with each other, loved, quarreled, but clung together desperately.

One day Uziel came to work in a befuddled condition. When Reb Michel reproved him, the young man declared his independence and announced that Fraydel and he had been plighted to each other and would be married.

The scene that followed was that of the outraged father driving the unwanted suitor from the house. But no amount of talk and no degree of wrath could induce Fraydel to leave the man she loved. She stood by him, disdaining the opinion of both friends and foes. Nobody sided with Fraydel. This was because in a Jewish community of her time (and long after) a drinking man was looked down upon with the utmost contempt. There was no smiling at him in indulgent amusement when he was befuddled, no forbearing helpfulness when he was drunk. He was avoided and despised. A habitual drinker was looked upon as a creature who had forsaken his power of mind, his human heritage, his oneness with the Almighty and had sunk to the level of a beast. He was a loathsome sight to his fellow men. And Fraydel— lovely, gifted Fraydel—had set her heart on such a man. No wonder she was the subject of discussion everywhere she went.

One day as she was walking along the main street of the town she saw an agitated crowd running after a man who was being dragged to jail by a policeman. She was told that the fellow had been arrested for stealing. The crowd jeered him lustily. Fraydel followed and saw that the man was

Uziel. He had taken something that belonged to his landlady. The woman had missed the object, traced it to the
tavern where it had been pawned, discovered the borrower
and raised such an outcry that half the town had come to her
side. Now Uziel was a self-confessed thief. Fraydel quietly
redeemed the pledge for the landlady and had Uziel released,
but she could not bear the disgrace he had brought upon
himself and her. She broke with her lover.

There was only one thing for Fraydel to do. Forget. There
were many men who desired her. She was beautiful, and gay
—when she wanted to be—and she was quick witted. She
must find someone else for herself.

It was at this point that she collided with her sister
Menye. As long as Fraydel had Uziel, she took no notice of
Menye and let her have as many admirers as she pleased.
But now, when she, Fraydel, was called upon to choose a
man from their circle, things took on a different aspect. She
quickly discovered that people who came to see her drifted
away in Menye's direction, that Menye held them as if by
magic power. Menye, who had that intimate way of looking
into people's eyes. Menye in whose own eyes there floated
those liquid fires that played havoc with men. She exerted
a force men could not resist. Menye would laugh in her own
hearty way. The more she laughed, the closer her admirers
came, the longer they stayed. It disturbed things for Fraydel.
It threatened her future.

I remember one occasion when a group had gathered at
our home to watch the rehearsal of a play my father was to
produce in Lubetzky's garden. Of course the Yiddish theater
was still under a ban, but a performance was smuggled in
occasionally with the help of the local chief of police; Pinsk,
Jewish and non-Jewish, loved the theater. It was considered
a great privilege to be invited to Shaikevitsch's house to see

and meet the theatrical folk and watch a production being created. Among the many people in the house were Fraydel and Menye.

As in all matters that required action, Fraydel arrived first; dark, flushed, slender, beautiful. Her entrance caused a little stir. Soon she had a group of young men around her. They smoked and laughed together and exchanged jokes. Then Menye came in, soft, white, and languorous. She passed through the crowd. She sat quietly. Before long Fraydel found her own crowd dispersing. Scarcely conscious of what they were about, the young men one by one wandered over to Menye. Fraydel was deserted.

Reproached for her behavior, Menye laughed her great deep laugh. What was she to do? Could she help it if people liked her? Didn't Fraydel see for herself that she, Menye, did nothing whatever to call attention to herself? Was there any crime in being attractive?

Perhaps you wonder why Menye had not won away Uziel. Probably it was because Menye had no use for his type of man. Boyish, intellectual—what good was he! She liked real men. To put it as she once did—she liked men who gave promise of becoming lions! She had no use for striplings and was amused at Fraydel's devotion to Uziel. But Menye was kind. Uziel was a weakling who needed affection; let Fraydel give it to him if that was her pleasure.

And now Uziel was removed from the scene. The two beautiful girls saw each other in a new light. They measured each other's powers. The struggle was an unequal one, for with all Fraydel's bravado, she still had Uziel in her heart.

When Menye went to Warsaw for a while to visit relatives and to learn to dance, Fraydel took herself in hand. She decided that she must not ruin her life through useless longing. Quickly she found herself a *chossen.* No matchmakers, no intermediaries. Just so, in a modern way, she cemented a friendship with a man she knew and admired—Layvick. He was the blond son of a good family, well provided for and quite a catch. He was much in love with Fraydel. They announced their betrothal.

When Menye heard the news she was overjoyed. At last Fraydel would be out of the way, and her own matrimonial path would be unobstructed. The old precept of no marriage for the younger daughter until the older one was settled still held sway.

But no sooner had the announcement of Fraydel's forthcoming marriage been made than things began to stir uneasily in grandfather's house—and in our own. All one could hear were whispered phrases containing the word Uziel. Was it that Fraydel still loved Uziel? That Layvick was jealous of Uziel? That Uziel was jealous of Layvick? There was no way of telling. Then one day the words came out sharp and clear: Uziel had taken an oath that he would kill Fraydel and Layvick. All the Bercinskys took the threat seriously.

I remember one night when Fraydel and Layvick were at our house. Mother ordered the shutters of the windows closed. We gathered about the table where the lamp was burning. The maid brought in the steaming samovar; someone poured the tea while mother passed the raspberry preserves. Fraydel was smoking. Layvick had folded his hands behind his blond head, his handsome face turned to the light. Suddenly there was a pounding on the shutter of the window. Someone rushed to lock the door. Mother quickly extinguished the lamp. The pounding was repeated. Silence. Once again the pounding came—this time on the door. Mother stepped up quickly but on tiptoe:

"Who is there?" she called in Russian.

Uziel's voice demanded sharply, "Is Fraydel there?"

"No," my mother said. "Why do you come pounding at the door? Why do you rouse people out of their sleep?" We listened breathlessly for Uziel's retreating footsteps. But we could not hear well enough. Had he gone or was he still there watching? The lamp was not relit. The samovar was allowed to grow cold. Fraydel stayed with us that night, and Layvick left stealthily through a back window. We all felt that Uziel was standing out in the dark—waiting.

Uziel was very ill at the time of his attack on our door. During his short prison stay and through the many months he had been separated from Fraydel, the unhappy man had drunk incessantly and developed a wracking cough. In his pitiful condition, without pride, he had exposed himself to insult, cold and shame. At last he put himself in the hands of a physician, but it was too late; he was in an advanced stage of tuberculosis. When the news reached Fraydel, she ran, wild-eyed, to his side. She nursed him day and night, never leaving him for an instant. The town shook its head in disapproval, but Fraydel cared nothing for opinion. She saw only Uziel, heard nothing but his dying cough. He died in her arms.

5

When she emerged from her long mourning for Uziel, Fraydel became aware of three facts: her beauty had faded; Menye was in a state of rebellion because she was not allowed to get married; she, Fraydel, stood an excellent chance of becoming a *farzesseneh*—"a woman left sitting," a spinster. But in Yiddish the word has another quality: it implies a dehydrated condition such as fruit reaches when it is left about. Once it got about that a woman was a *farzesseneh* things went badly for her. Even the marriage brokers abandoned her and dropped her from their eligible lists. Since the unmarried women of Fraydel's day had no economic independence, and since there were no avenues of self-expression except through marriage, the woman "left sitting" was in a desperate state.

Modern bachelor girls, who know something of the bitterness of being lonely and apart, can hardly guess the depths of unhappiness reached by the *farzesseneh* of Fraydel's generation. There was not only the bitterness to endure, but there was the scorn of the community to deal with; an old maid was the butt of everybody's humor.

Fraydel knew these things only too well; now she faced the possibility of entering the class of the dehydrated and undesirable. She by no means qualified under the first category; but was eminently fitted for the second. Had she not been the affianced of a drunkard and thief? Had she not deserted the honorable, decent Layvick to go back to the drunkard? One could not do such things with impunity. The town wagged its head in disapproval. Fraydel was in disgrace.

Fraydel listened to Menye as the younger sister grew righteously wrathful—in her own quiet way, of course. How long was Menye going to be kept in a single state by a sister who did all manner of idiotic things? What was to become of her if this sort of thing went on indefinitely? Was she to be sacrificed to Fraydel's folly? If that were the case, she, Menye, knew many ways in which to make her life enjoyable. If that was the sort of thing proud Michel Bercinsky wanted of his daughter. . . . But Menye did not get a chance to finish, for Fraydel had suddenly turned into a fire-spouting volcano—a true Bercinsky. After the explosion, Menye knew that she would have to wait her turn.

A period of calm followed the volcanic outburst. Then

Fraydel realized the validity of Menye's argument. She decided to do something about it for her own as well as for her sister's sake. Fraydel was still beautiful; but more than that —she was energetic. Now she was determined that come what might she would find a husband for herself. She could not appeal to her father, because he would have to appeal to the matchmakers, and with them she had no chance. She went about the matter on her own, and one day she came home with the tidings that she had a *chossen.* He was a stranger in the city, a well-to-do merchant who had come to Pinsk in his own steamboat, bearing a cargo of grain. How she met and where she captured this desirable man (I think his name was Baron) was nobody's business. But there he was, rich, in love and ready to marry.

While Menye was kept carefully out of sight, Baron was received in Reb Michel's house. There was much rejoicing, but the event was not noised about. Gossip might reach the *chossen*'s ears. Quietly a troth was plighted, promises exchanged and gifts presented. Since Baron had, happily, to go back to his home town to look after important business, it was decided that the marriage would take place immediately upon his return, which would be in three weeks. In this little space of time everything would be readied for the wedding. Fraydel already had a good part of her trousseau, originally intended for Layvick's wedding, assembled; the rest could be gotten together somehow. It was planned that right after the wedding, Fraydel and her husband should leave Pinsk to make their home in Baron's native town, where he was well established.

Baron took his leave. He sailed away as he had come, in his own steamboat.

Reb Michel's household heaved a great sigh of relief, for a calamity had been averted. Fraydel was indeed to be married—and married well! Wedding preparations were started without delay, and Reb Michel gave every *groschen* he had to set the plans in motion. He loved Fraydel. She had suffered and had made them all suffer, but now let her go in peace with his blessing; may she find the happiness she sought. God was good. The old *Chassid* raised his eyes to heaven. His heart was full of praise, and his house was full of mirth.

The short weeks of exciting preparations were hurrying by and the tension grew in my grandfather's house. No word had come from Baron. Importunate messages sent to him had remained unanswered. No one dared to speak the dreaded thought. Anxious days. Sleepless nights.

The day of Baron's expected arrival came, but not the man. Weeks went by. He never returned. There was no doubt now but that gossip had followed the man to his home. Fraydel was lost.

The only one who derived any satisfaction out of this tragedy was Dvayreh. She remembered her own desertion with undiminished bitterness.

6

In the days of despair that followed, Reb Michel came to a grave conclusion. It was better to sacrifice one daughter than two. He could no longer contend with the battling women or restrain Menye from her wish. If the younger daughter was to be married before the older one, then in God's name let it be done. Obviously it was His will.

Thus it happened that the old father listened to the tale of a seasoned old *shadchen* (matchmaker) who had come to propose a match for the younger daughter; but the conference was held in secret. There was no use of flaunting one's decision before unhappy Fraydel. The *shadchen*'s tale ran thus:

There was a certain Boruch Rubenstein, of the city of

Gomel, due to arrive in Pinsk within a few days. He was a man of parts, a widower, a stationer, a merchant of the first guild. (There were three merchant classes in Czarist Russia. The first was the most distinguished and carried with it many privileges, one of them, for a Jew, being the right to live outside the Pale, in any city he chose, a right denied most others.) The *shadchen* believed that because Rubenstein felt the loss of his wife very deeply, he would consider being comforted by way of marriage. The *shadchen* felt sure that Menye . . . but this was not the point. The point was that Rubenstein could get a thousand *kallehs* just for the asking. For a man in his position it was the easiest thing in the world to get a bride. What one had to consider was a wife who could bring him a dowry befitting his station. Was Reb Michel willing to entertain the proposition?

The old man who had just emptied his pockets for Fraydel's sake cut the *shadchen* short. There was no use making such a fuss about a mere merchant. He had seen them many times in his day. The matchmaker was asked to remember that Reb Michel had sons-in-law who had achieved fame through the printed word. He was further admonished not to talk money, dowry. If he had a fitting match to propose, let him do it. Other matters—trifles—could be considered in due course.

The *shadchen* looked puzzled. He chewed his beard. Well, really, if Reb Michel . . .

But he was again cut short. The *shadchen* had said that Rubenstein was due in Pinsk on business? Well, then, let him come to the house ostensibly on business; Reb Michel would look him over and then the matter could be discussed with some degree of intelligence.

The *shadchen* chewed his beard. Somehow Reb Michel had taken the wind out of his sails. Still, if that was the way the impetuous old man felt, all the *shadchen* could do was to see that the merchant of the first guild did as he was bid.

A few days later Reb Michel told his wife to prepare one of her special teas. He was expecting an important client. He then sent Fraydel on an elaborate errand that would take her a day to execute. He told Menye to wear her best clothes and be prepared to superintend the serving of tea when his client arrived. This done, he settled himself in his big armchair to smoke and to examine the papers of Rubenstein's affairs, which he already had in hand.

At the appointed hour his guest arrived. Counsellor and client sat down to talk of many things. In the end it was Rubenstein and not Reb Michel who was mightily impressed. While the younger man wondered at the older one's wisdom, Reb Michel found his client to be a merchant of the first guild, right enough, but otherwise quite an ordinary mortal. Yet as he looked at the blue-eyed, strapping man before him, he realized infinite possibilities for his daughter's happiness. To begin with, Rubenstein was of the leonine variety of man that Menye so much admired. Secondly, he was very good natured. And, finally, he was wealthy enough to keep her in the state of idleness to which she was accustomed. He was about ten years older than Menye, so that he would probably coddle and baby her—which was exactly what Menye most desired. There was no doubt but that here was the perfect match for the girl. As for the dowry—he had nothing to give her, nothing but the house he had built with so much toil; the house that had seen his glory, the house that still sheltered him and his old Yentel. But mortgaging the house would have to be considered. And then again—God was the father of all—God would help!

It was in the midst of these speculations that the servant

brought in the steaming samovar, and Menye came in to serve tea.

You already know of Menye's subtle flirtatious ways and what a fascination she held for the male of the species. Now she knew that she was getting on in years (she was twenty-four), that she would have to marry out of Pinsk to avoid Fraydel, and that the man before her was her big chance. As a result, she put so much into her smile as she looked into Rubenstein's eyes that he failed to take the proffered glass of tea from her hand, but stared at her openmouthed. This was not lost on Menye. She said something pleasant to the man, laughed in her own hearty way, and set the sparkling glass of deep red tea before him.

Rubenstein suddenly discovered that he had much business to transact in Pinsk and that it was most important that he see old Reb Michel every day. He also developed an inordinate thirst for tea, and Menye developed an unusual agility in serving it.

During all this time Fraydel was lost in a maze of errands which kept her out of the house for hours at a time. It seemed that age-old matters of neglected business had now urgently to be looked after.

Finally Rubenstein could stand the strain no longer. He had had enough of business and beverage. He sent for the *shadchen* and told him to conclude the arrangements. Businessman though he was, he could not talk dowry and gifts to Reb Michel. But the *shadchen* could and did.

I have heard it repeated time and again how the old father, now past seventy, paled at the thought of mortgaging his home, but how he had now determined to do it. Menye would not be allowed to miss her chance for happiness for want of money. But the girl herself stepped in and saved the day. As Rubenstein was leaving the house one day, she stopped him in the hallway.

"Would you let me say a few words to you?" she asked.

Would he indeed! The man beamed in delighted anticipation.

Menye looked into his eyes and said simply: "I know you want to marry me. My father has no money. If you want me, you will have to take me as I am. Just me." What would Rubenstein possibly want at that moment more than Menye, just Menye?

Pinsk was in a state. Michel Bercinsky's younger daughter Menye was going to marry before her older sister Fraydel!

There is no use in dwelling upon the confusion in grandfather's house when Menye's engagement was revealed, or in describing Fraydel's shame and misery. It is enough to say that she could bear neither. She left her father's house. She packed her things and fled the town. She sought refuge at Avrom's house in Minsk, where Soreh-Minye received her kindly. No doubt these two lovesick women wept together as one thought of Uziel and the other of the man who could never be her husband.

Menye was married quietly. For Fraydel's sake the festivities were subdued. There was no use in "pouring salt upon one's wounds." Menye did not miss the public celebration. She had waited so long, she had had so many flirtations, that she was glad at last to be settled and have a husband to take care of her. Besides, she had much to look forward to. She was going to a home where there was money aplenty, where servants would wait on her, where her word would be law, where she could indulge her love for ease and luxury.

"Lucky Menye," the town said.

But the town was not entirely right.

7

For several unhappy months Fraydel stayed in Minsk. Then Soreh-Minye did something only a fellow-sufferer could do. She arranged a match for Fraydel.

Soreh-Minye was worldly wise. Nobody in Minsk knew of Menye's marriage. Why inform them? They had no idea which of Bercinsky's daughters was the older. Why tell them? The business about Uziel, Layvick and Baron need never be revealed. Fraydel must clean her slate and begin over again. And she would have to get a man who had faith, one who would believe in her.

Soreh-Minye looked about carefully. All the men were too sophisticated, too much men of the world. They speculated and asked questions. One would need a beginner; an innocent.

Soreh-Minye found a very young man, a distant relative of hers—very undistinguished, but fine and gentle, shy and retiring. He saw Fraydel. He heard her bright talk. He was much impressed. What a woman she was! And she deigned to talk to him as an equal. She was young, too! No older than he was, they said, yet she knew much of life!

When the match was proposed, the young man was abashed. He was sure Fraydel wouldn't have him. But Soreh-Minye assured him to the contrary. She, Soreh-Minye, had herself arranged everything because the young man was her relative. And that was not all; this wonderful Fraydel had a remarkable father who would do all manner of things for his daughter and her husband.

When the couple settled in Pinsk, people said of Avrom Gruenberg, the husband, that "his mother's milk still lay on his lips." He looked that young and innocent. He was slender and dark, with great soft eyes and a small red mouth over which sprouted a downy mustache. His beard, just beginning to show, was soft.

Fraydel, sobered by all she had been through, devoted herself entirely to her husband. She concentrated on seeing that he was happy and making a home for him. But it was a desperate pull. How were they to live? Again the old father was called. He set the couple up in the stationery business. He opened a shop for them on "the big street." How he had secured the money, where he got the stock that filled the shelves, was nobody's business. Actually it was Menye's doing. She was rich now; the adored wife of a husband who carried out her every wish. And her wish, upon her father's request, was that Rubenstein help establish Fraydel and her young husband in business.

Fraydel had to accept her sister's help. She had to eat the bitter bread of humiliation out of her hand. Was there to be no end of Menye?

How Menye felt about all this is hard to say. When she came to Pinsk in grand style to adjust matters, she was kind and gracious. Too gracious. She indulged Fraydel and she smiled into Gruenberg's eyes. The young man never saw such beauty, such graciousness, he said.

Fraydel burned with mortification. The old struggle was on again. But Gruenberg must not know of the conflict that had raged between the two. He must never be told how his wife had been beaten and sidetracked. Fraydel powdered her face, lit a cigarette and smiled—a wan smile to be sure, but still a smile. Then she looked at her sister and told her secret: she was going to have a child. Menye was greatly moved. A child! Congratulations! She herself had two stepsons, but she had not been blessed with a child of her own. She was getting too fat inside to have a baby, the doctor said. Nonsense! Her mother Yentel had been fat all her life, but that had not prevented her from having twenty-four children. Nevertheless, Menye had not conceived, and Fraydel was going to have a child. Congratulations! For once Fraydel felt that she had bested her sister.

When Fraydel's little girl was born there was still no sign of a child for Menye. She had put on a little more weight, but that did not detract from her beauty. On the contrary, it added to her charm. It seems that at that time physical bulk and beauty were in a sense synonymous. I have heard it said of a woman: *"Zi is azay shain, as zi vet durch der tir nit durch gehen"*—"She is so beautiful that she cannot pass through the door."

8

At this point we took leave of Fraydel and Menye, as well as of grandfather and grandmother, and went to America. The distant rumbling of a widespread Jewish immigration had overtaken Pinsk. One day my father came home from Vilna and closeted himself with grandfather Reb Michel. When they emerged, their eyes were red with weeping. My father had secretly given him an insurance policy upon which to collect for Dinneh and the children were he, Nochim-Mayer, to be lost at sea. The troupe of actors who had left him in Odessa had, after much persuasion, induced him to leave Madame Romm's employ and join them in New York. So now he was going across "the seven lands and seven seas" that everybody was talking about; he was leaving his home, country, wife, children and mother, to join the procession of persecuted Russian Jews who were migrating to the golden land of promise.

A year later we were on our way to join him. We were packed among the stacks of books and mountains of featherbeds (there was persistent talk that there were no pillows or featherbeds in America, that the people there slept on hard planks or mattresses of a crude kind), in a wagon bound for the train. That train took us to another train, which took us to Warsaw, whence we went to Hamburg, were we boarded the steamship *Augusta Victoria* for a tempestuous voyage across the "seven seas." In our double bunk my mother, brother, Rose, Anna and I were all very sick. Between spells of nausea we sat up and looked out through the portholes at the mountainous waves that surrounded us and waited anxiously for the day when we would climb the golden stairs leading to the top of the American palace where father was supposed to live. There we would see with our own eyes how water was drawn from the wall, how people swung in the breeze when they hung their clothes out to dry on ropes suspended high in the air, how a fire was built in a curious iron contraption they called a stove, and where, it was said, there were more of those strange little lamps we saw on the ship, strange lamps which burned without oil or wick or even a match to light them.

We were going to a land of wonders, and we were prepared for all manner of miracles. There were very few women in America, we were told; people who lived there for a long time turned black, and, it was whispered, there was a class of Cyclops—people who had only one eye in the middle of their foreheads. It was a strange, wonderful land! We peered through the portholes into the blackness at night, into the teeth of the tempest and forgot our seasickness in anticipation of the wonders we were to behold.

When we sailed into the harbor, the crowd of Jewish immigrants who traveled steerage together wept with joy.

There were those who prayed, and those who recited the Psalms. But one and all dedicated their hearts to America. They had left nothing but tears and pain behind. Now they were America's, to do with as she chose.

Father met us at Castle Garden. We did not recognize him. He was not the man we knew. He had shaved off his full round beard and was changed beyond recognition. The miracles had begun to materialize!

While the transportation of our baggage was being arranged, we sat down and waited in Battery Park. Father bought us bananas. We had never seen the fruit before—and bit into it, skin and all. We were shocked. What sort of fruit was this? A black man passed us by. It was true, then, that people turned black in America. We looked at each other in anxiety, but we had not too much time for speculation. Father, looking ill and unhappy, put us into some sort of a conveyance—I don't remember just what kind it was—and we went "home" to what we children expected to be the American palace with flights of golden stairs. We came to an ugly old tenement in the heart of the Lower East Side. There were stairs to climb but they were not golden. The water came from the wall, the iron stove was there and so were those clothes lines suspended high up in the air.

9

When, some fifteen years later, Menye and Rubenstein together with Avrom and Dvayreh joined us in America, they had already been preceded by Haiye and Rosenberg, Fraydel and Gruenberg, David and Joshua. All the Bercinskys, then, except Reb Michel and Yentel, who by this time were dead, and Mayshe, who was living his last days somewhere in the region of Baku, had now been trans-

planted to America. The old conflict between Fraydel and
Menye had been suspended for a dozen years. Now it was
resumed again in a very delicate fashion.

Fraydel with her husband and two children had gone
through great hardships. Now, in the land of promise,
Avrom Gruenberg faced more challenges; he slaved in a
sweatshop and finally emerged as the secretary of an old
folks' home. Throughout all his struggles Fraydel had been
his constant helper. She still ran a little stationery shop and
a newspaper route to make ends meet. At five in the morning, while her husband was still asleep, Fraydel was up
supervising the distribution of newspapers. She was back at
home preparing breakfast by the time he arose. She saw that
he left for work looking spick and span. She saw the children
off to school with shining faces and immaculate clothes.
Fraydel had forgotten all about her beauty and her wit. She
submerged her life entirely in that of her family.

Fraydel was no longer beautiful. The hard years of toil
showed in her face, left lines on her cheeks, frayed her hair
and took the luster from her eyes. Her husband was very
handsome. To begin with, he was younger than she. And he
was well cared for by his wife.

When Menye set foot on American soil, Fraydel grew
wary. Menye on the horizon always spelled trouble; besides,
Gruenberg, remembering Menye's good offices and her
beauty, was still rhapsodic about her. Fraydel smiled her
wan smile and did not invite her younger sister to Philadelphia to visit. She wrote Menye friendly letters expressing
the hope of seeing her in New York.

They met at my wedding.

My wedding was not a very joyous affair. My father had
died only a month earlier. There was no dancing; the ceremony was simple, and dinner was served for the guests.

Many of them were my father's friends. It was, I think, the last time that the Bercinskys gathered about one table. For soon after that Avrom went back to Warsaw to die. Dvayreh crept into the dingy little tenement flat to take up her life with "Elephant." Haiye went back into seclusion and Rosenberg into his cellar printing shop. My mother, of course, had her own troubles.

The field was left to Fraydel and Menye. It was Menye who was now the unhappier of the two. She and her husband had come away from home not to escape the tyranny of the Czar, but to avoid violence at the hands of the revolutionists. Times had changed. After January 22, 1905—after Nicholas II had yielded to the advice of Pobyedonostsev and had his peaceful petitioners shot down in the square before the Winter Palace—the revolutionists started an uprising. It was then that Menye's stepson, Rubenstein's youngest boy by his previous marriage, appeared with his comrades in Rubenstein's shop and, with drawn revolver, called his father an exploiter of the working classes and demanded money for the revolution. Rubenstein yielded to their demands, but since he was in terror of being accused on the one hand of revolutionary activities and on the other of being murdered for exploitation of the working classes, he sold his business and went to America. Before he did so, however, he converted the ten thousand-odd rubles he had received for his business into down—yes, feather down. You see, the notion that there were no proper pillows or featherbeds in America still prevailed. Well then, he would bring goose down to America where it could be quickly transformed into a fortune. But the down was lost on the way, and a good part of Rubenstein's fortune disappeared with it. Now these two pampered, comfort-loving people found themselves in a land which said, "Work or starve."

They could or would do neither. They had some money left, but not much when converted into American dollars.

Menye and Rubenstein talked over their dilemma with Fraydel and Gruenberg. No matter what conclusions they arrived at, Menye saw that Gruenberg was young and handsome, and that he had a good position. Gruenberg saw that Rubenstein was a poor man, and rather old. He also saw that Menye, though considerably heavier, had retained her good looks and was still a charmer. Fraydel saw that Menye was as flirtatious as ever, and Rubenstein saw that America was no place for him.

A few months later Rubenstein and Menye turned their backs on America and went back to Gomel. They took care, however, to leave Rubenstein's troublemaking son safely in America. They were not going to be held up by anyone for money to support the Revolution. That was in 1906, eleven years before the Bolsheviki came into power.

10

After Fraydel and Gruenberg had struggled through their hardships, when they had saved enough money to buy themselves a little home, furnish it prettily and marry off their daughter, Fraydel died of pneumonia. She was overworked in setting up the new home and in preparing for her darling girl's wedding. She would not allow a doctor to be called because it would mean spending two of the dollars she and her husband had so carefully hoarded against the time when they would be alone together.

I saw Gruenberg a year after her death, but his eyes still held such sorrow that one could not bear to look into them.

"What do you think of what Fraydel did to me?" he asked. I did not quite understand.

"What?" I asked. "What did she do to you?"

"She died and left me behind," he said.

What could I say to the man? He left me where I stood. He did not care whom he met, what he saw or where he went. He wandered about forlornly, entirely lost without Fraydel.

For five long years he wandered about without purpose until Rubenstein died in Gomel. The end came to Rubenstein after he had been stripped of everything he had by the new Bolshevik power. Being a merchant of the first guild, he was naturally treated as a prime enemy of the state. The fortune he had rebuilt during the war, after his return from America, was considered proof positive that he was an exploiter. As he lay dying, soldiers entered his room to requisition the very bed he was resting on. Menye stood before them.

"You can shoot me," she said, "but I will not let you take my husband's bed."

She was roughly brushed aside. Rubenstein was deposited on the floor, and bed and bedding were taken away. The man died where he lay while Menye cried at his side.

Menye's cries for help carried across the sea to her kin in America. When they reached Gruenberg's ears they stirred in him an ancient dream of loveliness, a passion long denied.

Avrom Gruenberg came to New York in a fevered state. He had called a family conference. He was suave and circumspect, but full of fervor, nevertheless. What was this he had heard and about which the family was so complacent? Did they know that Menye was destitute? Did they realize that of all the Bercinskys, Menye alone was in Russia? How could they leave her in such a state? The family put their heads together. True, Menye was in a bad state.

Suave, silent Gruenberg spoke with unusual animation. If

the family had any sense of honor, love or loyalty, they would pool their offerings and bring Menye back to America. He would do it himself if. . . . Well, after all, he was only a brother-in-law. Besides he could not do it legally. The law prevented him. Otherwise—why not? After all this was Menye—Fraydel's dear sister.

We all felt something in the man's ardor that left us speechless. We knew how deeply Gruenberg felt about Fraydel's death. We saw how unhappy he was. And now this! Menye, what a woman she was! It had been a dozen years since he saw her last, and still. . . . Gruenberg was alone and unhappy and so was Menye. Indeed, why not bring her back to America?

We did not know that when Menye was on the high seas she was in constant communication with Gruenberg by wireless. The messages kept singing through the air, and as they did so they gained in ardor. By the time the boat neared shore the dispatches were those of young lovers waiting to fly into each other's arms. An ancient spark had been kindled into flame.

When the boat docked, Gruenberg was not there to greet his sister-in-law. No use disclosing one's state to the family. Let them think her coming over was all their doing. He would drop in discreetly during the evening. All that had been arranged by wireless.

We lived in Ardsley at the time Menye arrived. I could not get to New York in time to meet her at the boat. She was to stop at Anna's house for the night, so I hastened there as fast as I could. As I was coming up the stairs, Anna stood on the landing waiting for me.

"Well, how is she?" I asked.

"You'll be surprised," Anna said.

I did not know what she meant. One could never tell about Menye. She had been such a beauty, and I had not seen her for a dozen years. Who knew what time had done to her? Perhaps it had treated her kindly, as it had Gruenberg, who was handsomer now than ever. Perhaps it had not; Menye had suffered, lived through a revolution. A rush of speculation as I passed through the door, and there sat Menye!

Time and Menye had worked hand in hand. Time put the weight of years upon her; Menye through her love of ease had burdened herself with the weight of flesh. She now weighed over two hundred and fifty pounds. Her face was still rather attractive; the little flaming lights still danced in her eyes, but she had hardly any hair, and what she had straggled in ringlets about a head that was much too small for her enormous body. Her abdomen was mountainous, her legs heavy as pillars of rock. She wore shabby clothes, for she had no others. What would Gruenberg think?

We fussed about our aunt, and Anna delicately suggested to her that she go and fix herself up a bit; Gruenberg was coming. With his ecstatic messages in her purse, Menye raised her head and asked proudly:

"Are you afraid he wouldn't like me as I am?"

Then she laughed in her old remembered way, but as she did so her huge uncorseted body heaved. Anna and I stood speechless before her. Together we thought, "Menye, how could you have let yourself go this way!"

I was not there when Gruenberg arrived. Nor was I present when he took her—as he promised in his letters he would—for a visit to Philadelphia. The next time I saw Menye she was sitting rather crestfallen in Rose's office. She had just returned from the city of brotherly love.

11

In the lonely furnished room she now occupies, Menye sits heavily in her chair dreaming of what might have been. For a long time after the tragic denouement of her romance, she asked eagerly if Gruenberg mentioned her name in the letters he wrote to us or if he spoke of her when we saw him. He did not. He does not. The last time I saw him, which was not so very long ago, the sorrow in his eyes was deeper than ever.

I wonder which of two emotions would be paramount in Fraydel's mind: pity for her suffering husband or triumph over defeated Menye?

EIGHT

David

A SUMMER NIGHT in Pinsk. There are people visiting the house, but we children have been sent to bed. The conversation in the dining room becomes jumbled in my consciousness. I am about to fall asleep when I hear my brother Abe coming home with Dave. I nudge Rose, who is falling asleep beside me. Together we sit up and listen. The measured tread of Abe's and Dave's footsteps beats on the wooden sidewalk in front of the house. Dave is talking, in his excited way. Every little while he utters a snatch of song, a musical phrase, a bit of tune.

They come into the house. We don't know where they have been, but they are full of music. Rose and I wrap our blankets about us and steal unnoticed into the dining room.

Abe is much younger than Dave, but they are pals. Dave treats Abe as if they were of equal age. Perhaps that is because the younger boy is so mature, but Dave does not draw lines. He does not intimidate those beneath him. He hates superficialities. He likes real people. He loves music.

When they come in Dave does not stop to say good evening. He is singing. He steps across the threshold and addresses himself to the people in the room with his song. They greet him cheerily, laugh at him, but he does not stop to answer. He continues to sing; yet in the wave of his hand, in the direction of his voice, in the modulation of his phrases, he returns their greetings. Everybody loves Dave and is glad that he has come.

Now he stands in the middle of the room singing a moving melody. He stands among the people he loves and looks into their faces. His gesture is one of appeal. It says: "Do you understand the import of this song I sing?" Yes, they understand. They join in the singing. Avrom Gruenberg, that shy and silent man, joins in. So does my brother Abe, who nods his head in full appreciation of the melody. We children wrapped in our blankets gather around. We can't get the full significance of what Dave is about, but his voice, his look, his manner creep into our hearts. Soon our childish voices join the chorus. We are not scolded when discovered, nor are we pushed away. We are drawn tenderly into the singing ring.

Dave is singing again, this time passages from the Sabbath services as interpreted by Pinsk's remarkable cantor, Yale-Zelig. A strange beauty fills the air. Until the end of their days, no matter where they were, the Bercinskys responded to Dave's melodies.

He is gone now. For the Bercinskys, Yale-Zelig's divine chants died with him, as did certain Russian romances and even some of the songs of your grandfather Zunser. It is not that these things have ceased to be, but that they can never again be as strange and beautiful as Dave made them.

It is a day in New York, forty years ago: Our father and mother and we children are sitting together around the supper table in our curious parlor floor and basement apartment on Madison Street. We have been completely disillusioned about America. We no longer dream of palaces, and we no longer expect miracles. We have accepted the drab reality of our daily existence and tried to make the best of it. In our ignorance of New York we have been moving from one tenement to another seeking light and air and space. Every time we move my father's printing shop moves with us. Oh, yes, my father had a printing shop where he published a monthly magazine called *Der Menshen Freind*—"The Friend of the People." But the magazine failed, the printing shop was sold to Uncle Rosenberg and my poor father sat about wondering what to do next. What he could do, of course, was the only thing possible for him to do—to write; but there was no Madame Romm to buy his products. He had to be his own publisher—until the printing shop was sold.

Father was very unhappy. So was my mother. So were we children. Abe knocked about somehow, and we three little girls found solace in two things: school and giving plays. We loved school. It seemed to fill every gap in our hungry hearts. Because we were of different ages, we were in different classes. We made the most of school by telling each other at the end of the day what each of us had done, and that gave Rose a chance to use her imagination again. She told me that her teacher, Miss Boland, dressed in a red velvet gown with a long flowing train, and sat on a throne of gold when she taught. The classroom was full of palm and date trees.

We indulged our love for giving plays on evenings when father and mother went out. We would rush up to our cold parlor floor and get into action. The first thing we did was to bring out dozens of volumes of "The Friend of the People." These we laid out on the floor in tiers to form a mountain range. Then we opened up an old trunk of stage costumes, dressed up and proceeded to give Goldfaden's operetta *Shulamith*, which we knew by heart in every detail.

The mountains were necessary for Shulamith to get lost in during the first act. I sang the lead. I had a voice then. Anna, younger and smaller than I, sang the leading male role, Avsholem. Rose played every other part in the play. In the first act she was my old father, then she was the half-tamed savage slave and comedian and finally she was the chorus. She also was the prompter and the director of the play as well as all the stage hands rolled into one.

Well, as we sat around the supper table in our home on Madison Street, a messenger brought us a cablegram. We were all on our feet. The message was from Dave and Gruenberg, who were stranded in Hamburg. They were on their way to America but they had no money for steamship tickets. "Hurry," the message read, "send us steamship tickets before we die of starvation." Perhaps these were not the exact words, but they conveyed that they were starving in Hamburg. Nobody had even known that they had left Pinsk or that they had contemplated coming to America, and now they were in Hamburg and hungry.

My father went to the steamship company that had brought us and so many thousands of other people across the sea, and procured two steamship tickets on the installment plan. These were sent to the starving men in the hope that they would survive.

Weeks of wondering and waiting passed. No news. No response of any kind. Then one day two gaunt, heavily bearded, bedraggled men stalked into our house. We looked at them in amazement. Then from behind one of these beards came Dave's cheerful voice:

"How are you, Dinneh?"

Shouts and tears and laughter and embraces. Here they were, those two starving men. And they certainly looked starved. What on earth? . . . but we did not have to ask. Dave's speech filled our ears. We rocked with laughter, we wept and we relived with Dave his experiences from the time he left Pinsk until he found his brother-in-law unexpectedly in Hamburg.

2

When Dave became eligible for military service he determined that he would not be a burden to his father. He hated the tyrannical Czar and his government, but if a man had to serve, well, then, there was nothing to do but serve. It was a matter of three or four years to be torn out of one's life and given to a cruel despot, but what could one do about it? He would not cheat, he would not lie, he would not have his father buy him out. He told the old man that if he was called upon to go into the army he would go. That enraged Reb Michel. No son of his was to be subjected to humiliations or made to eat the soldiers' filthy porridge. While the old man steeped himself in legal and illegal intricacies for the liberation of his son, Dave ran away to the recruiting office and offered himself for military duty.

While Reb Michel stormed at home, Dave raged inwardly at the examination office. But all the froth and fury of the two were quite unnecessary, for without much ado Dave was rejected by the examining officers because he was nearsighted. He was told that he would have to wear eyeglasses and that these would prove a serious handicap for service in the army.

Dave's joy did not last long. He did not know what to do with himself. He had had a row with one of the teachers at the *gymnasium* (high school) and so had discontinued his studies there. He had wanted to study medicine, but that was definitely out of his reach not only because of the quarrelsome teacher, but because of the hardships placed in the path of any Jewish student at a university in Russia. He would not go into business because he hated everything connected with it. He could not become a workingman because to do so would humiliate his father.

And now, to make things harder, all about him there was secret revolutionary activity aimed at the overthrow of the Czar and his government. All his sympathies were with the revolutionists. He was yielding to their call, but he could not join them because of the love he bore his father. The possible vision of Siberia for himself did not frighten him so much as the tortures that would be visited upon the old man. Well, then, what was he to do with himself? He turned his face to the west.

One day Dave packed a few things in a little bag, put on his hat and coat and told his father that he would run out to Warsaw to see if he could find something to do. As he took his old father in his arms his heart was sore, for he might never see him again. Perhaps Reb Michel felt the struggle that was going on in his son's heart, for the old man wept. "Good-bye, my son!"

Then Dave kissed his mother good-bye. "Poor old creature. Just a *Yiddene* [ordinary Jewish woman]! Goodbye, Dvayreh—my unfortunate sister! You are young, you are strong, you are brilliant. Be brave, Joshua—and take care of those three helpless ones. . . . I'll be back soon. . . . Well, good-bye all. Wait for me, all of you!"

By the time Dave got to Warsaw he was minus his hat and overcoat. He had given them away to a stranger he found lying under one of the benches on the train. In Warsaw he sold his extra suit of clothing, the watch out of his pocket and everything that could be turned into money and made his way to Hamburg, whence the great vessels sailed for America. He never stopped to consider how he would cross the ocean. He would find a way.

When he reached Hamburg, Dave was thin and gaunt. His stomach was empty. His pockets were empty, too. He walked the streets in astonishment. Was it really he who was wandering the streets of a strange city without a *groschen* in his pockets, without a friend, with no shelter? Was it really David Bercinsky going about everywhere asking for work of any kind and being turned away? He stared into the faces of people. He saw that many of them were homeless wanderers like himself. He stopped one of them. If one is starving, where does one get something to eat? The man, who happened to be a Galician Jew, pointed in a certain direction and said in his own particular dialect: *"Geitz ahin"!* ("Go there"!) At the other end of the city, it seemed, a Jewish philanthropic organization had opened a kitchen where bread and soup were dispensed to hungry Jewish immigrants who were passing through Hamburg on their way to other lands. Dave almost hugged that stranger. He pulled himself together, told his stomach to be good enough to wait just a little longer, and started on his long walk to the other end of town.

Sure enough, there was the kitchen where one could get bread and soup! But how did one go about asking since there were scores of people waiting their turn to be served? The answer was "Go to the end of the line and wait. When your turn comes you will get what you want." Dave did as he was told with a feeling of shame and pride. Shame, because he was a beggar standing in a breadline; pride, because he saw himself as a true son of his people, a people who were forced to wander but who would not die. If he were not so hungry he could bear his position with hauteur.

The line moved forward. It took such a long time, but still it moved. Then, as he looked at the line behind him, he thought he saw a familiar face. Surely it could not be! "Avrom!" he yelled, "Avrom Gruenberg!"

The man at the end of the line started at the cry of his name. Dave rushed for his brother-in-law and they fell into each other's arms. But when they recovered from their surprise Dave found that he had lost his place in the line. The long wait for bread and soup had to be started all over again.

Things had not been going well for Avrom. His business had failed. So he had taken courage and, following Dave's example, had made a dash for America. He had very little money with him—so little, indeed, that he feared it would not cover his stay in Hamburg and the price of a steamship ticket. Hence his presence in the breadline.

Happy as they were at being together, the two men were much disturbed by the gnawing of their stomachs. With the smell of food in their nostrils, their appetites were whetted beyond endurance. But the line moved along, and finally food tickets were put into their hands. Their turn finally came, but they had to enter one at a time. Gruenberg went through the door while Dave remained on the sidewalk. He looked at his ticket and danced with impatience. How long it took those people to eat! Why didn't they hurry a bit? To make himself feel better and to encourage those behind him, Dave held his ticket aloft and shouted:

"Look! I am going to eat! So are you!"

Just then a man, not in line, but standing near Dave, fell to the sidewalk.

"He fainted with hunger!" "He is starving to death!" Impetuously, Dave ran to the man, pushed the precious food ticket into his hand and dragged him to the kitchen door:

"Let this man eat," he shouted to the guard, "or his death

will be on your head!" With that he pushed the man into the kitchen. What surprised Dave was the agility with which the stricken man rose and used his legs once he was inside the kitchen door. Not until that moment did Dave realize that he had been duped. The bright vision of bread and soup faded. Cheated and abashed, he stood on the sidewalk waiting for Gruenberg to reappear. Finally Avrom did so, smiling and happy. Dave poured out his tale of woe. Gruenberg laughed in his own quiet way.

"Good soup," he said, wiping his mouth with his handkerchief.

The little money that Gruenberg had went for a cablegram to the Bercinskys in America and for keeping the two alive somehow until the steamship tickets arrived.

Now in New York, the two hollow-eyed, black-bearded men laughed. They had conquered the storm-tossed seas; they had survived hunger and want; they had reached America! Their happiness was boundless. But Dave broke this mood suddenly. He thought of his father. "Well, Reb Michel Bercinsky, I left you just as you left your own father. You don't really blame me, do you?" He paused for an answer. But Reb Michel did not answer. He was four thousand miles away, and Dave's self-defense ended in a bitter tone of self-reproach.

In the early nineties most Russian and Polish immigrants to America worked in the sweatshops of New York. When a boatload of immigrants arrived at Castle Garden, sweatshop owners or their agents were waiting to receive them with offers of immediate work. Many of the bosses were newcomers to America who had opened little shops and felt righteous about giving their own countrymen a chance to earn a living. Many of them did not realize that they were

exploiting their *landsleit,* but they did so nevertheless. Dozens of shops in filthy tenement houses or in dingy lofts held
staggering numbers of forlorn Russian or Polish Jews. Filled
with the glorious legends of the "new land" these harassed
men considered the opportunities for immediate work part
of the miracles they had heard about, and so fell easily into
the hands of the unscrupulous.

Dave and, for a time, Gruenberg, escaped the sweatshops
only because they believed that the great Shomer and the
learned Rosenberg had been appreciated in America. In this
land where every "nobody" made his way, these two shining stars would be acclaimed for their worth; soon, no doubt,
they would even be in a position to help their troubled kin.
Dave and Gruenberg had no way of knowing that the more
learning and culture a man had, the harder he would find it
to adjust to the environment later called the "melting pot."
The sooner a man melted his personality and mixed it with
the other elements in the seething cauldron of disintegra-
tion, the sooner he would emerge as the new type of American citizen. It was a process thousands of people could not
survive. But neither Dave nor Gruenberg realized this at that
time. It became clear only in retrospect, when the work was
done; when the remains of the sacrificed lay discarded in a
heap and the shout of the newly emerged filled our ears with
their din.

A few weeks after Dave came to America, he blew into
our house in breezy American fashion. He looked at us with
glittering eyes, pointed down his throat and with elaborate
workings of the lips said, "I . . . vant . . . to eat!"

This was the first English sentence he learned, and no
wonder—he was still hungry. Delighted with his speech, we
children emptied every cupboard in the house for him. He

ate all he could hold, borrowed two cents from us for cigarettes and announced that he had started in business; he was
peddling suspenders. But when mother went to Hester
Street to see him, she found that the suspender business had
already been suspended and that her intellectual brother
was selling herring and eggs to the *coshenierkes* of that marketplace. (*Coshenierke* is a word in the Yiddish of New York,
probably derived from "connoisseur." It means a female
bargain hunter or one who haggles about the price of
things.) Mother was horrified. Dave selling herring! What
would his father say? But Dave appreciated the humor of
the situation and enjoyed himself immensely as he held a
herring on high by its tail and allowed the *coshenierkes* to view
it from every angle. His boss did not seem to appreciate his
attitude or enthusiasm, however. He discharged the indefatigable young man, who immediately bought himself a
pushcart and sold remnants of dress goods to a new set of
coshenierkes. Here he had a fine time watching them smuggle
pieces of cloth into their market baskets. Some he held up
to public disgrace, while others—the very poor ones—he
encouraged to take something worthwhile.

After the total collapse of the remnant business because
of the thieving *coshenierkes,* Dave became a banker. Yes, a
banker. A friend of his by the name of Kolodne had arrived from Pinsk with a considerable amount of money.
With true business acumen the greenhorn chose Dave as
his partner in the banking business he wished to establish.
Since Kolodne depended upon Dave for his knowledge of
America and American business methods, it wasn't long
before Kolodne went back to Pinsk utterly disgusted with
American business ways. Dave then became a window-
and bottle washer in a corner drugstore. It was a fine sight
to see the erstwhile banker standing on the sidewalk with

a bucket of water swabbing the windows of the shop.

But Dave was not in the least embarrassed. Hadn't he told Kolodne that he hated business? Now Kolodne had a chance to hate it himself. As for window washing, at least it was constructive. Besides, he was now in a drug store. With the smell of medicine in his nostrils he felt close to his heart's desire. He wanted to study medicine.

It was about this time that Dave fell in love with Nancy Davidson and joined the "Counts" of East Broadway. Nancy, of course, would not consider him. Why should she? Such a crazy lanky fellow, a banker one day and a bottle washer the next! But Dave had made up his mind. It would be medicine at Yale University, and it would be Nancy Davidson.

But I must explain the "Counts" of East Broadway. Then, as now, before one could enter a college or university, certain entrance requirements had to be met. In comparison to the requirements of today those of the time I speak of were minimal. Still, they had to be met. For those who had no opportunity to take the regular prescribed courses at recognized schools there was a way out of the difficulty by taking the examinations given by the New York State Board of Regents. These were held three or four times a year and were open to all comers regardless of how, when and where they received their education. Every subject passed meant so many "counts" or points. A given number of counts entitled one to a certificate or to a diploma, which insured entrance in the desired college.

On the Lower East Side of New York, newly Americanized Russian and Polish Jews fell eagerly upon the opportunity of educating and making something of themselves. In the lands from which they had come every possible barrier had been placed between them and the liberal professions.

Now, after a long day of toil in dark, airless sweatshops, many young men eagerly engaged in the pursuit of knowledge, which could be turned into "counts"—toward entering universities. Thus it happened that the host of pale, serious young men who emerged at midnight on East Broadway with their books under their arms seeking a breath of air and serious discussion, came to be known as the "Counts of East Broadway." Dave and his brother Joshua, who had by this time joined him, belonged to this new aristocracy. Dave was making his way toward Nancy and Yale.

3

It is several years later, a day in autumn, a high holy day —the Day of Atonement. The house is hushed. Mother has just come home from *shul* for a little rest. The tall Yom Kippur candle she lit the night before at the setting of the sun still burns in its pot of earth, shedding its melancholy light. On Yom Kippur mother always thinks of her "old home" in Pinsk. There the whole town was steeped in solemn fear. No one took a morsel of food or even a drink of water for twenty-four hours. The men were in *shul* all day standing in their stockinged feet and wearing the shrouds in which they would someday be buried. The cries of the women in the gallery rent the heavens. All were atoning for the sins they might have committed during the past year. All beat their breasts, forgave their enemies, clasped their friends to their hearts, and asked the Lord to be merciful to them, to forgive them their trespasses and to grant them life and happiness for the coming year.

Mother regretted that things were so different in New York. The Jewish community in the city was divided against itself. There were those who observed the day, but there

were also those who called themselves anarchists and deliberately desecrated the day by eating in public on the very
night when *Kol Nidre* was sung in the synagogues. In our
house Jewish traditions were observed only to a certain extent. My father, though an ardent nationalist, was not an
observant Jew. He recognized our holidays as events in Jewish history and celebrated them without going to *shul*. In
consequence, in the observance of Jewish holidays and holy
days we were jovial or solemn, as the occasion required, but
there was none of that ecstatic jubilation or solemn awe that
rose from orthodox conviction.

On the Yom Kippur day in question, we were balancing
our souls on the scales of the past and present when there
was a quick knock at the door and Dave came in—all excitement. It was not an appropriate mood on the Day of Atonement, but Dave had good reason to be in that state. He was
going to get married; he was leaving New York; he was
opening a drug store; he was entering Yale. All this in one
breath without a moment of preparation. Naturally, he
brought upon himself an avalanche of questions. When was
all this to happen? Who was the girl? Why a drug store?
Why Yale?

Dave looked at us. Don't you know that the girl is Nancy?
He had quite forgotten that we had not seen him for months
and that he hadn't kept us informed. They were going to
New Haven, and he would enter the medical school. Oh,
yes, he had his "counts"! What were they to live on? The
drug store, of course, which he and Nancy would operate
together. They were qualified; the "counts" seemed to have
taken care of that, too. And when would the marriage take
place? Why that very day!

The clamor suddenly ceased. We were simply speechless.
Then mother: "Today! Why it is Yom Kippur!" But Dave's

eyes were blazing. Yes, that very day! At sundown when Nancy's father returned from *shul.*

"But old man Davidson is a strictly orthodox Jew! He is fasting, wearing a shroud and going about in his stockinged feet! Has he consented to his daughter's being married on Yom Kippur night?"

Dave was more excited than ever. How should he know if Davidson would consent or not; he hadn't been asked yet!

This was too much. My mother exploded. Who ever heard of such a thing? The old man was in *shul* praying and fasting and here was Dave planning to surprise him by marrying his first-born child, his lovely daughter Nancy, that very night. It was perfectly absurd! The word did not in the least frighten Dave. There was no use talking to him. He would have his way no matter what was said. "Well, then, good luck! Get married and may happiness be yours!"

The torrent of words ceased. Dave was touched by everyone's solicitude. His excitement gave way to tenderness and a deeply touching mood. We understood. *"Der tatte!"* ("Father.") Reb Michel would not be there when the son of his heart, Dave, took his bride to the *chuppe.* Dave would not have his beloved father with him in this great moment of his life. There were tears in his eyes. In a moment Pinsk had him in its grip. Grandfather, grandmother, the house, the town, the people—how far away they were! How remote, like the centuries of the past. All were embraced in the one word he uttered with longing: *"Tatte!"*

Dave took off his glasses, wiped the mist that had gathered on them and became suddenly pugnacious. What was this? Why was he standing about talking sentimentalities? He was getting married that night, wasn't he? Well, then, he had better be on his way and see that it was so. As for his father, surely the man would not die. He would wait. . . .

4

But the time came when Reb Michel could no longer wait to die. He came home from *shul* one day and sat down at the great deserted table to his lonely meal with Yentel. Before taking any food he inquired about the town lunatic whom he had been feeding all through the winter. The man had not put in an appearance for two days and Reb Michel was worried about him. Where could he possibly be? He was not admitted or fed anywhere except in the kitchen of Reb Michel's house, and now he had not been seen for forty-eight hours. Just then the water carrier came with news: "Reb Michel, that lunatic of yours, that crazy Berke was found frozen stiff on the riverbank!"

The spoon dropped from grandfather's hand. He fell from his chair to the floor. It was a stroke from which he did not recover. Two days later he died. He was eighty-four.

In a few months Yentel followed him. She could not abide the house without her Michel. She went about from room to room calling his name. He had been her husband for seventy years and she could not live without him. She was not buried at his side but in another part of the cemetery, because among orthodox Jews men and women may not mingle, even in death.

When news of grandfather's passing reached America, Dave came down from New Haven to sit with us in silence. Somehow the two most talkative Bercinskys, my mother and Dave, had become speechless. Together they sat and wept. Mother rent her garments and Dave did not protest when she cut the lapel of his coat. He went as silently as he had come.

5

Some years after your father and I were married, we visited Dave and Nancy at their home. It was plain and unadorned, but it was not poor; it was lovely. The bookshelves, the little pots of geraniums, the portrait bust of Nancy's mother made by her brother Jo before he went to Paris, his little statue of the biblical David, which first attracted the notice of critics and the public—these were part of their peaceful home. Then there were the simple, comfortable chairs, the rough reading table, the couch with its spotless monk's cloth covering and the cushions made by the indefatigable hands of old Mrs. Davidson, Nancy's mother. And among all these the enlarged photographs of Reb Michel and Yentel. How strange they looked in their new surroundings! But there they were, looking down upon the daughter-in-law whom they did not know, and upon Dave, who could call upon them to bear witness to what he was —their truly begotten son who was carrying on his father's tradition in word and deed, making a place for himself in the hearts of his fellow men.

That little visit with Dave and Nancy lingers in my mind because of the spirit of festivity that surrounded us. Dave felt our intimacy, and he talked, and sang and filled our hearts with happiness.

Nancy went about on her dainty feet, chattering in her spirited way, and having an awful time with Dave. It was all right for him to sit there in an endless flow of conversation, but an office full of patients was waiting for him. Nancy pulled at his sleeve, tugged at his coat, but he continued to talk. The poor girl, though used to his ways, did not quite know what to do with him. She scolded him roundly and went back to the patients with all sorts of excuses for the doctor's absence. At last Dave told us to wait —just a few minutes—and made his way into the office. The few minutes extended themselves into hours with no sign of Dave; for now that he was with his patients he had forgotten us completely.

We were seated at the table one day when the telephone rang. Nancy answered.

"Dave, Mrs. Cohen called again."

Dave made no answer but continued to talk.

"It's the fifth time, Dave," Nancy said in despair. "She says she will die if you don't come."

"That woman!" Dave cried excitedly. "That woman will be the death of me first!"

He leaned back in his chair studying us critically. Up went an eyebrow in characteristic fashion (like grandmother's when she is angry), and he swung his leg with impatience.

"The woman came into my office one day: 'Doctor, the medicine you gave me made me nauseous.' "

"How do you know it was the medicine? Maybe it was the rice or beans or potatoes you were eating?"

" '*I* was eating potatoes? *When* was I eating potatoes?' "

" 'Yesterday, I suppose.' "

" 'Yesterday I only ate noodles with cheese.' "

" 'Well, then, maybe the noodles made you nauseous.' "

" 'Why should the *noodles* make me nauseous, and not the *cheese?*' "

" 'Maybe the cheese, too. I told you not to eat starches and cheese.' "

" '*I* eat starch! Why don't you say that I eat *soap?*' " (Evidently she was thinking of the laundry.)

" 'Because you don't eat soap. You eat starch when you eat flour.' "

" 'Who *told* you I eat flour? What! am I *crazy*? *Who* eats flour?' "

" 'Don't you make noodles of flour?' "

" 'What *then* shall I make them of—*stones?*' "

" 'Well, if you make the noodles out of flour and you eat it, don't you eat flour?' "

" 'No, doctor!' " (Dave said that at this point the woman laughed hilariously.) "Men don't know *anything!* When you take *flour* and put in *eggs* and cut it *up* and *boil it,* you don't eat *flour,* you eat *noodles!* "

Dave's face for the moment was Mrs. Cohen's, and he entertained us magnificently. But Nancy burned with impatience:

"Mrs. Kaplan called. Her Bessele is very sick. Choking, she says. If you don't go at once—"

But Dave was already on his feet, and in a moment he was out of the house.

When he returned he was a picture of disheveled triumph. His coat was rumpled, his tie awry, his hair, as always when he was excited, stood on end.

Bessele was certainly sick, with an acute case of diphtheria. He had sent the mother to the nearest drug store for serum, while he had taken out the hypodermic needle and started to prepare the child for an antitoxin injection. But instead of doing as she was told, the mother had begun to howl. What? He was going to stick a needle full of poison into her baby! She would not let him do it. To assure herself that the doctor would not carry out his murderous intent upon the child, the woman had raised a cry that had brought her neighbors rushing to her side. The women had surrounded him, and there was nothing for the man to do but run breathlessly to the drug store. Soon he was back among the astonished women, but they had not let him approach the child. Thereupon he had taken off his coat and made excellent use of the strength he had gathered since Nancy began taking care of him. One after the other he had thrown the screaming women out of the room, locked the door, and given Bessele the necessary treatment.

Of course, Nancy was delighted as we all were, but she quickly guessed that Dave would not be paid for his services and that he had paid for the serum out of his own pocket.

Some years later, when we were again with Nancy and Dave, we found them having the same argument:

"Dave, you know you were not the doctor engaged in this case. You were just called in because it was an emergency."

Nancy was referring to the delivery of a nine-pound baby Dave had just made.

"I hope you were paid."

Dave was eating an apple and snorting angrily.

"Were you, Dave? Or, do you expect to be?"

"No," he answered angrily, swallowing a big bite.

"But why?" Nancy was vexed.

"Because she is a poor woman."

"But we are poor, too. You must do something about this, Dave."

"What do you want me to do? Put the child back where it came from? I have already thrown away the placenta and cut away the umbilical cord!"

The last time we saw Dave was at our own house. It was on Purim. For some reason I developed a longing to be with all that was left of the Bercinskys, and I brought them together. Grandma was there, and Menye, Dave, and Nancy. Other friends came in. Soon they fell to talking about Pinsk and to telling stories, but it was mother and Dave whose tales silenced the rest. You know how these two were. They loved nothing quite so much as holding forth. The rivalry between them was keen, and it was hard to tell which was the greater storyteller.

A few short weeks later Dave was gone forever. A little lump on his foot, a blood clot, negligence. The clot disappeared, passed on into his bloodstream and reached his heart.

NINE

Joshua

WHAT I HAVE TO TELL YOU of Joshua's story is merely a brief
account of his prematurely disrupted life. It had very little
to do with the Bercinsky family as such. Yet, in retrospect,
Joshua's isolation as an individual becomes rather significant. It bears witness to the many changes that took place
in the nearly forty years between his birth and that of his
brother Mayshe, who was the first of Reb Michel's sons.
Joshua, as you know, was the last. In Mayshe's time the
Bercinsky family was a unit that centered about Reb Michel.
In Joshua's day it was a scattered tribe living in many cities
of Russia and America. Mayshe was the very heart of his
family, but he had no voice in important matters. In keeping
with the tradition of his time, he had to submit to the judgment of his father even in the choice of a wife, for that too
was a family matter rather than a personal affair, since it
affected the house of Bercinsky. In contrast, Joshua considered his affairs strictly his own and was concerned with no
one but himself. He asked for no opinion and valued none
but his own. The lives of those of Reb Michel's children who
thrived in the period between these two sons mark the many

stages of transition from the one manner of life to the other.

Mayshe, you will remember, never saw the woman he was to marry until the actual moment—a tragic one for him —when the marriage ceremony was performed. My mother, Dinneh, made some progress when she was permitted to see her *chossen* before the betrothal bonds were sealed. Haiye went so far as to fall in love and fight for the right to marry the man of her choice even if in the end she had to do as she was told. Avrom took a long step away from custom when he married the woman he was allowed to court. Fraydel struggled with her father's wishes, and acted against them. Menye yielded to them only because they coincided with her own. David did not even consult Reb Michel on what course he was to take in life, and Joshua openly scoffed at his parent's opinion and did only what he pleased. Vast changes had occurred in the time between Mayshe's and Joshua's coming of age.

You already know that Joshua was Reb Michel's and Yentel's twenty-fourth child. At the time of his birth, his mother was several times a grandmother.

As a boy, Joshua, unlike Dave, loved study. He lived by it, thrived on it. One could think of David as romping in the fields, skating on the frozen river, riding bareback on any old horse; but one could not think of Joshua without a book in his hand or examination papers on the table before him. He was passed along quickly from one teacher to another because of the rapidity with which he outgrew them. He devoured the Talmudic courses and at an early age was able to perform a curious trick practiced at that time among exceptional students. It consisted of being able to tell what words a pin pierced when struck at random through any word on any page of any of the Five Books of Moses. Joshua knew the Torah by heart. He remembered the look of every page and the succession of every line.

Naturally Reb Michel rejoiced in his son. At last the family would possess a great scholar, perhaps a great rabbi. But it soon became clear that the boy could not be held down to Talmudic studies only. His quick mind had caught the Russian that was now current in the house and in the town; it caught a visitor's German and the neighboring doctor's Polish. Soon, too, he was interested in science, mathematics and philosophy. There was only one place for a boy of this type—the *gymnasium,* or high school. *Gymnasium* it was for both David and Joshua.

Before long they were wearing the school uniform with its brass buttons and peaked cap, their books and tablets strapped across their backs. This was certainly a new note in the Bercinsky house, within whose walls Reb Michel's father once rent his garments and uttered the prayer for the dead, because his son was found reading a Russian book.

Under Nicholas I and Alexander II the Jews were coaxed or forcibly driven into the state schools for study and Russification. Now, under Alexander III, every obstacle was put in the way of their attending these public institutions of learning. It was no easy task for a Jewish boy to enter the *gymnasium* or to go through all its forms. If a boy surmounted the difficulties he met before he could enter the *gymnasium,* he had to maintain a high standard of excellence in order to remain there. Joshua found himself at the head of every class he attended. His future seemed bright. But fate seemed to have something quite different in store for him.

Among the non-Jewish students in the school there were some who were far from bright. Since no very high standard of excellence was required for them to continue their studies, many a dullard found his place in classes where he did

not rightly belong. There was one in particular at the *gymnasium* who had plenty of money. He was the pampered son
of a *pomestchik* (rich landowner) who was worried about his
son's inability to learn. With examinations looming ahead,
the *pomestchik* decided that something drastic would have to
be done. He looked about carefully for a tutor. Joshua
seemed to be a young man who could be depended on to
shepherd his son through exams. Accordingly, the landowner approached Joshua with the following proposition: if
he would come to the *pomestchik*'s estate for the summer to
teach his son, he would receive three hundred rubles in cash.
He would also share the son's apartment and his luxurious
way of life and could count on the *pomestchik*'s promise of
many future favors. All this seemed the very pinnacle of
attainment for Joshua—a fortune. Prospects for the future.
And best of all, life in grand style. For a young man who had
never left his home town and had seen no other way of life,
this last part of the offer was the most enticing. But it was
just this that Reb Michel objected to most strenuously. Everything would be well enough, but a Jew could not live at
a Gentile's home and share his life. There were such things
as dietary laws and the Sabbath to observe, and there were
rules and regulations for one's personal conduct which the
pomestchik's son certainly knew nothing of. But young Joshua
disregarded his seventy-year-old father. The old man would
have to understand that times had changed.

So it happened that one day when his father was not at
home, the precocious young man of eighteen waved a blithe
good-bye to the women and rode away in the *pomestchik*'s
carriage with the pampered son.

At the end of the summer Joshua returned, but he did not
seem happy and carefree. As a matter of fact, he was pale
and troubled. He said little when questioned, and went

about rather morosely grooming himself and attending to the many suits of clothes he had bought. There was no doubt but that he looked handsome in his new attire, but there was also no denying that an anxious expression had crept into his face, and that his curious secretive ways did not add elegance to his deportment. Silently Joshua prepared for his return to school. The strangeness of his manner aroused the family's concern; he sought seclusion, avoided being questioned, slept badly and was obviously much worried.

School started and it was evident that Joshua's mind was not on his work. Then reports came in that he was falling behind in his studies. The family became seriously alarmed. What was the matter? The young man simply would not talk. He kept to himself more than ever, refused to see his friends and avoided the family. One day it was discovered that Joshua could no longer study; then he failed his examinations. The family was shocked, but when they looked into his eyes for an explanation they were horrified. Joshua's burning, furious stare was that of a madman.

Medical examination showed that the young man had contracted a venereal disease that had affected his mind. It was a temporary condition, the doctors said.

At the time we left Pinsk, Joshua had recovered from his illness, but he never returned to the *gymnasium.* He had lost his place there and lacked the heart to try for readmission. It was all too humiliating. He did clerical work for his father and felt demeaned by it. I don't know if he was told the nature of his trouble. He was only nineteen years old at this time, and already a great calamity had descended upon him. Military service loomed two years ahead. Joshua did not seem troubled by the thought of it. Perhaps he regarded it as a way out of a difficult situation.

About a year after Dave came to America we received a letter from grandfather revealing that Joshua had been drafted into the army. Of all his sons, the brilliant Joshua was the only one to actually serve the Czar. From Reb Michel's description it was easy to see that his big house was now a lonely place. One after another his many children had left for different parts of the world. The only one who remained with him and Yentel was the scarred, muttering Dvayreh. The two old people went about the empty rooms listening to echoes of the past. Everywhere there were signs of the days that had been, of the people who had filled them. All that was left now were memories and a few photographs hanging on the walls. A lonesome old age awaited in spite of the many children the couple had brought into the world, in spite of the largeness of the life they had lived. All they looked forward to now was Menye's occasional visit and to Joshua's return. In three or four years he would be back. But they were old . . . would they live to see him again?

Joshua never came back. He deserted the army and escaped to America.

I recall a scene at my father's printing shop in the basement of a tenement house on Madison Street. My father sits at his desk writing. Joshua stands over the little printing press, feeding it circulars announcing the opening of a butcher shop around the corner. He is no hurry about turning out his work. My father casts anxious glances in his direction, because the job has been promised for a certain time, but Joshua is entirely unconcerned. He stops the press, lights a cigarette and starts singing a melancholy Russian air. Father picks up his high silk hat and leaves the office hurriedly to avoid showing his irritation. Joshua continues to sing. He fills the dingy shop with his sorrowful music.

Hellman the compositor puts down the job he is setting and gazes at Joshua. There is something sad about the man, and his song is compelling. Soon the compositor is singing; he, too, is a sad exile from Russia—forced to flee the country because of his political activities. Both of my father's "workingmen" sing while their tasks wait. My brother Abe comes down the basement stairs. The pressman and the compositor return to their work, though not very energetically. Abe takes off his coat and starts setting a job. But the singing has not stopped. Presently Abe joins the dismal chorus. He is seventeen now, without any knowledge of America and with no one to turn to for guidance. Father cannot help him because he is himself lost in the new country. Abe works in the shop at all hours, helping father with the printing. He undertakes tasks that are too great for a boy his age. He is able and ambitious, and quite unhappy. So the voices of the three young men rise in mournful song and fill the wretched cellar which houses Shomer's printing establishment.

Presently Shomer himself returns. He lays aside his silk hat and walking stick; he turns back the skirt of his Prince Albert frock coat and sits down again at his desk. No, he does not prepare the copy for his industrious workmen— that is Abe's business; but he has to turn out copy for the three novels he is writing simultaneously, and which are appearing in serial form. Two of these novels have been commissioned by Katzenelenbogen and Kantrovitsch's publishing house; the third he is putting out himself. The money father receives from his publishers goes toward the upkeep of the printing shop, for that does not pay for itself. Why, then, bother about running it? Nobody seems quite to know;

but it forestalls the possibility of father's not having a publisher. Yet the shop eats up his earnings, so things are not
good at all.

Yes, indeed, the basement printing establishment is a sad
place. Once in a while Dave rests his pushcart (these are his
remnant days) on the sidewalk and comes down to take a
look at the boys and to cheer them up. But even he cannot
dispel their gloom.

Joshua avoided his family as much as possible. If he
worked for my father, it was only because he could find
nothing else to do. One night he came to our home very
much upset. He demanded to see father, who happened to
be out. Mother was frightened. She asked him to rest awhile.
But he began pounding the table and talking nonsense. In
terror mother realized that he was again out of his mind. She
sent for Dave, who was the only one who could control
Joshua. But before Dave arrived Joshua had fled.

The next day, while Dave and the family sat in troubled
conference, Joshua rushed into the house. He was in a worse
state and threatened violence to Dave unless Dave returned
his fortune of many millions at once. Dave said quietly that
he would and left the house. As we all sat anxiously by,
Joshua's rage subsided; then he burst into song. There was
such heartrending appeal in the tender passages of his song
that we children lost our fear of him. We put our arms about
him and tried to comfort him. For a moment he became as
submissive as a child. Just then there was much commotion
in the hall. Joshua jumped to his feet in terror. He knew at
once that Dave had come back with people to subdue him.
With a cry he rushed about the room trying to escape, but
there was no way out of the apartment except through the
door by which the men were entering. In despair Joshua ran

to the bathroom and locked himself in. But the hospital attendant soon broke through the door. Joshua was put into a straitjacket and led screaming to the ambulance downstairs.

A year later Joshua was released from the asylum. It was at this point that the worst tragedy of his life began, for now he was fully aware of what ailed him and where he had been. No doubt he also knew the recurrent nature of his disease, but for the time being he again had the use of his mind.

During these hard times Dave and my brother Abe took care of him, I believe. Later, on the rare occasions when Joshua visited us, we learned that he was supporting himself by teaching languages, mathematics, physics and other subjects. The "Counts of East Broadway" were making good use of him and paying him well. But he did not like teaching. He had hoped for the university himself. Had he not shown promise of great things? Now all the man could do was to prepare others for careers he himself was afraid to approach.

To hide his pain, he put on a laughing, nonchalant air and ignored his doom by taking examinations—any kind of examinations. What difference did it make if he had no reasons for taking them? It was fun to enter the regents' great examination hall, pick up some question papers, answer the number required on each paper in no time at all, and stalk proudly out of the room while all the others sat as if glued to their seats, sweating over the tasks before them. Invariably he would pass with "honors"—that is, with ninety percent or more correct answers. It pleased him to do so. Once, after receiving several nineties, he walked to the mirror, looked at himself keenly and said: "A bright man this, and a good-looking one, too." Then he said, bitterly, to those who observed him: "Isn't that so?"

Joshua was handsome. He was well built and muscular, his features were small and fine, his brown hair soft and silky, and warm little lights like Menye's danced in the depths of his eyes.

Once Joshua indulged his love for both examinations and singing to an extraordinary degree. He walked into an examination hall, quite unprepared, and took the competitive test for a full medical scholarship offered by Cornell University in honor of the opening of its medical school. Then, that very day, he went to the Metropolitan Opera House and took a test for admission into its chorus. He won both the scholarship and the chorus job.

Joshua laughed sadly when he entered upon his studies as a medical student at Cornell. Perhaps he would yet be that great something-or-other people had expected him to be.

He rarely saw his relatives and seldom wrote to his father and mother, but he had pride. No matter what misfortune had befallen him, he was still Joshua Bercinsky, or now, Joshua Behring. He had cast off his father's name; he was not to be part of a tribe, but a new entity.

For two years Joshua held his head high. All went well in school, and the many students he continued to tutor paid him more than ever. We rarely saw him, but reports reached us from many sources that Joshua was thriving. Then one day we received a message from Mr. Behring's landlady saying that all was not quite well with her lodger and asking that someone come to see him. Mother asked me to go.

When I came to Joshua's room he was lying on his bed fully dressed, his face turned to the wall. I quietly called his name. He turned abruptly and looked at me. Then he sat up, pale and trembling. With one hand he covered his blazing eyes; with the other he clutched nervously at the coverlet. He was not feeling well, he said in a rather jocular tone, trying to make light of his state, and doing everything possible to hide his eyes. Would I please go into the kitchen and fetch him a cup of tea?

I hastened to do so. When I returned he was standing before the mirror combing his hair. He had put on dark glasses. He addressed me without turning around, saying, with a rather nervous laugh, that one must not appear in a disheveled condition before a young lady. He kept grooming himself; as he did I noticed how curiously he twisted his arms and hands. This and the eyes I had seen a moment before filled me with terror. Finally Joshua finished his toilet and came to sit beside me. From behind the dark glasses, which set off sharply the extreme pallor of his face, he watched me closely as we spoke. I don't know in what way I betrayed my discomfiture, for he suddenly stopped.

"You are not listening," he said.

I assured him that I was.

"But you are afraid of me?"

"Of course not! Why should I be?"

"Come," he said, "I'll show you why."

He led me to the mirror.

"Look!" he said, standing beside me in front of the mirror and taking off his glasses. He pointed at his reflection. Once again I saw those terrifying eyes.

"Lunatic!" Joshua suddenly shrieked at his image. Then with his fist he smashed the mirror. I fled from the room.

The same evening Joshua joined my family for dinner. He made much of his coming, and we did everything possible to hide the anxiety we felt for him. We tried hard to carry on a normal conversation, but it was not normal at all, for Joshua was talking at the top of his voice, trying to explain things for which there was no explanation. Without doubt he knew his condition. He realized that he was again drifting into insanity and tried desperately to hold on to his reason.

The more the man argued, the more involved he became, and the more furious. The fund of knowledge upon which he drew became a grotesque labyrinth of distorted facts from which he could find no way out. Exhausted by the violence of his effort, exasperated by the words that jumbled in his mouth, Joshua pounded the table and screamed that we were not intelligent enough to follow his arguments. Suddenly he became aware of the deathly stillness in the room. He realized that he alone was talking, screaming, and that we sat like figures of stone anxiously watching him. Shrieking, he tore out of the room. No one had the heart to overtake him.

When Abe called at his room that night, he was not there. He had not returned by morning. Dave and Abe ran about everywhere looking for him. Several days later a policeman picked him up on an empty lot in Brooklyn, where he was disrobing and calling for his royal raiment and proclaiming himself a king.

Joshua died some years later in an insane asylum. He was in his early thirties, but I am told he looked like a beaten, broken man of eighty.

This was the sorry end of Joshua, the most promising son of Reb Michel and Yentel, the last in the long line of their children.

The house in which your great-grandfather Reb Michel lived still stands in Pinsk. About four years ago your father and I had the chance to see both the house and the town, but we did not do it. We were then in Vilna, only a few hours' journey from Pinsk. We wanted very much to see the old place and to mark the graves of my grandfather and grandmother. But we were told by those who knew that we would find no trace of the graves. It seems that the cemetery of Pinsk had been used as a battleground during the Great War. The ancient burial place was no longer consecrated ground. It was just a disrupted heap of earth and dust of which Reb Michel's and Yentel's remains were a part. Their bones, as well as those of their children, had been tossed up on the raging battlefield by the plunging horses of the Russians, Germans and Poles.

We had not the heart to go to Pinsk. We came back to our beloved America.

Postscript
by Emily Wortis Leider

WHEN MY GRANDMOTHER died in 1951, she was sixty-eight and I thirteen. My firsthand recollections of her are naturally those of a child. She was heavy and had long dark hair, which she wore piled on top of her head. Her nose was prominent, her eyes alert. She dressed in black most of the time (maybe because she thought it would minimize her weight) and wore the kind of glasses that are now called "granny glasses." Her smile was both warm and sardonic, her voice soft, her speech precise. There was no trace of a foreign accent. She looked like, and I think she was, a wise-woman.

People often came to her for advice and leaned on her for support. In *Yesterday* she is the one who visits pathetic, be-reaved Dvayreh on her family's behalf, and again, it is she who is sent to call on mad Joshua. She liked to be and often was defender, protector, helpmate.

She could also be impatient, imperious, arrogant. She ex-pected others to be what she was: hardworking, intelligent, gifted, interesting.

I can see her arriving with my grandfather at our house in

Brooklyn, laden with string-tied bakery boxes full of cakes. I can picture her playing chess with my father at the dining-room table after dinner. ("She liked to win," my father says.) I can hear her remonstrating on the telephone in her apartment, acting as peacemaker in the umpteenth quarrel between my grandfather and one of her sisters: "He says he's sorry."

I used to pay a weekly visit to their Seventy-fifth Street Manhattan apartment after my piano lesson. It pleased her that I was musical; it was a link between us.

Miriam Shomer Zunser was born Manya Shaikevitsch on November 25, 1882, in Odessa, Russia. At that time her father, a popular and prolific writer of *shund* (trashy) novels in Yiddish under the pen name Shomer, was writing plays for the Maryinsky Theater, in which he was a partner with Joseph Lerner and Abraham Goldfaden. (Later, in New York, the red velvet curtain from that theater was used to make party dresses—the only ones they owned—for Manya and her two sisters, Rose and Anna.) At the age of three she moved to her mother's home village, Pinsk. The Yiddish theater in Odessa had been closed by Alexander III in the despotic aftermath of the assassination of the more permissive Alexander II. Shomer sent his wife and children back to Pinsk and returned to Vilna, where he wrote for the publishing house of Madame Romm. In 1889 his Odessa theater friends sent him money to join them in New York as a playwright for the Rumanian Opera House. He came, and a year later his family—my grandmother among them—followed.

Manya attended a Manhattan public school where her Yiddish name was converted to "Minnie." She always disliked the name, but it stuck. "Miriam" was her name on paper, "Minnie" what people called her, and she identified with it enough to make me change my cat's name from "Minnie" (after a character in the Danny Kaye song "Minnie the Moocher") to "Moochie."

She never forgot what it was like to be a "greenhorn" and as a woman in her sixties could still reproduce the garbled English of the first American song she learned:

> How my har was beechy
> For the old samechee
> Swinka in the ol applechee,

which should have been

> How my heart was beating
> for the old time greeting
> swinging in the old apple tree.

The family, which in Pinsk had had servants and spacious quarters, was now poor. New York's Yiddish theater community could offer Shomer production of his plays but not a living. He was forced to open his own printing business, which produced handbills for Lower East Side merchants as well as a magazine, *Der Menshen Freind* (The Friend of the People), and Shomer's novels. The family moved frequently from one tenement to another, finally settling in a place on Madison Street with the printing shop in the basement.

Shomer's literary fortunes had fallen too. His once celebrated novels were now out of fashion. Worse, they had been attacked in print by no less a figure than Sholom Aleichem in *Shomer on Trial,* a pamphlet published in 1888 in Russia. Aleichem accused his literary predecessor of writing escapist junk without relevance to actual Jewish life. First lionized, then vilified, the gentle and unworldly Shomer always aroused a fierce protectiveness in his grown children. My grandmother, known for her hardnosed practicality, verged on the histrionic when she described him.

Minnie loved school and excelled there, but had to fight for a higher education because her mother forbade it. Dinneh, the once-spirited, rebellious daughter of Reb Michel, who had so bridled with resentment at being denied the first-rate education her brothers received, now became as prejudiced against her own girls. She had three daughters who were expected to serve her while she indulged and coddled her only son, Abe. My grandmother attended high school at night, was admitted to Hunter College and fervently wished to attend. Instead, she took a job as a librarian and leader of girls' clubs at the Hebrew Educational Society. At night she studied drawing and art history at the Educational Alliance. Her teacher there, Henry McBride, was impressed by her talent as an artist and encouraged her to become a professional. He trained her as an art teacher, and she began to give her own classes at the Alliance and to lecture for the Board of Education on classical Greek and Roman art. During this period (she was in her early twenties) she also published, for the first time, occasional columns for the English section of the Yiddish newspaper *Tageblat.*

At seventeen she had met Charles Zunser, a handsome young man with curls, blue eyes, a Byronic cape, and literary aspirations, whom she married in 1905. Charles was the son of Elyakum Zunser, a Minsk songwriter, folk poet and performer at weddings *(badkhen),* who was well known in the Yiddish-speaking world. For their whole married life, the daughter of Shomer and the son of Elyakum Zunser paid homage to the memory and work of their fathers. It was actually because of their fathers that they met.

Zunser had contributed some poems to the journal that Shomer edited and printed. Shomer took the liberty of changing a rhyme without consulting the poet. Zunser responded with an angry letter, and the two were on the outs. Some years later, Dinneh Shaikevitsch (Madame Shomer) passed Elyakum Zunser in front of his printing shop on East Broadway. I will give you my grandmother's own account (from an article she published about her wedding party):

"The old man" (he was thus called because of his gray hair) sat in his chair on the sidewalk, as was his custom. My mother had been an admirer of Zunser from her earliest days. She used to sing his songs with great feeling and often with tears in her eyes. When she saw Zunser in his chair she approached him.

"What is this business of being mad?" she said in her usual quick manner. "Cut out the anger! Enough of it. I shall go at once and bring over here my Nochim-Mayer."

Father happened to be across the street in the editorial office of the *Tageblat*. When he was through with his business, mother began to persuade him to go over to Zunser. She persisted in her demand and father yielded.

The reconciliation between the two friends ended with an invitation to our home in Bayonne, where we spent that summer. The Zunsers came on the following Sunday and brought along their second son, the eighteen-year-old Charles. . . . During the few hours that his parents spent in our house, young Zunser poured out a stream of English poetry. He knew by heart scores of poems by Poe, Shelley and Keats. We embarked on a somewhat complicated romance. Our wedding photograph was taken over six years after our first meeting.

Shomer's death in November 1905 caused the wedding to be postponed for a month and cast a shadow over the event when it did take place. In the photograph of the wedding feast his portrait, draped in black, can be seen hanging on the wall behind the banquet table. There was none of the dancing and singing traditional at Jewish weddings, but, as the photograph attests, there was abundant food and drink. (Those are seltzer siphons on the table, along with wine bottles.)

The wedding brought together members of the Bercinsky

family who were never to meet again. Menye was to return to Russia and Dvayreh to her isolated life with "Elephant." It was also an important social event in the world of the New York Jewish intelligentsia. Elyakum Zunser, of course, was there. So were Abraham Goldfaden, playwright and founder of the Yiddish theater in Odessa, Johann Paley, editor of the *Tageblat,* and Rose Pastor Stokes, a radical activist who wrote for the *Tageblat* and had married a millionaire.

My mother, Helen, was born less than a year after the wedding. She was the first of three children born to Charles and Miriam within five years. Grandfather, doubtful of ever supporting his family by writing, had gone to law school and set up a faltering law practice in the Brownsville section of Brooklyn. Money was short, and continued to be, even after Charles began work at the National Desertion Bureau. The young family moved frequently, an average of once a year, partly (according to my mother) "due to my father's difficulties in establishing himself, but also to mother's restlessness." They did not really settle down until they bought a house after thirteen years of marriage.

Before each move my grandmother would draw a diagram on which the position of all the furniture was marked. The movers would then know exactly where to place the sofa, table, piano. The sewing machine was usually put in the kitchen, where Minnie could quickly set about the task of making curtains. According to my mother, she did all the repairs and laid all the carpets herself:

She could change washers, wire lamps, replace fuses, glue chair legs, install curtain rods and window shades. She cut up the old carpets to fit the new rooms. She had her own tool box.

Grandma, it should be clear, was immensely competent, a great "doer," with wonderful hands that were always occupied with fixing or creating. She hated idleness.

While her children were young her main work was at home. She did translations (from Yiddish to English), editing and writing—tasks she could combine with mothering and housekeeping. One of her jobs, the occasion of much family mirth, was on a version of *Hamlet* for the Yiddish theater, "enlarged and improved" by its New York adapter.

She edited and wrote columns for both the children's page and the women's page of a publication called *The American Weekly Jewish News*. Her women's columns often addressed feminist issues. It was the time of the women's suffrage movement, in which she participated at least to the extent of marching in a 1917 parade. In one column she wrote:

Our [women's] powers will be curtailed just so long as we do not understand ourselves, past and present. We have a history, though it is generally unrecorded. (June 14, 1918)

In another piece she spoke of the frustration of a woman confined to the role of housewife despite training and competence for a position outside the home. For this woman, "who silently eats her heart out" as her "cultivated faculties nag for expression," she urged some degree of economic independence and some time "saved for self development, self expression."

The granddaughter of a woman who had married at age twelve a man she'd never seen, who despite twenty-four pregnancies had remained so ignorant she could never tell time, Minnie rejoiced that woman's "usefulness, her intelligence, her integrity are at last being called into play":

The shackles which held woman in bondage for thousands of years are dropping off as if by magic. . . . It is not only her political station that is being changed, but her social and moral status. It is not only the freedom to cast her ballot that she will obtain but the freedom to cast her life and destiny. (March 15, 1918)

For reasons I don't know, my grandmother's editorship of the women's page lasted only about six months, though she continued to edit and write for the children's page. The paper itself folded after about two years.

At about that time my grandparents became active Zionists. Grandma was a delegate to the first American Jewish Congress, an organization founded by her brother, Abe. Henrietta Szold had established the women's Zionist organization Hadassah, and my grandmother, now beginning to be active outside her home, founded a Brooklyn chapter. For three years she headed the New York organization.

In 1919 the family was in its third year in Borough Park, Brooklyn, having moved there from various locations in the Bronx and Manhattan. There was again a feeling of "move" in the air, with vague talk of settling in Palestine. The three children, Helen, Flossie (Florence) and Shomer (named for his grandfather) longed to live in the country and begged to move there. All extra change was collected in a cardboard box on the bedroom shelf to be put toward the purchase of a country house. Shomer's illness—he was recovering from encephalitis—may have contributed to the desire to move to a healthier and more serene environment. And, too, my grandparents were determined to bring their children up as assimilated Americans rather than as marked "greenhorns." They were unhappy that their children spoke with the singsong Yiddish intonation. Perhaps in the country, surrounded by "real American" speech, they would lose the unwanted inflection.

The move became a reality after my grandfather took a job as a district organizer for John Purroy Mitchell, a reform mayor of New York who was running for reelection. Mitchell was trounced, but for his work on the campaign my grandfather earned two hundred dollars, enough to make a down payment on a small Sears, Roebuck prefab house in Ardsley, Westchester County, next door to some family friends. They moved in in the spring of 1919.

Since the Ardsley house was not sold until 1945, I have firsthand recollections of it. By the time I was visiting it, the house was used as a summer and weekend place by my grandparents, who had moved back into a city apartment. The grounds, to me, were a paradise. There was a beautifully tended (by my grandfather) rolling lawn, a lush flower garden (my grandmother's province), many fruit trees (under one of which was a swing, my favorite haunt) and an outcropping of rock that was perfect for the castle games we children used to play. Each of the three Zunser children and seven grandchildren had a special tree planted on the lawn.

By the 1940s Ardsley was an affluent suburb, but at the time my grandparents moved there it was rural, remote and not accustomed to Jews. The Zunsers were only the third Jewish family in town. Poised for anti-Semitic attack, they weren't surprised when a group of young caddies on their way to the golf course threw stones at the house and shouted, "Dirty Jew." Others were friendlier to the new family, but when a Presbyterian minister called one afternoon to greet the recently arrived residents, my grandmother engaged him in a long talk in which she explained why the Zunsers, as Jews, could not fully participate in the community. She then went on to discuss with him the theological and philosophical differences between Christianity and Judaism.

The Zunser home in Ardsley was open to many guests. Family and friends came up from the city, some for long stays. But in Ardsley my grandmother always felt socially isolated. Although she organized the first hot-lunch program in the school and started the town's first public library, her community activities failed to cultivate friendships. To relieve her loneliness she depended on weekly visits to New York City, always hurried because she had to return in time to put dinner on the table.

In Ardsley she began to seriously pursue a career as a playwright for the Yiddish theater, a world into which she had been born. Her father had written plays. Her mother, too, had been involved in the theater—managing the house and selecting the actors in Odessa. As children, Minnie and her sisters knew Goldfaden scripts by heart and played at performing them. And her brother, Abe, had written a series of hits in New York—*The Yellow Passport, The Green Millionaire, At Sea and Ellis Island.* He had many contacts and had kept the name Shomer before the Yiddish-speaking public. As "the Shomer sisters," Grandma and her sister Rose collaborated on a play, *One of the Many (Eine fun Volk),* which was to be both a critical and a financial success. The family became accustomed to the sight of her, wrapped in a gray flannel bathrobe, writing at night at the kitchen table, her long black braid hanging down her back, a light dangling overhead.

The actress Bertha Kalich starred in *One of the Many* and contributed greatly to its success. She was making her return to the Yiddish stage after a series of appearances on Broadway and a nervous breakdown, which forced her into temporary retirement. As the play's opening in October 1921 approached, the Yiddish press lavished attention on it and its leading lady. Kalich told one interviewer (Leon Elmer, in the *Jewish Times,* Baltimore, September 2, 1921) that her return to the Yiddish theater was like coming back, after an absence, to her native land. And she enthused about the play she was using as the vehicle for her comeback:

I have succeeded at last in securing a play by two women authors which treats of family life of today, abounds in poignant and humorous situations, and what is more gives a clear and unequivocal solution to the burning questions that are of utmost importance to every married—and unmarried—man and woman.

One of the Many, touted in the press as "the first Yiddish play by women," concerns a noble, neglected wife, devoted to her children, who has married the wrong man —a failed musician who does not understand or appreciate her and is involved with other women. The wife, Esther, full of unfulfilled ambition and suppressed rage, resembled the frustrated housewife who appeared in my grandmother's columns for *The American Weekly Jewish News,* and undoubtedly resembled my grandmother herself. She cries out:

It was decreed that a woman who had a home and children should be contented. I was not contented. My heart rebelled against the crushing drudgery.

Esther seizes an opportunity to do useful work at a settlement house run by the man she really loves, who returns her love and offers to marry her. But at home her children are suffering in her absence, and when her husband sees how close he has come to losing her, he repents. She goes back to him, but as a woman who has asserted her independence and who commands respect.

Kalich took this melodrama as serious literature and felt it had something important to say. She told Dr. L. B. Lazarus, who wrote a column for the *Hebrew Standard:*

The new play is not a piece which gives one a chance to display beautiful gowns or to indulge in grandiloquence, but it is what I would call a drama of heart and soul.

When I made up my mind to give a few Yiddish performances this season, . . . I promised to myself that it will not be a play translated from Russian or Hungarian or adapted from any other literature but that it would be a Yiddish play, written in Yiddish by a Jewish author and dealing with the problems of our present life.

The Shomer sisters made some money, perhaps a few thousand dollars each, on the play. At last Grandma felt she'd achieved the recognition she craved. Like her heroine, she was now more free and independent. When the play was in rehearsal she had traveled into the city almost daily. On opening night she and Rose held court at the Café Royale, as family and friends gathered round. With her earnings she treated the family to previously out-of-reach luxuries. She made the down payment on a Model-T Ford, bought new furnishings for the house, was able to pay the tuition for my mother's freshman year at N.Y.U.

The Zunsers moved back to the city, which Grandma emphatically preferred—but only briefly, for my mother contracted tuberculosis, and her mother determined to nurse her at home, in Ardsley. For two years Grandma endured a confinement more absolute than any she had previously known. She rarely left the house. When she could she worked (again in collaboration with Rose) on a new play. Amazingly, it was a light comedy, *Circus Girl,* which opened in 1928, with music by Rumshinsky and starring Molly Picon. It was the second triumph for the Shomer sisters. The *New York Times'* Brooks Atkinson, who knew not a word of Yiddish, urged others equally ignorant of the language to make the trip down to the Kessler Second Avenue Theater for a guaranteed good time. As bait he offered this description of Picon portraying an actress from a traveling company who masquerades as a child:

As a little girl Miss Picon is at her best, behaving for all the world like a brat, innocently flipping up her short dresses in the rear, snatching expensive ornaments from the royal raiment of an imposing upper-class snob, clinging pathetically to a stalwart tenor hero whom she saves from a wretched marriage. . . . For random divertissement she interpolates stunts. She performs card tricks and feats of magic. She clogs "The March of the Wooden Soldiers." She impersonates great musicians on the violin and the piano. And finally, in true acrobatic style, she dangles by one foot from a rope and daringly mocks the impertinence of Newton's naive law of science. (October 21, 1928)

The play was clearly a vehicle for Miss Picon, with just enough plot and dialogue to provide occasions for her to display her full bag of tricks. Audiences loved it. Several months after the play opened Grandma wrote to my mother (who had recovered sufficiently to have gone to Europe) that "the house has been so full all the time that I could not get passes for our friends."

Again Minnie returned with the family to the city. The younger children were now grown and getting ready to leave home. She and Rose worked on another play, *The Singing Thief,* for comedian Ludwig Satz, in which Satz was a night-club performer and would-be burglar disguised as a housemaid. It opened, got panned and closed immediately. And, as far as I know, it was the last of Grandma's plays to be produced.

In the 1930s it became clear that the Yiddish theater in New York was dying. Immigration quotas had successfully cut the influx of Yiddish speakers who had comprised its eager New York audience. The Jews who had arrived earlier were moving out of the Lower East Side, and were hesitant to travel to and from week-night performances. A second generation of Jews was coming of age. They spoke English and patronized the Broadway stage. Attempting to change with the times, Grandma wrote several plays in English, including one, *Goldenlocks and The Bears,* that was commissioned for Broadway by Arthur Hopkins.

Between 1932 and 1942 she devoted considerable time

and energy to MAILAMM, an organization she helped found and presided over, which was devoted to supporting, performing and developing Jewish music in Palestine and America. It raised money for research on deciphering the cantillation (chanting) of the Bible, aided in the formation of the music department at Hebrew University and presented monthly concerts of Jewish music in New York. A West Coast branch of MAILAMM was founded, at Grandma's urging, by her sister Rose. MAILAMM and its successor, the Jewish Music Forum, allowed Grandma to exercise her ability as an organizer and administrator. It brought her into contact with celebrities of the music world, which she enjoyed, and encouraged her to turn her home into a meeting place for the Jewish cultural elite. My aunt Flossie (Florence Saltz) describes the salon atmosphere:

Friday nights became traditional "open house"—the samovar boiling away, trays of *peroshki, blini, rugeloch* (nut cookies), bowls of *schi* (Russian cabbage soup), plates of chopped liver and *gefulte* fish. The evenings became increasingly music filled. Musicians of every type would be on hand regularly. I remember particularly one, who had been a leading opera conductor pre-Hitler, whose forte was to have a guest give him a theme which he would develop extemporaneously in the style of any composer we wanted. There was frequently a string quartet, any number of singers and pianists. Mother was a marvelous hostess and the evenings became legendary.

Rose was now living in Los Angeles. She'd moved there at the invitation of her brother, Abe, who had a contract to direct a movie *(Today)* in Hollywood. In order to accept Abe's invitation Rose had had to leave behind not only her business, a translation and typing bureau, but also a husband she'd hastily acquired and never had much use for. In Los Angeles Abe introduced her to a wealthy businessman and sparks flew. They decided to marry, but the wronged husband in New York, previously quiescent, balked. He sued his rival for "alienation of affections." There were headlines, court battles and finally an expensive settlement. Through all of this, Rose got to play the heroine in a romantic melodrama, a role she adored, just as her aunts Haiye and Fraydel had enjoyed their dramatic love triangles. In traditional Jewish culture, a love drama offered one of the few chances for a woman to hold center stage.

Without Rose as a partner or the Yiddish stage as a focus, Grandma cast about for another outlet for her creativity and ambition. She began to explore her gifts in the visual arts, which had lain dormant since the days before her marriage when she had studied and then taught art at the Educational Alliance. She started to study ceramics, experimenting with different types of glazes, firings, colors and designs, and traveling several times a week from her apartment to a kiln in Greenwich Village. Then she announced she'd had enough of vases and bowls and began to make sculpture. She did several impressive portrait busts of family members. Her son Shomer, himself a watercolorist, without her knowledge submitted one of her figures to a jury selecting works for a show at the Brooklyn Museum. She was jubilant and surprised to hear it had been chosen for the exhibition. She wrote Rose: "I am going to be represented in a regular artists' show, and that given by a museum! Wonder of wonders!" Shortly after this she showed two pieces at an exhibit of the Society of Independent Artists at the American Fine Arts Gallery in New York.

At the same time she was sculpting, while in her fifties, she began to write *Yesterday*. She had always loved telling, and her children hearing, stories about her mother's family in Russia. Hers was a family of storytellers. The vitality, the folk quality of *Yesterday* springs from this oral tradition. Many of the stories in it must be versions told to my grandmother by her mother or another family member. In writing them down she was acknowledging her own mortality, looking ahead to the time when she wouldn't be around to tell them in person. Her children had urged her to make a written record, and she complied. My aunt's manuscript copy of the book is inscribed, "These are the stories you asked for."

The book was published by Stackpole in the ominous year 1939. The dust jacket of the original edition bears an advertisement for *Mein Kampf* and a promise that the royalties from the sale of that book will go not to Hitler but to refugees. An ad for *Yesterday* reads:

In a day when the Jewish people are discussed as an alien race and their culture hysterically attacked as superstition and cabalistic doctrine, it is important that normal, human Jewish life be presented to thinking people everywhere. It is important that Jews themselves know the richness and beauty of their own background.

In 1939 no one could respond to the book without awareness of what was happening to the European Jews who had not come to America, who had stayed behind.

Grandma kept a scrapbook of letters from *Yesterday*'s first readers. Many thanked her for reminding them of something they too remembered—the Sabbath nights, the many-stranded candles. One person remarked: "How those people had the courage to last through what they did! Will we be as courageous in living through what is coming?"

Dedicated "to my children," *Yesterday* had to be written in English, not Yiddish, if those children were to read it. Helen, Flossie and Shomer, the grandchildren of two well-known Yiddish writers, were never taught to read Yiddish and barely understood the spoken language. At the time they were growing up, the big push was to become American, to assimilate. Too late, my grandparents realized that Yiddish was a dying language, but by that time their children had already moved out into the world without it.

What they did have was a taste for English literature, which their parents had cultivated. Grafting English literary culture onto Yiddish may seem odd, but it was very much a reality, and not that unusual. When my grandparents first met, still in their teens, Charles was spouting Keats and Shelley and trying to write poetry in the English romantic tradition. My mother describes a book her parents created before their marriage, containing poems by Charles and illustrations by Miriam, "replete with graves, lilies, willow trees and sorrowing maidens." They raised their children on English novels, particularly Dickens. My grandmother and Rose even wrote a play, *The Master of Thornfield,* based on *Jane Eyre.* In *Yesterday* the British infusion shows up in sentences like "I was ready for a vision of Reb Michel stepping forth like the Pied Piper of Hamelin," or (my favorite): "He was sitting around at his Uncle Vigodsky's house waiting, Micawber-like, for something to turn up."

In embracing English culture, this Jewish family and others were continuing what nineteenth-century *Haskalah,* or enlightenment, had begun. Reb Michel had read Russian books on the sly, disobeying the injunction against study for other than religious purposes. His son-in-law Nochim-Mayer had devoured Russian, Polish and German books, also in secret. Now it was no longer necessary to sneak, but the fears of conservative Jews were borne out: Judaism's hold *was* weakened when it was no longer the sole cultural influence.

Jewish identification (cultural, not religious) came first for my grandparents. For me, for my brothers and cousins, it does not. The part of my grandparents' value system that does carry over is their emphasis on family closeness, and the high value placed on artistic and intellectual achievement. Grandma was an elitist, not about money (which she never had much of) but about mind and talent. I think that bias still exists among her descendants in my generation. The Yiddish word *yiches,* meaning family prestige, may not be used any more, but what it describes continues to flourish. It's no accident that one grandchild of Miriam Shomer Zunser writes novels for children and another directs plays for a repertory theater company.

In our family I'm the one with a reputation for sympathy with the past. For that reason, I was given the old red plush photo album, weak in the spine, with the photographs of our relatives as dwellers in the old country and as recent immigrants in New York. I'm the one who has my great-grandfather's inlaid-wood writing chest (the design, of dark wood set in light, is of birds on leafy branches), his brass inkstand and pen brush. My great-aunt's samovar came to me, and so did the beautifully preserved shawl, made of the finest wool challis, that decorated my grandmother's piano. But a receiver must also pass things on. Out of print for more than thirty years, *Yesterday* has been a private mission of mine. Now it has a present, and a future.

BIBLIOGRAPHICAL NOTE

Material for this essay was drawn in part from the following sources:

BACHELIS, ROSE SHOMER. "The Story of MAILAMM, The American Palestine Music Organization (1932–1942)." Typescript.
MADISON, CHARLES. *Yiddish Literature.* New York: Schocken Books, 1971.
SANDERS, RONALD. *The Downtown Jews.* New York: Harper & Row, 1969.
SALTZ, FLORENCE ZUNSER. Conversation, letters.
WORTIS, HELEN ZUNSER. Conversation, letters and unpublished autobiographical essay.
ZUNSER, JESSE AND MARY. Conversation.

ZUNSER, MIRIAM SHOMER. "The Jewish Literary Scene in New York at the Beginning of the Century," *Yivo Annual of Jewish Social Science,* Vol. VII, 1952, pp. 277–295.

ZUNSER, MIRIAM SHOMER, WITH ROSE SHOMER, *One of the Many.* Typescript, New York Public Library, Library of the Performing Arts at Lincoln Center.

Glossary of Terms

alter. old man
avek. away
badkhen. entertainer at weddings
beholoh. fright or panic, pogrom
bobbe. grandmother
bock. goat
brayges tanz. folk dance
Brilliantenshtayn. brilliant stone
Brith Milah. covenant of circumcision
broit. bride
caftan. gabardine coat
capelles. band
challe. loaf of white Sabbath bread
calle nehmen. setting aside a portion of dough to be burnt as an offering
Chassid. member of a Jewish sect known mainly for the strict observance
  of ritual law
Chassidism. practices and beliefs of the Chassidim
chayder. Hebrew school
chazzan. cantor
chossen. bridegroom-to-be
Chumesh. Pentateuch
chuppe. wedding canopy
coshenierke. female bargain hunter or haggler
Der Menshen Freind. "The Friend of the People" (publication)
der shodt meshugener. the town lunatic

Deutschmarish. Yiddish with a mixture of German words and style

diadka. "little uncle," a Russian to whom a Jewish boy was sent to live by the authorities, as part of the policy of Russification in the first half of the nineteenth century.

Diamantenshtayn. diamond stone

duma. town council

-e, -ke, -le, -el. Yiddish diminutives

-er. "belonging to"

erev Shabas. eve of the Sabbath

es vet kumen der goy. the Gentile will come

ethrog. citrus fruit used during the Feast of Tabernacles

farzesseneh. spinster

feldsher. barber-surgeon, or unlicensed medical practitioner

fetter. uncle

gebrakevet. rejected

gefullte fish. dish of stewed or baked fish

Gemoreh keppel. "Talmud head"—a mind that displays aptitude for Talmudic and rabbinic lore

Goldshtayn. gold stone

golva. head of the town council

gospodin. mister

goy, goyish. Gentile

gragers. noisemakers

groschen. coin

gymnasium. high school

hachnosses kalleh. money collected as dowry for a poor girl who could not otherwise get married

Ha-Melitz. Hebrew journal

Haskalah. enlightenment

Havdalah. ceremony marking the end of the Sabbath

heidim deidem. a folk dance

hetter. permission

Homantaschen. Purim cakes filled with poppyseeds or prunes boiled in honey

Hoveve Zion. Lovers of Zion

kaddish. prayer for the dead

kalleh. bride-to-be

kashruth. Jewish dietary laws

kaylitsch. braided loaf of white bread

kest. obligation usually assumed by the parents of a bride to provide the newly married couple with room and board at the bride's father's house for a given length of time, usually a year

kichlach. yeast cakes filled with chopped almonds, raisins and cinnamon

killeh. rupture, hernia

klezmer. band of musicians

klois. coventicle

Kol Nidre. prayer chanted in the synagogue on the eve of Yom Kippur
kosher tanz. a folk dance
kuchen. cake
kugel. pudding
kreplach. patties stuffed with spiced chopped meat
kvater. young man and woman who carry baby to circumcision ceremony; godparent
kvitantzie. certificate of exemption from military service
landsleit. countrymen
laptches. foot coverings without heel, made of cloth or felt
lebensbilder. "pictures of life"; dramas
licht benchen. blessing of the Sabbath candles
Listcher Vald. forest of Listch
Maftir. a portion of the Bible read on Sabbaths and holidays
marshaloch. wedding jester
maskilim. apostles of the Hebrew enlightenment
mazeltov. good luck
mechautonim. in-laws
Melamed. Hebrew teacher
meshugeneh. lunatic
meshummad. apostate
mikva. ritual bath
mitzvah tanz. a folk dance
mohel. man who performs a circumcision
monolach. Purim sweetmeats made of poppyseeds cooked in honey
muchinetze. female sufferer
niyaw. giddyap
orchim. guests
Ozar ha-Shemot. encyclopedia of the Bible
patch tanz. a folk dance
pazharne komande. volunteer fire brigade
podradchik. commission merchant
pomestchik. rich landowner
porocheth. ornamental curtain suspended before the Ark of the Law
postoles. foot coverings without heel, made of cloth or felt
pripechuk. contraption in front and to one side of oven used for quick cooking over an open fire
prisive. medical examination by draft board
Purim. Jewish holiday commemorating the deliverance of the Jews from the massacre plotted by Haman
Rabbiner. government rabbi
Rabbiner-schulen. rabbinical crown schools
Rashi. eleventh-century commentator on the Pentateuch and Talmud
rayfeh. barber-surgeon, or unlicensed medical practitioner
Reb. reverential title applied to men with Talmudic learning
Reb Yid. "Mr. or Sir Jew", a common appellation

roman. novel
romanen. romances
Rov. rabbi
salle. livingroom
sandik. man in whose lap a newborn baby is circumcised
Seder. service including feast at Passover
shadchen. matchmaker
shalach-mones. Purim cooked meats and other foods given to one's
    friends as well as to poor people
shpiel. play
shpiller. actor
shudduch. match
shul. synagogue
shund. trashy
shtodt. town
shtreimel. great round fur hat worn on special occasions
Sibir. Siberia
sofar. scribe of Scrolls of the Torah
tatte. father
Teitsch Chumesh. the *Ze'enah-U-Re'enah*
torba. bag in which a peasant carried tobacco, coins, and food
tscholent. meat, potatoe and bean dish
tzad. family; literally, family side
tzaddik. holy man
tzaztke. toy or doll
tzimmes. cooked carrot dish
ukaz. edict
vach-nacht. night of watching before the ceremony of circumcision
vatnik. cotton-wool seller
yeshivah. Talmudic academy
yeshuvnize. Jewish peasant woman; ignorant female
yiches. prestige, pedigree
Yiddene. ordinary Jewish woman
Ze'enah-U-Re'enah. Yiddish paraphrase of the Five Books of Moses
Zogerke. female reader of the Hebrew service in the women's section of
    the shul